118

Cultural Critique

Winter
2023

v Editorial Statement

1 *Yijun Sun* The Desire to See: Binary Systems, Architectural Space, and the Ontology of Being-with

23 *Briankle G. Chang* Seeing . . . What? Four Images and Their (In)Visibility

56 *G Douglas Barrett* Technological Catastrophe and the Robots of Nam June Paik

83 *Jennifer Wang* Embryonic Citizenship: Disidentifications of Asian Racialized Settlerhood

115 *Erin Nunoda* Lotus Flower's Colors: Interracial Autoeroticism and *The Toll of the Sea*

Review Essays

155 Politically Red
The Benjamin Files by Fredric Jameson
Eduardo L. Cadava and Sara Nadal-Melsió

172 Parting Ways: With Werner Hamacher
Give the Word: Responses to Werner Hamacher's 95 Theses on Philology edited by Ann Smock and Gerhard Richter *Kevin Newmark*

Book Review

219 "The Mad (wo)Man in Black Studies"
Black Madness: Mad Blackness
by Therí Alyce Pickens *Megan Finch*

229 Books Received

EDITORIAL STATEMENT

Cultural Critique provides a forum for creative and provocative scholarship in the theoretical humanities and humanistic social sciences. Transnational in scope and transdisciplinary in orientation, the journal strives to spark and galvanize intellectual debates as well as to attract and foster critical investigations regarding any aspect of culture as it expresses itself in words, images, and sounds, across both time and space. The journal is especially keen to support scholarship that engages the ways in which cultural production, cultural practices, and cultural forms constitute and manifest the nexus between the aesthetic, the psychic, the economic, the political, and the ethical intended in their widest senses. While informed by the diverse traditions of historical materialism as well as by the numerous critiques of such traditions from various parts of the globe, the journal welcomes contributions based on a variety of theoretical-methodological paradigms.

Cultural Critique appears four times a year. General issues, including essays, book reviews, and thematic sections, as well as entire issues devoted to special topics, are regularly published. The editors welcome the submission of freestanding essays, special issue proposals on topics of interest to the journal, as well as reviews of relevant, new, and not-so-new books.

In 2022, the journal launched its online section hosted by Manifold, the open-access platform of the University of Minnesota Press. *Cultural Critique Online* on Manifold expands *Cultural Critique's* existing web presence to include new open-access book reviews, short articles, interviews, and more. For more, please visit https://z.umn.edu/7p7i or scan the QR code below.

Cultural Critique Books is the companion series of the journal. It seeks to attract work by those scholars across the humanities and social sciences who continue to draw inspiration from, and seek to contribute to, the theoretical movements and debates so long nurtured at Minnesota. Book proposals should be addressed to one of the five senior editors at: *Cultural Critique,* Department of Cultural Studies and Comparative Literature, 235 Nicholson Hall, 216 Pillsbury Drive S.E., University of Minnesota, Minneapolis, MN 55455–0229, U.S.A., or via email to cultcrit@umn.edu.

THE DESIRE TO SEE
BINARY SYSTEMS, ARCHITECTURAL SPACE,
AND THE ONTOLOGY OF BEING-WITH

Yijun Sun

> *There is never a pure access to a single object; vision is always multiple,*
> *adjacent to and overlapping with other objects, desires and vectors.*
>
> —Jonathan Crary, *Techniques of the Observer*

In 1771, Claude-Nicholas Ledoux was appointed by Louis XV as administrator and architect adjunct to the *inspectur des salines* for Lorraine and France-Comté to survey the existing saltworks[1] in Arc-et-Senans in eastern France. His task was simple—to make recommendations as to their repair and to draw up plans for new manufactures (Ledoux and Vidler, iv). Since the extraction of salt required the vaporization of salt water extracted from *saline* wells in furnaces fueled by wood, two locations were fundamental to the saltworks: the well and the forest. Ledoux decided to move the factory to the nearby forest of Chaux instead of the site near the wells, with the idea that it would be easier to transport water than wood. And this is how this design was given the name Saline de Chaux.

Ledoux understood his task was to build a model factory to bring all resources together and to more efficiently organize the labor. After the survey, he believed that the existing *saline* was far from a productive enterprise for its heterogeneous plans and disordered spatial organizations. To improve it, he attempted to invent an industrial architecture with a "language that might speak to the workers, didactically and directly, of the dignity of their occupations, and on behalf of the managers in their surveillance labor" (v). Ledoux's intention was to reform not only the production of salt but also the administration of that production by means of constructing an entire manufacturing community. In 1774, he drew the final schematic plan, transforming the old *saline* into a new one with a semicircular core. Luckily, this semicircular core of the saltwork got actually built between 1774 and 1778, though with modifications and compromises.

The most obvious change of Ledoux's design was the shift from a disordered square to a semicircular complex,[2] with the specific separation of pavilions grouping areas by use. It demonstrated a change in the institutional conception of the factory as a whole. Instead of the old plan combining all activities in one building, he separated the different functions of the *saline* and accommodated them in detached buildings. In this architectural complex, the director's house, together with the chapel, was situated at the center of the straight diameter, which brought together at a clear center all the constituent parts; while the vast semicircular open space surrounded by ten buildings at the periphery was divided into stable cells, each one of them functioning as a component of the whole system. This was later proved to be a highly efficient scheme—by the design of light paths, the power of gaze was introduced into this space.

Emil Kaufmann sees Ledoux as the paradigmatic figure in the shift from Classicism to Neoclassicism (Vidler 2002, 18). The breakdown of the project into functionally defined and formally expressed units is an indication of the "principle of isolation" (19). For Kaufmann, the emergence of an "architecture of isolation" can be likened to the emergence of the modern "individual" consciousness. He believes that Ledoux used these designs as expressions of "autonomy"—the social ideas of the new bourgeoisie and the political ideas of the Enlightenment as developed by Jean-Jacques Rousseau's idea of individual freedom (18).[3] We see the entanglement of light and reason in architecture in the prominence of the Enlightenment ideology whose motto says, "Dare to know!" The awareness of the deliberately designed light path and corresponding power regimes are the preconditions of these transforming architectural spaces.

Ledoux never intended to build a surveillance machine. In accordance with Kantian philosophy, he emphasized geometry as a calculated control of form or use. For him, Saline de Chaux was a concrete utopia[4] to exercise the rationality of the plan, which informed the construction of the central ideas of the "Ideal City of Chaux," a project of a utopian city twenty years after the salt factory. However, the rationality of space and the calculation of control for common good cannot be separated from absolute sovereignty.[5] Upon the building of this model, it doesn't matter who is in the position of the overseer's place or if there is an overseer at all; it is a language that directly speaks to the corporeality of bodies, turning them into docile components under the collaboration of self-censorship. Saline de Chaux's achieved efficiency makes it similar to an optical machine that runs automatically.[6] As incorporated factors, bodies in this architectural enclosure can be easily rendered under the control of the eminent, present gaze illuminating from the center.[7]

This anticipation of a new form of surveillance was perfected in Jeremy Bentham's panopticon schemes of the 1790s as a model of a single gaze constantly surveilling everything. The panopticon became a model of surveillance for Michel Foucault as the embodiment of the desire to construct a perfect disciplinary apparatus. In his reading of Foucault, Gilles Deleuze argues "the ideal project of these environments of enclosure, particularly visible within the factory" is "to concentrate; to distribute in space; to order in time; to compose a productive force within the dimension of space-time whose effect will be greater than the sum of its component forces" (3). The central point in the design was, meanwhile, the source of light illuminating all, as well as the place of convergence for everything that should be known. These designs reflected the world whose image was built on discoveries from Galileo Galilei to Isaac Newton that gave people faith in an established relationship between vision and knowledge.[8]

The panoptic mechanism arranges spatial unities in a way that makes the unobstructed gaze see constantly and immediately. Hence the intimate state of conscious and permanent visibility assures the automatic function of power (Foucault 1995, 176). A hierarchical apparatus is established on the architectural practice in the preference for ovals over squares, which erects the privileged central position of the observing subjects and the unobstructed lines of light radiating from the center. It shares the topology with other architectural designs where the binary division of a center and a periphery facilitates the possibility of seeing and hearing. In parallel with surveillance, a similar construction of vision—panorama with the aim of spectatorship—comes to our view.

SURVEILLANCE OR SPECTACLE?

Kaufmann parallels the French architecture of the Enlightenment and Revolutionary Era with the already well-established German Neoclassicism represented by Karl Friedrich Schinkel. They share similarities in the awareness of light design. At the beginning of the nineteenth century, Schinkel was among the highly accomplished architects who transformed Berlin through their redefinition of buildings. One manifestation of his talents was shown in his clear awareness of the visual aspect in his architectural thinking. One of Schinkel's most widely reproduced plates in *Sammlung Architektonischer Entwürfe* showed the "perspective view from the staircase gallery in the museum, seen through the porticos and across the Lustgarten square and its surroundings" (Forster 1983, 63). In this plate, twelve spectators were walking around in the space, exploring views from different perspectives between the artifacts and the city (63). The vision of this image was based on a deliberately exaggerated scope: it was a wide and deep scope in which everything was vying for attention (63). When Kurt Walter Forster describes the intention of this design, he writes, "The viewer is assumed to stand in the rear corner of the stairwell gallery—deep in the cavity of the building—so that his panoramically extended view embraces in one sweep paintings, sculptures, the architectural members of the building, and a quadrant of the cityscape beyond, including the royal palace, public gardens, burgher houses, and Schinkel's own church at Werder" (63).

It is not without connection to Schinkel's interest in his design of panoramas. In the plate of the staircase, the observing bodies are necessary components of this vision machine, which is also the case of panoramas with the difference that spectators are freed from walking around. Panorama is the machine of seeing; it has an imaginary spectator at the center that rises above the city. All the scenes around are rendered as immense images presented to the central viewer.[9] Seeing from this center position, the individual dominates everything visible, the eyes wandering through trees and squares. The scenery is presented as a whole ensemble, and all details of this immense perspective are rendered to the observer (68).

Panorama received significant general recognition in Europe during this time.[10] Preferred themes of historical events and the topography of famous towns contributed to this success (68). After Schinkel's visit to Palermo in 1804, he decided to build a panorama to show the entirety of this city's majestic view, with the sea beyond the mountains descending from two sides from the height of the Norman villas (68). Schinkel described the view as a "vast amphitheater."[11] The popular success of panoramic cityscapes coincided with the wake of souvenir pictures and urban vedette paintings, which in part depended on the techniques of the panoramic image.

Panorama later became the embodiment of a new form of vision— spectatorship. It is an instrumentalized way of seeing that is only possible in a binary apparatus with a clear definition of the center and the periphery. Forster describes the viewers' experience in a panorama in detail: "Upon entering the enclosure of a panorama, the first impression one gains is that of an immense, but confusing view in which all points overwhelm the eyes at once and without apparent order; this effect is inevitable for it is brought about by the brusque and instantaneous transition of the appearance of nature to that of its image" (68). The structure of a panorama is a conjunction of topography with theatrical potential (68–69). Theater, the older origin of the spectatorship, relates to this binary system of seeing in one way or another. In panoramas, "The viewer's eyes will do the walking, but extended movement is intrinsic to the very structure of the images" (75). The center of the panorama is almost an imaginary viewpoint that brings the spectator a sort of "urban CinemaScope" in which "proximity and distance, appearance and disappearance, together spell out a dynamic architectural order far beyond the visually obvious" (75).[12]

An intriguing contradiction appears when we read in line with Foucault. In *Discipline and Punish*'s discussion of the appearance of Bentham's panopticon as a fulfilled historical process, Foucault concludes that we are not in the amphitheater nor on stage but in a panoptic machine; our society is not one of spectacle but of surveillance (217). Through this differentiation, Foucault implies that surveillance works on the concrete corporeality of bodies while spectacle stays under the abstract surface of images. He concludes that individuals are not amputated, repressed, altered by the social order but are being carefully fabricated in it through techniques of force and body. However, this argument, aiming to highlight a difference between the power relations in antiquity and modernity, seems to overlook the effect of power that brings together the regimes of surveillance and spectacle (Crary, 18). It can hardly be ignored that spectacle and surveillance both emerge from the need for seeing, while this need is made possible on a set of embodied optical operations in a binary system constructed by spatial instruments that capture bodies and create the desired subjects. As Jonathan Crary points out, what shouldn't be ignored is that in the regularity of vision, upon the operations in optical apparatus, vision itself becomes a kind of discipline (18). The question left unanswered here is this: how does this optical power operate upon individuals? To be more specific, are there any essential differences between the seeing and the seen?

The answer to this question may be found in another panoramic facility associated with Schinkel in the 1820s—the reflective *Granitschale*[13] in front of the Altes Museum in Berlin. In this design of the granite basin, the panoramic view showed its fascination again: spectators were amused to see themselves in the panoramic image being reflected.[14] This optical design can be clearly seen from Johann Erdmann Hummel's 1831 painting, *Die Granitschale im Lustgarten zu Berlin*. In this painting, "Encircled by admiring passers-by, the double curvature of the basin reflects viewers twice, once head-on, and a second time upside down, leaving out nothing and no one, certainly not the dog, and never the technical expert proudly standing at its side, posing in elegant attire next to his masterpiece" (Forster 2018, 142). When Foucault criticizes the dissymmetry and disequilibrium of this machinery, he notices this particular power dynamic between the seeing and the being seen. Addressing the invisibility of individuals kept in the periphery, he believes that the supervised individuals are the ones seen but who do not see and that they are the objects of information but not the subjects in communication. However, the tricky question is: how do individuals know they are being seen if they cannot see?

The reflection on the panoramic basin at Lustgarten shows us a possible way out of this dilemma—individuals experience the dominant power by seeing the image of themselves from the imaginary position of the center. This visibility needs to remain opaque—individuals captured are not able to see through the center of the machine where the mechanism is located but amused and fascinated by the reflection of themselves. It turns out to be an almost straightforward physical manifestation of the internalized surveillance, telling us that the subject of spectator and the object of surveillance are not as distinct as we once perceived. Instead of invisibility as the guarantee of order explained by Foucault (1995, 200), a new invisible visibility is constructed; instead of individuals rendered as objects, a subject-object position comes into form.[15]

AMPHITHEATER OR PANOPTIC MACHINE?

There is another pair of concepts Foucault brings up in his discussion of spectator and surveillance that points the way for our following discussion: the amphitheater and the panoptic machine. If surveillance and spectator, as constructed visions, are just two sides of the same coin, how do we understand the material part of this construction, that is, the architectural space that makes seeing possible?

Located at the beginning of light manipulation in architectural history, theater naturally bears the consciousness of light and gaze in design. It is a place of seeing, a building type in which performance is given before the audience. The evolving design of theater has always been determined by the spectator's physical requirements for seeing and hearing the performers. Étienne-Louis Boullée's discussions on the construction of theaters offer us a general principle of theater design:

> I have made the inside of my auditorium in the shape of a semicircle . . . Moreover, this is the only shape suitable for a Theater. It is necessary to be able to see and hear perfectly and what shape fulfills these two requirements better than the one whose exactly equal radii give the ear and eye the greatest and most equitably distributed freedom; where no point hides another and where, for this reason, all spectators on the same level can see and hear equally well. Moreover, this shape enabled me to enclose my auditorium with spherical vaulting which not only has the advantage of being a simple form of decoration in good taste, but which is also the most favorable from an acoustic point of view. (Rosenau, 96–97)

This logic of space arrangement is almost a duplicate of what appears in Saline de Chaux and Bentham's panopticon—as every seat has to have a view of the stage, the area occupied by the seating is confined to a semicircle.

Anthony Vidler regards Saline de Chaux as the theater of production. He argues that "perhaps the most persuasive of sources Ledoux

drew from the tradition of architecture itself, joining, in his imagination, all functional and aesthetic requirements in a single, powerful
symbol of the kind of community he envisaged for the *saline*: that
of an antique theater" (Vidler 1990, 98). For a long time, people were
misled by the notion that Ledoux's semicircular structure of the *saline*
was merely the first half of the unfinished oval town. Instead of an
"incomplete form," Vidler sees it as a complete and finite entity at first.
He believes that "a comparison of the general and detailed geometries
of Perrault's reconstruction of Vitruvius's theaters with those of the
plan of the *saline* shows this to be an unambiguous analogy" (98).

> Only the theater, with its semicircular auditorium facing a proscenium
> across the diagonal, shares this typology. As the type and as metaphor,
> it controlled and gave substance to Ledoux's complex political and social
> idealism, balanced between a pre-panoptical symbolism of surveillance
> and a model of a community; it also unified his decorative devices and
> supplied an appropriate allegory for the "production" of salt. In the event,
> the near simultaneity of Ledoux's projects for the *Saline de Chaux* and the
> Theater of *Besançon* was thus a coincidence of great formal significance.
> (98–99)

We already know that a binary system operates in theaters. Indeed, it
is in the act of setting up separate spaces for performer and spectator that the theater emerges, which echoes a more general need for
mass participation. But how does this theatrical binary division have
anything to do with the apparatus of surveillance or spectator? The
answer lies in the structure of the desire to see—the desire of invisibility, of not being seen while seeing. It is this possibility of asymmetry
in seeing that enhances the power already embedded in the essence of
the binary theatrical space. What would happen if bodies in this space
are not being regulated? There would be no theater at all—only chaos.
The inequality of position and condition between those whose bodies
are present and those whose bodies are absent but whose visions are
omnipresent is embedded in the structure that keeps the theater functioning. Alain Badiou draws political theatricality to our attention.[16]
He writes that "the theatricality of politics is self-evident: there is an
organic relationship between theatre and politics, all the more strong
since theatre is a public institution and since the State still involves
itself in the situation of the theatre" (Badiou, 71). There is "the perma-
nence of the interest of states in the theatre, often taking the form of a

surveillance, simply because one gathers there to listen to remarks and discussions which are perhaps uncontrolled" (73).

Yet the theater, as a practice of community, has another side. In the process of controlling massive bodies, it creates subjects through its mechanism of spectatorship. As Badiou beautifully writes in *In Praise of Theater*, the transference that exists in theaters "transforms subjectivity through a kind of mental incorporation into the dialectic of the theatre" (33). The theater is a machine that continuously produces spectacles. Spectacle blurs separation and bears the quality of transcendence that the spectators, being fascinated, are not totally passive but are merged into this newly constructed subjectivity as a community, even if they remain seated in their designated spots. The theater is a perfect technical system that seeks the power of abolishing barriers; it is a representation of the whole of the multitudes that are present. Individuals, as spectators, become one community in this sense.

For Badiou, theater is an art of spectacle that uses the power of imagery in a sophisticated way (50); it is a result of the negotiation between the symbolic, the imaginary, and most importantly the real, which encounters the phantom of ideas physically (59). As a corporeal presentation, it is situated between transcendence and immanence.[17] The theater always requests the presence of living bodies; it sits between the tension of the transcendence of the idea and its immanent action in a contingent subjectivity (59). The existence of the public/audience is constitutive of the theater (50).

Perhaps Ledoux's design of the *Coup d'oeil* in the theater of Besançon tells everything. As Ledoux's only fully realized public theater, it was conceived in 1775 and built between 1778 to 1784 near Besançon in France. Ledoux published an engraving of *Coup d'oeil du théâtre de Besançon* in 1804, featuring a haunting human eye in whose pupil the auditorium in the interior of the theater was reflected. This engraving was widely reprinted and can still be easily seen online from all sorts of art print retailers. The position of the eye was supposed to serve as the curtain on stage, which was at the right-center of the theater. Situated in the center of the curtain on stage facing in front of the auditorium, this reflecting pupil showed the semicircular theatrical space from an outsized human eye. Vidler sees a paradoxical duality in Ledoux's design, which "suggests a view through a transparent pupil to the empty auditorium as well as its reflection" (177); it is this reflection that gives structure to the mechanism of theater as a seeing machine.

What Ledoux's engraving reveals is almost an ontological manifestation of what he thinks the theater is. Individuals, seated in the auditorium in the semicircular periphery, see nothing but their own reflections. This is a twist of light paths. The vision of the audience in the theater becomes incorporeal, that is, no longer derived from the position of its body but from the monocular eye at the center of the optical apparatus. No matter where the audiences are, they all see from this imaginary center. Only functioning in this way of seeing is a collective theatrical experience possible. Once the machine is operating, the huge pupil in the middle of the stage facing the auditorium will be the only seeing position, where nothing can be seen except the individuals themselves. In this sense, being both the ones seeing and the ones being seen, individuals in this space are captured and turned into both objects and subjects: invisibility and visibility operate simultaneously.[18] It reminds us that visibility is only possible on a set of predetermined invisibility fulfilled by certain technical conditions. What functions at the very bottom of transparency is namely the hidden opacity.

Thus, the human eye from the center of the curtain reveals the often-concealed dominant power in theaters, the always-hidden mechanism that constructs the optical machine. The same set of optical designs links the *Granitschale* and the theater together. The reflection of the theater that we see from *Coup d'oeil* reveals to us that the stage, which promises unobstructed transparency, is perhaps a one-way mirror. The curtain, which is the same surface of the presentation of visibility, conceals the machine that is modeling us and observing us through the illusion of reunification. The theater sees us.[19] We audiences are captured and turned into the subjects of the community desired from the center of the theater, while our bodies are positioned in uniform, clearly zoned, symmetrical spaces in the periphery with clear boundaries.[20] The *Coup d'oeil* itself is the visual representation of this collective subject—the single representation of this community—constructed in the theater to capture all these natural bodies, turning them into an image. In this eye, barriers are abolished, contractions are absorbed. Just as Badiou understands it, the theater is both transcendent and immanent: it is an art of the collective (57–70).

Upon a series of systematic operations, a practice of community emerges. Badiou claims that "the theatre unavoidably takes the form of an event: it takes place, it happens . . . the theatre is the site of the idea's living appearance" (62–63); it is the process of making-appear. We arrive at the conclusion that the theater is the event of thought; it has a spatial-temporal dimension. The theater is always about being-with; it is about coappearance at the-same-time-in-the-same-place (Nancy, 35). With this understanding, it is not hard to notice that community is always at the center of theater design. When Vitruvius Pollio discusses the plan of the theater, he writes:

> The plan of the theatre itself is to be constructed as follows. Having fixed upon the principal centre, draw a line of circumference equivalent to what is to be the perimeter at the bottom, and in it inscribe four equilateral triangles, at equal distances apart and touching the boundary line of the circle, as the astrologers do in a figure of the twelve signs of the zodiac, when they are making computations from the musical harmony of the stars. (146)

The dimension of coexistence appears when we combine the control machine with the theatrical space, which eventually leads us to the question of what community we wanted to build and what individuals we needed for this community back at the beginning of the Enlightenment.

ON SURVEILLANCE AND COMMUNITY

In December 1784, German periodical *Berlinische Monatsschrift* published a response from Immanuel Kant to the question posed a year earlier: *Was ist Aufklärung?* His response, which later became the motto of the Enlightenment, is well known—"Enlightenment is man's emergence from his self-imposed nonage . . . Dare to know!" (Kant 1963, 3). The concept of *Enlightenment* takes on a suspicious role in Foucault's writing on the same question. As pointed out by Foucault, "Kant defines *Aufklärung* in an almost entirely negative way, as an *Ausgang*, an 'exit,' a 'way out.' . . . In the text on *Aufklärung*, he deals with the question of contemporary reality alone. He is not seeking to understand the present on the basis of a totality or of a future achievement. He is looking for a difference: What difference does today introduce with respect to yesterday?" (Foucault 1984, 34). As noticed by Foucault, this way out described by Kant is rather ambiguous. In Kant's explanation, "Enlightenment must be considered both as a process in which men participate collectively and as an act of courage to be accomplished personally. Men are at once elements and agents of a single process. They may be actors in the process to the extent that they participate in it; and the process occurs to the extent that men decide to be its voluntary actors" (35). What is also problematic in Kant's text is his use of the word "mankind," *Menschheit*. Foucault poses this question to us: "Are we to understand that it involves a change affecting what constitutes the humanity of human beings?" (35). In any case, beneath the answer's deceptive simplicity, it is rather complex. The use of reason must be free and public. But how is a public use of that reason to be assured?

Foucault forthrightly speaks out about the dilemma embedded in the Enlightenment ideology that is still prevalent today: that is, the relationship between the multitude of natural bodies and the single representation of the subject. The question of how to incorporate natural material bodies into a collective image of the whole society was what practitioners of the Enlightenment worked hard to figure out. These endeavors were recorded in the architectural space they tried to build beginning in the late eighteenth century mindful of the fact that architecture offers the material possibilities of being-together. In the process of transforming people, the need of the Enlightenment inevitably took on a surveillance appearance.

As a microcosm of community practice, theater has offered us many details in the operation of this larger machine called society. Crary argues that "though obviously one who sees, an observer is more importantly one who sees within a prescribed set of possibilities, one who is embedded in a system of conventions and limitations" (6). To discuss this in more detail, I will use an example—Boullée's conception of the cenotaph for Newton.

This imaginary cenotaph[21] was designed in 1784 in honor of Isaac Newton, who has long been a symbol of Enlightenment ideals. It was mainly designed as an expansive spherical monument rising up high to complement the light Newton brought to this world that created order and reason. To pay homage to Newton, Boullée admitted that he could not find a better way than to envelop Newton in his own self

(Rosenau, 107). To achieve this, he created an interior that inverted the exterior lighting condition through a light positioned at the center of the sphere, so that the light of the monument at night could resemble the star shining on the planet in the daytime. As explained by Boullée, "This form of lighting the monument is a perfect reproduction and the effect of the stars could not be more brilliant" (107). Likely, Peters writes, "If the eye is the light of the body, then the great star—the sun—as Dante says, is the light of the intelligence" (Peters, 16). There is no doubt that for Boullée, Newton, who decried the shape of the earth, represented the ideal individual of the Enlightenment. The ceno-taph for Newton was a spatial manifestation of the Enlightenment ideology itself.

Like panoramas and theaters, the Enlightenment as a spectator is what this design tells us. In the interior of the cenotaph, Newton's divine system was used to create the sepulchral lamp that lights the tomb. Boullée wanted to give him the "immortal resting place, the Heavens" (107). What he did was to make the interior of the monu-ment a vast sphere so that individuals entering this space could see nothing but a continuous surface out of their reach. No matter which side spectators looked at, there was neither beginning nor end in this curve; the more they looked at it, the larger it appeared.[22] Boullée made the tomb the only material object (107). It was designed to be unap-proachable, which means individuals were asked to stay in the place assigned to them (i.e., the center of the vast space) to maintain an appro-priate distance in order to appreciate this illusion.

It might be appropriate to arrive at the conclusion now that the power that constitutes spectatorship in this designed space, as well as in other binary machines, is specifically the detachment of vision from the position of bodies. Crary believes that the breach between tangi-bility and visuality was an event of the remapping of the body in the nineteenth century.

The loss of touch as a conceptual component of vision meant the un-loosening of the eye from the network of referentiality incarnated in tac-tility and its subjective relation to perceived space. This automatization of sight, occurring in many different domains, was a historical condition for the rebuilding of an observer fitted for the tasks of "spectacular" con-sumption. Not only did the empirical isolation of vision allow its quanti-fication and homogenization but it also enabled the new objects of vision (whether commodities, photographs, to the act of perception itself) to assume a mystified and abstract identity, sundered from any relation to the observer's position within a cognitively unified field. (19)

By detaching vision from touch and projecting/exteriorizing it into the center of buildings, the nineteenth-century designs merge spectatorship and surveillance. Operating upon the dualistic logic of the multitude of natural bodies and the single representation of the subject, theater shares the topology with control machines of the sovereign state. From this we know that ever since the appearance of individuals in history, surveillance has coexisted with pleasure and entertainment. It was never just a modern product solely of the digital age.[23]

As has been discussed in the uniformity of the theatrical space, architecture offers us an environment of the enclosure, a space of co-appearance, "the space in which we live, which draws us out of ourselves, in which the erosion of our lives, our time and our history occurs, the space that claws and gnaws at us" (Foucault and Miskowiec, 23). We do not live in a void but in a heterogeneous space with a set of relations. As Jean-Luc Nancy famously claims, "Being is singularly plural and plurally singular," (28) Being is being-with[24] and being-with is the sharing of space-time (35). Furthermore, he argues:

> If being-with is the sharing of a simultaneous space-time, then it involves a presentation of this space-time as such. In order to say "we," one must present the "here and now" of this "we." Or rather, saying "we" brings about the presentation of a "here and now," however it is determined: as a room, a region, a group of friends, an association, a "people" . . . What is presented in this way, each time, is a stage [scène] on which several [people] can say "I," each on his own account, each in turn. (65)

Being gives itself as singular plural and organizes itself as its own stage in this way (67). There is no society without the spectacle of society, in the sense that society is the spectacle of itself (67).[25]

This condition is discussed in depth by Giorgio Agamben in *Stasis*. The Leviathan represents the paradox between the single representation of people and the multitude of natural bodies.[26] "The gigantic body of the Leviathan formed by innumerable tiny figures is not a reality, however artificial, but an optical illusion—'a meer phantasme'" (Agamben 2015, 38–41). If we approach it more closely, we will find that the Leviathan is nothing but an artifact, an automaton and optical device that shares the same topology with theater. Sovereign is an artificial person whose unity is the effect of an optical contraption or a mask.[27] The same optical illusion in the architectural space after the late eighteenth century contributes to the collective representation of the singular plural spectator conceived by the Enlightenment community.[28] Individuals, unlike what the Enlightenment ideology perceives, are part of the spectacle of the society itself.

Why does architectural space matter? What are the relations of political to the spatial and temporal factors? In the words of Samuel Weber, politics is related to "the organization of space through the assigning of places, and to the organization of time through the regulation of past, present and future"[29] (Weber, 716). Architecture, as established codes of articulation, visualizes the grids within which actions and interpretations are situated. Architectural space of the past will serve as an interface for our understanding of the present as well as the future. As Felicity D. Scott notes, "Design involves projections, a throwing forward of images and ideas, utopian or otherwise. Architecture thus opens onto a future, but the nature of that future is under question" (Scott, 280).

Bernard E. Harcourt reminds us that we lack the presentation that would help us better understand how contemporary neoliberalism distributes power and how the digitalization of neoliberalism affects those distributions of relations; we are faced with the problem that neither spectacle nor surveillance was fitted to the present (Harcourt, 4).[30] Instead of being stuck with or completely dissolving these two concepts, we should perhaps notice the complexities in the blending of surveillance and entertainment and conceive them as the sites of struggle. By exhibiting the different layers of meanings of the architectural heterotopias,[31] and by detailing the ambiguities between reality and virtuality, we may better acknowledge the dangers as well as possibilities in our age.

Yijun Sun is a Ph.D. candidate in the Department of Communication at the University of Massachusetts at Amherst. Her research focuses on media histories and media theories. Yijun is writing a dissertation on the media archaeology of vacuum tubes in telecommunication history.

Notes

I would like to extend my deepest thanks to Burcu Baykurt and Briankle G. Chang for their guidance and encouragement throughout the writing of this paper. My thanks also go to Henry Geddes, Shawn Shimpach, and Timothy M. Rohan who have read and offered helpful suggestions on an earlier draft of this work. A draft of this paper was presented at 4S-EASST Conference 2020. I'm grateful to the anonymous readers and the editors of *Cultural Critique* for their helpful comments on this work.

1. Salt was then a very valuable and essential commodity on which the heavy tax served as an important source of income for the French king.

2. Ledoux's design went through several stages as his plan developed. It was in the second plan that he designed this semicircular complex. Based on this he came up with a complete plan of the "Ideal City of Chaux," which was never built other than the diameter and semicircular buildings of the saltworks.

3. Kaufmann exalts Kant as the founding father of modern bourgeois society. Vidler notes in "The Ledoux Effect" that "where the Frankfurt school sociologists were already looking at the paradoxes and problematics of Kantian idealism, and Cassirer himself was struggling with the difficulty of reconciling Rousseau and Kant in essays published in 1932, Kaufmann apparently blithely ignored such questions in favor of a generalized appeal to Rousseau/Kant as signifying an Enlightenment unified enough to provide an intellectual base, both for Ledoux, and for his interpretation" (22).

4. Henry Lefebvre in *Toward an Architecture of Enjoyment* argues for the differentiation between "abstract utopia" and "concrete utopia." He believes that the "abstract utopia" was inspired by philosophical and cosmological considerations that projected a presentation of space into the urban core, while the "concrete utopia" was located in spatial practice that made a space of representation take shape (141). Similarly, Samuel Weber argues that "there is a difference in being 'political' at the level of propositional statement (i.e., making declarations, signing petitions, etc.) and being political at the level of the established codes of articulation to which one is necessarily submitted, but which are also susceptible to change" (714).

5. Adorno, for example, sees Kantian autonomy as a double-edged sword. He questions the implications of appeals to "reason" that had exhibited their "dark side" of the bourgeois society.

6. In the pages that follow, I intend to argue that the architectural space constructed after the Enlightenment offers a material and instrumental perspective to reflect on surveillance and community. My purpose is not to offer an alternative narration of architecture history in any sense. Architectures discussed here serve as technical occasions, material apparatuses that make the assemblage of space-time coexistence possible and in turn capture and transform living beings into subjects. This article's discussion is in line with Agamben, taking architecture not only

as single-authored art piece but, more importantly, as abstract machine that exists as the material trace of cultural practices. It takes an external instead of an internal perspective of architecture.

7. Vidler notes that Ledoux's discourse is more moderate than Bentham's model in the sense that the panopticon brought the symbolic presence of power to a material functionalization of visual control. He believes Ledoux's design showed a blend of social and political idealism, which stood between the prepanoptic symbolism of surveillance and the proto-Rousseauist model of community (2002, 56). Rousseau's ideas about communities have been widely critiqued for being proto-totalitarian and providing the foundation for nationalism even though he never endorsed it. This essay argues for an understanding of community deriving from Nancy, which will be discussed in the latter part of the essay.

8. For a discussion on Galileo's telescope and the visibility and invisibility in the process of becoming-media, see, for example, Vogl's "Becoming-Media, Galileo's Telescope."

9. More details can be found in Forster's writings: "The first panorama to be seen in Paris was executed under Foucault's direction; it represents a view of this immense city: the spectator is seemingly raised on the roof platform of the central pavilion of the Tuileries; from this point his view encompasses an immense horizon containing not only Paris but also part of its surrounding countryside; he dominants everything, seems to glide over it, his eyes follow the embankments of the Seine, move through the trees of the Tuileries Gardens, or wander through the trees and squares; and wherever he fixes his gaze he is struck by the truthfulness with which the whole ensemble and the details of this immense perspective have been rendered" (1983, 68).

10. "Panoramas were patented by Robert Barker in 1787 and within a few years became the most sensational commercial attraction after theaters and fairs of various kinds" (Forster, 67).

11. Forster writes: "It is again the conjunction of topography with theatrical potential that kindled Schinkel's interest, rather than the vicarious satisfaction of wanderlust and a mild curiosity about faraway places" (1983, 68–69).

12. Forster argues that "the tempo of early modern life and the desire for an instant visual grasp of complex rapports prompted Schinkel to impart panoramic qualities to the static relationship among buildings" (75).

13. The *Granitschale* was an important artifact due to the complex background stories of its geological origin, its transport to the city, and its process of transformation. It was ordered by King Friedrich Wilhelm III in 1826. Schinkel proposed to locate the basin in the rotunda of the Altes Museum, which had been under construction since 1824. And for a variety of technical and aesthetic reasons, the *Granitschale* was to find its place in front of the Altes Museum, raised on a pedestal in the Lustgarten (Forster 2018, 138). The *Granitschale* was the form of artifact Schinkel used to seek a reconciliation between architecture and nature, which significantly added to the "topographical *imaginaire*" (126).

14. The basin was grounded into shape and polished to a mirrorlike quality on the eastern side of the Altes Museum that took as long as two and a half years. This whole process became a public spectacle even before its final installation a year later (Forster 2018, 140).

15. For more on the image, seeing image, and subject, see Mondzain, "What Does Seeing an Image Mean?"

16. Badiou writes: "There is a political theatricality, or a politics of theatricality, which comes together around the figure of the rally" (70).

17. Badiou writes: "The theatre, when it takes place, is a representation of the idea: What the theatre shows is the tension between the transcendence and the immanence of the idea. This is the only subject of the theatre" (57–58).

18. More discussions on the intersection between visibility and invisibility can be found in Chang's "Seeing Goddess in Typhoons" and his recent translation "An Interview with Marie-José Mondzain: What is an Image?" For example: "According to Mondzain, images are not visual objects we may or may not see; rather they are the site where the visible and its invisibility crisscross each other in opening the field of presence. Images, as Mondzain says in the interview, are cracks or leaks in being. They are where lights first come in and where man and beings are born to each other in their being-in-the world, that is, in their truth" (2019, 483).

19. Here I intentionally use these wordings to engage with Kittler's discussion on digital technology. As Winthrop-Young Geoffrey beautifully puts it, "Operating systems, especially those with names like 'Windows', promise unobstructed transparency but are in fact one-way mirrors. Like invisible police investigators examining a suspect, the computer sees us; looking at the computer, we only see ourselves" (77).

20. By saying this, I do not intend to make a sharp division of subject and object here but instead focus on discussing a new subjective position that merged spectatorship and surveillance on its dual operations on the concrete corporeality of bodies and the abstract surface of images. In line with Crary, I argue that the mechanism of this subjective position operates on the arrangement of vision, space, and body.

21. It is never a fulfilled design that is totally visionary.

22. As explained by Boullée, "The form of the interior of this monument is, as you can see, that of a vast sphere. The center of gravity is reached by an opening in the base on which the Tomb is placed. The unique advantage of this form is that from whichever side we look at it (as in nature) we see only a continuous surface which has neither beginning nor end and the more we look at it, the larger it appears. This form has never been utilized and it is the only one appropriate to this monument, for its curve ensures that the onlooker cannot approach what he is looking at; he is forced as if by one hundred different circumstances outside his control, to remain in the place assigned to him and which, since it occupies the centre, keeps him at a sufficient distance to contribute to the illusion. He delights in it, without being able to destroy the effect by wanting to come too close in order

to satisfy his empty curiosity. He stands alone and his eyes can behold nothing but the immensity of the sky. The tomb is the only material object" (Rosenau, 107).

23. A relevant discussion on the blend of theater, performance, and digital surveillance, including drones, CCTV cameras, GPS tracking systems, medical surveillance equipment, and a host of other commercially available technologies, can be seen in Morrison, *Discipline and Desire: Surveillance Technologies in Performance*. Discussion on surveillance in modern society and new surveillance technologies can also be found in, for example, Lyon's *Electronic Eye: The Rise of Surveillance Society*. Studies of surveillance and the overhanging gaze of drones can be found in chapters of Chamayou's *A Theory of the Drone*.

24. In the human condition, Nancy reveals, Being is being separate from one another, and this separation is at the center of sharing. This does not in any sense indicate a failure of the unification of preexisting individuals but is the very condition of the existence of individuals. "We are only individuals as a collective" (Krämer, 53). To put it in another way, "It is the separation that makes community itself possible" (53). The community itself is this "with," this thirdness of mediality.

25. Many more identical expressions can be found in Nancy's discussions on this question. For example: "The theater as the place of the symbolic-imaginary appropriation of collective existence, appearing to us as the 'one' presentation of being-together, yet as a presentation where the condition for its possibility is the irreducible and institutive distance of representation" (71).

26. For a discussion of the optical unconscious of Hobbes's *Leviathan*, see, for example, Reinhardt, "Vision's Unseen: On Sovereignty, Race, and the Optical Unconscious."

27. As Agamben writes, "The unification of the multitude of citizens in a single person is something like a perspectival illusion; political representation is only an optical representation" (2015, 41).

28. Community is understood as this "distant closeness"; it is this matrix of sharing and communication that presupposes and reinforces the idea of separation. In line with Krämer, communication is not only the understanding of ideas. It takes on a more fundamental role in our social being, in the sense that it simultaneously bridges and maintains differences between heterogeneous worlds (16). "The medium neither annihilates the distance between the sender and the receiver nor enables any unmediated 'contact' between them; rather, it establishes a connection despite and in the distance that separates them" (23). What the claims of architecture in the aim of transforming people revealed is this dilemma of ambiguity embedded in the community itself—does it lead individuals toward emancipation or alienation? This philosophy on mediality based on community-building reveals a basic divide that constitutes our very existence as communal beings, as well as the effort to bridge the unbridgeable as a collective agent. Meanwhile, it shows us that the immaterial ideas are transmissible only through embodiment and incarnation.

29. Instead of a consensual understanding of the question of what is meant by "political," Samuel Weber suggests asking the following questions: "Is the political necessarily tied to the state? To society? Is it primarily a question of Power? Of the Common Good? The General Will? Community? Is it manifest primarily in 'action'? In strategies? In policies? Is it necessarily bound up with 'subjects,' in either the philosophical, grammatical, or social sense of the word? What is its relation to spatial and temporal factors: to the organization of space through the assigning of places, and to the organization of time through the regulation of past, present, and future?" (716).

30. He therefore suggests a third form of power relation beyond the classic form of spectacle and surveillance—the exhibition. Harcourt believes that the exhibition surpassed spectacle and surveillance and that we as digital persons give ourselves up voluntarily in a mad frenzy of disclosure (11).

31. Foucault distinguishes "utopias" from "heterotopias." Utopias represent society itself brought to perfection or its reverse; they are not real arrangements with spaces. Heterotopias, on the other side, are both real and unreal. They constitute a sort of counter-arrangement of realities through their virtuality (Foucault and Miskowiec, 3). This essay argues that the utopian architectures constitute this kind of real and effective heterotopia space that has reconstitutive power over reality in their virtuality. In line with Foucault, heterotopias, in relation to the rest of space, have a function that takes place between two opposite poles. One is to create a space of illusion that reveals how real space is more illusory. The other is to form another space, as in another real space (6).

Works Cited

Agamben, Giorgio. 2009. *What is An Apparatus? And Other Essays*. Translated by David Kishik and Stefan Pedatella. Stanford: Stanford University Press.

———. 2015. *Stasis: Civil War as a Political Paradigm*. Translated by Nicholas Heron. Stanford: Stanford University Press.

Badiou, Alain, and Nicolas Truong. 2015. *In Praise of Theatre*. Translated by Andrew Bielski. Cambridge: Policy Press.

Chamayou, Grégoire. 2015. *A Theory of the Drone*. Translated by Janet Lloyd. New York: New Press.

Chang, Briankle. 2019. "An Interview with Marie-José Mondzain: What Is an Image?" *Inter-Asia Cultural Studies* 20, no. 3:483–86.

———. 2018. "Seeing Goddess in Typhoons." *Differences: A Journal of Feminist Cultural Studies* 29, no. 3:1–32.

Crary, Jonathan. 1990. *Techniques of the Observer: On Vision and Modernity in the Nineteenth Century*. Cambridge, Mass.: MIT Press.

Deleuze, Gilles. 1992. "Postscript on the Societies of Control." *October* 59:3–7.

Foucault, Michel. 2012. *Discipline and Punish: The Birth of the Prison*. Translated by Alan Sheridan. New York: Vintage.

———. 1984. "What Is Enlightenment?" In *The Foucault Reader*, edited by Paul Rabinow, 32–50. New York: Pantheon.

Foucault, Michel, and Jay Miskowiec. 1986. "Of Other Spaces." *Diacritics* 16, no. 1:22–27.

Forster, Kurt W. 1983. "Schinkel's Panoramic Planning of Central Berlin." *Modulus: the University of Virginia School of Architecture Review* 16:62–77.

———. 2018. *Schinkel: A Meander through His Life and Work*. Badel: Birkhäuser.

Geoffrey, Winthrop-Young. 2011. *Kittler and the Media*. Cambridge: Polity Press.

Harcourt, Bernard E. 2014. "Digital Security in the Expository Society: Spectacle, Surveillance, and Exhibition in the Neoliberal Age of Big Data." APSA 2014 Annual Meeting Paper *Columbia Public Law Research Paper* no. 14–404. https://scholarship.law.columbia.edu/faculty_scholarship/1865.

Kant, Immanuel. 1963. "What Is Enlightenment?" *On History*, 3–10. Translated by Lewis White Beck. Indianapolis: Bobbs-Merrill.

Krämer, Sybille. 2015. *Medium, Messenger, Transmission: An Approach to Media Philosophy*. Translated by Anthony Enns. Amsterdam: Amsterdam University Press.

Ledoux, Claude-Nicolas, and Anthony Vidler. 1983. *Architecture de C.N. Ledoux, Premier Volume*. New York: Princeton Architectural Press.

Lefebvre, Henri. 2014. *Toward an Architecture of Enjoyment*. Translated by Robert Bononno. Minneapolis: University of Minnesota Press.

Lemagny, Jean-Claude. 1968. *Visionary Architects: Boullée, Ledoux, Lequeu*. Houston: University of St. Thomas.

Lyon, David. 1994. *Electronic Eye: The Rise of Surveillance Society*. Minneapolis: University of Minnesota Press.

Mondzain, Marie-José. 2010. "What Does Seeing an Image Mean?" *Journal of Visual Culture* 9, no. 3:307–15.

Morrison, Elise. 2016. *Discipline and Desire: Surveillance Technologies in Performance*. Ann Arbor: University of Michigan Press.

Nancy, Jean-Luc. 2000. *Being Singular Plural*. Translated by Robert D. Richardson and Anne E. O'Byrne. Stanford: Stanford University Press.

Peters, John. 2010. "Introduction: Friedrich Kittler's Light Show." In *Optical Media: Berlin Lectures 1999*, edited by Friedrich Kittler, 1–17. Translated by Anthony Enns. Cambridge: Polity Press.

Pollio, Vitruvius. 1914. *Vitruvius: The Ten Books on Architecture*. Translated by Morris Hicky Morgan. Cambridge, Mass.: Harvard University Press.

Reinhardt, Mark. 2017. "Vision's Unseen: On Sovereignty, Race, and the Optical Unconscious." In *Photography and the Optical Unconscious*, edited by Shawn Michelle Smith and Sharon Sliwinski, 174–221. Durham: Duke University Press.

Rosenau, Helen. 1976. *Boullée and Visionary Architecture, Including Boullée's Architecture, Essay on Art*. New York: Harmony.

Scott, Felicity D. 2007. *Architecture or Techno-utopia: Politics after Modernism*. Cambridge, Mass.: MIT Press.

Vidler, Anthony. 1990. *Claude-Nicolas Ledoux: Architecture and Social Reform at the End of the Ancien Régime*. Cambridge, Mass.: MIT Press.

——. 2002. "The Ledoux Effect: Emil Kaufmann and the Claims of Kantian Autonomy." *Perspecta* 33:16–29.

Vogl, Joseph. 2008. "Becoming-Media: Galileo's Telescope." *Grey Room* 29:14–25.

Weber, Samuel, Simon Wortham, and Gary Hall. 2002. "Responding: A Discussion with Samuel Weber." *South Atlantic Quarterly* 101, no. 3:695–724.

SEEING . . . WHAT?
FOUR IMAGES AND THEIR (IN)VISIBILITY

Briankle G. Chang

To see, is it simply looking?

—Marie-José Mondzain, *What Is an Image?*

There are many things we see and cannot fail to see, but only at a few of them we go on to look. That which we saw before may or may not be seen again, and that which we looked at earlier may or may not reappear and attract our attention. Seeing and looking thus complicate each other, circumscribing and (de)fining, that is, making finite a field of the visible, which because of this complication is always haunted by what exceeds it, by what remains, now or then, invisible. It is out of this complication that vision unfolds as images of further folds and further images. Surely and always, to see is not only to see what is readily open to view but also to cross to the invisible, which, as just mentioned, haunts the things seen and circumscribes the visible. In other words, because seeing is always (a) crossing (to) the (in)visible, the image seen in each instance, which is always of the visible, necessarily frustrates or foils itself the moment it is materialized. Consequently, looking may turn out to be a mere side effect of seeing and, as a side effect, matters little in the end.

We see things, and we see images. To see things is to see them as images. And to see images is to open ourselves to the world in which we can also see our own images amid all the things there to see. The world, we could say, comes to see itself through us; it sees itself as much as we see it. It is like a web of fluttering images: by ourselves seeing, by ourselves looking.

To see and to look, we and the things we see must already be in the visible. Moreover, thrown to and trapped in the visible, we appear as images to ourselves much as images show themselves to us on their own. But where exactly are we when we see things? And where are we when we look at them? In the clarity of being, as common sense suggests? In the opacity of nonbeing, as artists and philosophers recognize? What is the difference, if any, between seeing images and looking at them? Moreover, in what way and to what extent does it makes sense to say, as I did above, that looking is secondary to seeing? These questions, still ill-defined notwithstanding, launch us on a search for a better understanding of the complication of seeing and looking, an understanding that will help make sense of the claim I wish to make: to see is not simply to look; it is to see the invisible. In the following, I look at four examples, each of which is a moment of seeing in which something can also be looked at. An example is an exception, an instance taken out of a generality, a token of a type, as it were, upon which it sheds light and by virtue of which a general and generalizable idea can be grasped more clearly. A good example exemplifies and, by exemplifying, something otherwise obscure may be unclouded. By looking at four images in turn, I intend to show how images work and, therefore, what images can say (or fail to say) about seeing when we look at them closely.

DUCK OR RABBIT

The eye sees what it wants to see.

—Claude Monet

If an image is there, then . . . vision comes to take up things.

—John Sallis

A simple line drawing may appear to look like two things, a rabbit and a duck, as in figure 1. The same occurs with a Necker cube and many other pictures as well. The experience of and ability to see one thing in multiple ways is called "aspect-seeing."[1] It is something we undergo and perform without much trouble and with little afterthought.

The key point to note in cases of aspect-seeing is that the picture in question cannot be two images at the same time: one sees *either* a rabbit *or* a duck, not both at once.[2] To see a duck/rabbit as a rabbit is

Figure 1. Rabbit Duck Image.

to be blind to it as a duck, and the reverse is the case as well. To see, as is commonly recognized, is to see something *as* something and, for this very reason, is also to become blind to what is apparently visible but is nonetheless not seen. Seeing, in other words, is fundamentally "seeing aspect(s)," and it means, as just said, suffering from a certain aspect-blindness, in which "aspect-dawning"—the emergence and grasping of an alternative to the perceived aspect—lies in wait in constituting the visual experiences in full. Knowingly or not, we see what the mind chooses for us what is there to see, while keeping at bay what is admittedly also visible. As Stanley Cavell remarks,

> We may say that the rabbit aspect is hidden from us when we fail to see it. But what hides it is then obviously not the picture (that reveals it), but our (prior) way of taking it, namely in its duck-aspect. What hides one aspect is another aspect, something at the same level. So we might say: what hides the mind is not the body but the mind itself—his his, or mine his, and *contrawise*.[3]

It is the mind, not the eye, that sees; the eye merely senses what the mind has already grasped. At the same time, however, the mind's eye is also the cause of a certain blindness, a typhlosis to the aspect that is "at the same level" but is momentarily hidden. The principle of seeing therefore complicates the reality of vision by its own seemly activities. Indeed, not only is there always more available to see than meets the eye in the instance, but there might also be less behind or in what one sees than what unmistakably appears to be out there. We see, somehow, by not seeing, and we bring ourselves to look at what we, in some way, have already seen or detected.

If seeing always means seeing aspect(s), then it also means that seeing implies seeing more than one aspect of the object in view. When seeing a tabletop, for example, one also apperceives the underside and other parts of the table, even if and when they are blocked from sight. Seeing is as active as it is passive, driving as well as driven by the desire to see beyond the visible. It is to discover what the eye may succeed in registering but nonetheless fails to capture or identify. This explains why it may take a bit of trying before one can discern the rabbit *and/or* the duck in an image that one also recognizes to be unchanged. The same happens when one views a Necker cube or other wire frames of optical illusion as pointed out earlier. Extending the idea further, we can say that it is *an* aspect of the world that first connects us to the world, a connection that is itself *an* aspect of our relation to the world at large.

Recall that I described the rabbit / duck image as a simple line drawing. However it is perceived and whatever it is taken to be, a wayward line forms an image, bringing off against a blank background a certain uniformity that cannot be obtained independently of the uniformity of an image. Exceeding the form, the calm surface of representation, the image is actively *imagined*, yielding a recognizable presence out of absence. An image, a figure, suddenly shines forth. A rabbit, but also a duck.[4]

When an image is operative, it does something that writing and speech cannot. Nonnarrative and presemiotic, an image signifies directly, that is, by the immediate impression it imparts. Whether strange, interesting, recognizable, or otherwise—and regardless of how and why it affects the viewer—an image drawn leads us beyond the lines that compose it. In *drawing*, says Jean-Luc Nancy, there takes place the opening of form, namely, "exactly what must *not* have exactly been given in a form in order to form itself."[5] In the lines drawn, a gesture, a desire, a concern, an anticipation, is in formation but is not (yet) formed. "That a form comes" is drawing's truth and principle, and this truth implies "a way of being exposed to what comes, to an unexpected occurrence, or to a surprise that no prior formality will have been able to precede or perform."[6] A drawing—an image in potentia—performs what is to take form by it, by what is yet to be formed. With a duck, a rabbit comes smiling, and vice versa. Is this not what the painter tries to achieve when they draw? Is that what they wish to see in drawing? Is this not also what we, the viewers, hope to see when we look at the lines traced or drawn? Is this not, finally, the very source of the pleasure of drawing? To see is to draw (out) the invisible, the not-yet-visible. To draw is to give the invisible a presence, a form, a face. In drawing and in looking at what is drawn, one sees the invisible, the only thing that is worth seeing and awaits to be seen.

Is seeing simply looking?[7] There are plenty of things we can see and wish to look at, but one may hesitate to say what may actually be seen when we turn to look at them. With one thing drawn, other drawings may emerge. To someone who has never seen or been shown a duck, the rabbit/duck drawing cannot be a picture of a duck. But to someone who knows neither duck nor rabbit, the image can resemble whatever they take it to be: a paleontological crustacean, a badly damaged flower, a plainly meaningless ink wire, or many other things. And all these possibilities may change each time they look at it and in ways no one can predict. Image must be imagined, as said earlier, but it may set imagination free and trump itself as imagined.

Do we really see what we are looking at? Can we fail to look at what is manifestly visible? One can look into a mirror and see one's own eyes. But one can never see one's own eyes *seeing*.[8] The pair of eyes we see in the mirror is but an image, one hardly different from any other objects in our visual field. An image of an eye does not and cannot see; it is something that is *seen* rather than *seeing*, as just noted. Indeed, it is this *seeing eye* that sees *absolutely*, and seeing absolutely, that is, freely and from a separate place, it drives the eye and forces it to open. Perhaps it is this *seeing eye* in us—the mind's eye, as we say— that every act of seeing, always keeping itself in reserve and already escaping our gaze, wishes to see and, in its frustrated state, decides for us what we end up looking at. To see is not simply to look, for to look is to stop short of netting what seeing will have (but also may not have) made manifest. When something is seen, we see and do not see it. To see, after all, is (yet) to see the invisible.[9]

ZEBRA STRIPES AT A DISTANCE

See and to be seen.

—Ben Jonson, *Epithalamion*

Wildlife biologists have impressive eyesight, aptly sensitive to movements and shapes in the surroundings while scouting in the field. Not only do they watch animals and nature with more care than we do, but they also ask informed questions before zooming in to look at their targets that an untrained eye would likely miss. When they see the stripes on zebras, for instance, they wonder why equids have them on their coat and why these stripes are shaped the way they are (and other related questions).[10] More impressive still, they go to great lengths to bring home firsthand materials through which amateur nature lovers can learn about the subject matter in ways that curiosity or ecological consciousness alone does not match.

In an interesting study in wildlife ecology, a team of scientists shares with readers a suite of field photographs showing, as its title indicates, how a zebra appears to humans, zebras, lions, and hyenas respectively[11] (see figure 2). Taken in broad daylight, these pictures enable readers to see how a zebra would appear to us humans, relative to what a lion and a hyena would see under the same circumstances. In view of the four images, laid out one next to the other, it seems clear that under photopic conditions, we humans have a perceivably sharper vision of a zebra than lions, hyenas, or zebras do, when viewing the zebra from a distance of 6.4 meters in the African plains.

Photography is widely used in scientific research across disciplines. "Copying" nature, photochemically, digitally, or otherwise, photographs keep what does not last and bring near what is far away, providing direct evidence that illustrates and supports research findings with force well beyond what is testimonial or narrative in nature. Through the photographs, we can see, so we think rightly, what the scientist-photographers see or have seen and are thus led to lend credence to the research writing that they support and in turn anchors them. Seeing is believing, as we say: to the extent that scientific inquiry is essentially ocularcentric—arguably scopophilic at root— photographic images respond directly to science's desire for the truth

Figure 2. Images of a solitary zebra at a distance of 6.4 meters as it might appear to a human, zebra, lion, and spotted hyena under photopic conditions. Note: As shown, stripes are detectable to all species at this distance. The caption is as it appears in the source. Photo by Tim Caro.

behind appearance, at the same time satisfying the demand for objectivity we expect of scientists. The strength of photographic evidence, in the case of this zebra study as in numerous others, appears as strong as the inclusion of field data and is as effective in gaining readers' confidence in the study's value and validity.

Snapped in situ of a lone zebra in the African grassland, the four photos presented by the researchers appear to speak for themselves. Looking at them side by side, one will have no trouble appreciating why they are included in the report. But their purported evidentiary force notwithstanding, do they really support the claim made by the scientists? On what ground and in what sense are we to understand that these images represent "human view," "zebra view," "lion view," and "hyena view," as the labels indicate? Indeed, how do wildlife biologists, looking at and taking pictures of these animals much as we do, come to know that these images reflect the views of lions, zebras, and hyenas, whose vision and cognition most of us know little about?

It goes without saying that the four photos in the frame, labeled respectively as views of human, zebra, lion, and hyena, are views made *for* and *by* humans rather than *by* the animals under study *for* themselves. Lions, hyenas, and zebras do not take pictures and do not use photos the way we do: even if they did, there remains the question of how they would view the pictures they take and how they would view them when they (re)appear in print, on a screen, or anywhere other than in the viewfinder where the shots were first taken. After all, photography is a uniquely human practice, and regarding photographic images as "iconic," namely, realistic and transparent, is predicated more on sociosemiotic conventions than on physiology, neurochemistry in the brain, optics, or the like. While we may debate whether lions, hyenas, and zebras are as visually centered as we are, it is an unwarranted leap from the belief in and knowledge about animal vision to the claim that "*as shown*, stripes are detectable to all species." In any event, the "points of view" enabling the four photos are that of a camera, which sees a zebra on behalf of the researcher and, by extension, us the readers. It is not and cannot be the view taken by, or available to, the three animals in question.

Lions, hyenas, and zebras roam the African plains. They watch one another and wait for the opportunity to either strike or flee. Moreover, from where they are, not only can they see us watching them and pointing what we call a "camera" at them, but they can also see us taking pictures of them or something else in the vicinity. But it is not certain what we see when looking at a zebra bears any resemblance to what they see when looking at the same zebra, still less what (and how) they would see (in) a *photograph* of a zebra. At issue here is the (im)possibility of taking the point of view of others, especially those as alien as animals in the wild, despite the fact that we tend to regard photographs as self-explanatory and self-evident.

As is commonly understood, the "point of view" deployed in photography is predicated on the simple principle "one point, one view," dictated by what is called "central projection." Accordingly, since one point in space corresponds only to one view opened up thereby at a particular moment, a view of an object implies one position in space, which cannot be taken by two individuals at the same time and cannot be taken by the same individual at different times, however close they are to one another.[12] How and what the scientist-photographer sees in the field and subsequently captures with their camera at any given moment is tied to the condition of that moment and the instrument in use in that instance, and therefore it cannot be (re)produced by another photographic act, however hard the photographer tries to reproduce the prior capture. Since photography writes the light, and light comes to pass and changes unfailingly, a photograph is always *of* the past, of the object no longer present, and thus the presence of an absence. As long as point of view cannot be replicated, the four photographs taken by the biologist remain short of achieving their intended purposes. The great care with which they are collected on site merely serves to attest to our unquestioning belief in the verity of visual data rather than reflecting how things are actually perceived by various kinds of viewers (let alone our animal others).

Related to, and no less troubling than the problem of point of view, is the further complication created by the incompatibility of viewing dispositions as it bears upon *looking at* photographs, which, like picture taking, is a context-specific, situational-driven act. A photograph of a thing is an image—a mode, a nonfluctuating aspect, we could say—of the thing; it is not the thing itself and is certainly not made by the thing photographed, although one may resemble the other in some respect. Moreover, like picture *taking*, *seeing* or *looking at* a picture is the act of a viewer who is seeing or looking at the image, not someone else or another act. Accordingly, a photograph of a zebra is a picture of a zebra, a technology-dependent one at that; it is not a zebra in person and is not produced by a zebra or anyone else, although it may look to us like a zebra. And, like seeing or looking at any image, looking at a photograph of a zebra is tied to the viewer and the conditions in which the viewing takes place: conditions that are irreproducible, however approximate or similar they seem to the original perception.

Although requiring no special training, looking at and making sense of photographs like those in figure 2 in reality are complex acts. Enabled by competence entirely conventional in nature, they are at root an exercise in anthropocentric bias: while we, the readers, are looking at pictures of a zebra taken a while ago in Africa by someone we hardly know and are doing so in print or on a screen here and now, a lion or a hyena was actually looking at living prey there and then and doing so in their own nonhuman way. As Thibaut De Myer observes, "The fact that we would only see the results through human eyes would already encompass a bias: we would only see the point of view of the lion through the point of view of a human, whereas the lion directly perceives the content of its perception."[13] After all, the three photos in figure 2 described respectively as "lion view," "zebra view," and "hyena view" are artifactual, two-dimensional representations produced to document the "facts" by a research act and, by the time they become available for our viewing, are already several removes from the original scene. Photographs are proven documents across multiple fields of inquiry, adopted for their demonstrative power when evidence or proof is needed. But, in this case, they end up demonstrating the scientist's trusted method of data collection rather than animal vision as such. Photographs do not lie, as we say time and again. But the truths they tell are of our own making; they are not those of the animals. If photographs tell the truth, the truth told stays with and within our telling it. It is not told and cannot be told by animals, however we picture them.

When images are present, they do things that writing and speech cannot.[14] However, as we consider the photos in figure 2 against the captions, the images and words can be seen to work at cross-purposes: the words on their own say much more than what the pictures do and can do, and the four photographs, taken as such, do not and cannot support what the captions say in that they mean something other than what the scientist uses them to mean. Strictly speaking, lenses and optical mechanisms do not *see* anything; they write the light, not words, which are to be *read*, not merely to be seen or looked at. To see zebras and lions in the wild, one goes to Africa and looks for them. To find out how lions and hyenas see zebras, one begins by watching the former as they watch the latter. Zebras, lions, and hyenas are all there for us to see and to look at closely. But seeing a zebra as a lion does is not something that photographs of a zebra can do or prove. Indeed, to see as an other does, to see an object in the way that the other does, is strictly impossible. Anthropocentrism aside, the belief that we can see an animal as another animal does implies, among other things, a reduction in the differences between ourselves and the animal other, a difference that obliterates individuality, the multiple viewing dispositions and variable sense-making activities involved, as well as the conditions under which the viewing occurs. Further still, not only is it unjust to others like us, but it is also unjust to the animal others, whose life is more often than not in danger when we put it in the crosshairs.

To see—is it simply looking? We can see things but fail to look at them, and we may look at things without seeing anything in particular. We can look at a photograph and see, so we think, what the photographer must be seeing or looking at. But can we see what a zebra sees, even if it appears to stare at the same thing that we are looking at? Looking at the photo on the upper right in figure 2, we have reasons to think that a zebra is looking back at the photographer taking the shot. However, while we can reasonably assume the zebras can see everything in our field of vision, one might still wonder precisely what they see. For instance, do they see the camera held by the photographer? Do they see it as a camera, or as a chunk of mud, part of a dead elephant's body, the extremity of the photographer's arm, or anything else? Moreover, when we realize that we are being stared back at, that is, when we are in their eyeshot (which touches us and against which we have little protection), we might feel strangely anxious, even jarringly unsettled—all the more so when we do not know what it is they are seeing or looking at. It is in this uncertainty in the look of an other that one faces the fundamental question that haunts the reality of vision: How can we know for sure what others see? How can we know for sure whether what others see out there looks the same to them as to us, assuming that we are all looking at the same scene? If this question could be raised with regard to our fellow human beings, how can one ever say of a photo that it shows how an animal sees another animal? The research on a zebra's stripes by wildlife biologists is interesting and their effort praiseworthy. But that should not stop us from being skeptical about their claims. Always immanent to the search for truth, a certain skepticism might be in order, even if it mars the findings that appear welcome at first.

Seeing is not simply looking. Although they unfold in their own way, seeing and looking work in tandem to cast a wide field of visibility. Thus opens a world that is ours, but that world is also more than human, one that we share with others of many kinds. When we look at this world, it also looks back at us in that we map ourselves in it, in that we see ourselves through the others whom, we recognize, also see from within the same visual field. Seeing is premised upon seeing oneself seeing, and it orbits around ourselves being seen at the same time. This return look of the other, which involves the self as one among many viewers in the scene, opens and anchors what is called the "gaze"—a look at us that is more than our own, one that enables us to see precisely because it, always and already part of the picture we see, is no more our own than of an other, who is also the self. Image, photographic or not, is a crack in being, as Mondzain remarks.[15] It is a hole in the whole that, keeping at a distance what it at once brings close, lets out the light before the world and configures its presence. Inasmuch as there is a crack in being that opens (us) to what we then see, making sense of what we see is forever haunted by what is excluded from vision by what is prevented from becoming fully visible.

To see is to (want to) see the invisible; it is to see what is there *invisibly.* It is to see what is hidden but is also nevertheless in plain sight. Wildlife biologists have good eyesight, as demonstrated by the fine photos they take. In the wild, they are capable of detecting more things than we are. But, like us, they cannot see the invisible. In the wild, we can follow the biologists and watch animals watching us. But we cannot really tell what the animals see when they watch us. More likely than not, our field of vision is but one theater of the visible among many, that our point of view is but one method (meta-hodos), or way (hodos), of looking and of seeing among many possible paths or viewpoints. Looking at the photos of a zebra taken by a wildlife biologist, we face the enigma of vision, a bottomless wanting-to-see, thanks to which zebras are made to stand still, and we think we can see like a lion.

A DOUGHNUT IN THE SKY

The whole universe disappears if neither circumscribability nor image exists.

—Patriach Nikephoros, *Antirrhetics*, I, 244 D

Entering and exiting, that is what makes the image: appearing and disappearing.

—Jean-Luc Nancy, *The Ground of the Image*

Whereas wildlife biologists observe nature and animals and study the interaction between them, astronomers look deep into space and wonder what lies beyond the observable sky. Aided by mighty vision machines unmatched by wildlife biologists' cameras, astrophysicists undertake to see what even the most technologically advanced cameras would not be able to capture. So it was with great fanfare that on April 10, 2019, NASA announced that an international team of researchers had succeeded in taking a picture of a black hole.[16] One week later, the "first-ever image" of a black hole was made available on NASA's website (see figure 3), accompanied by a caption that reads, "Scientists have obtained the first image of a black hole, using Event Horizon Telescope observations of the center of the galaxy M87. The image shows a bright ring formed as light bends in the intense gravity around a black hole that is 6.5 billion times more massive than the Sun."[17] A hitherto invisible phenomenon or object deep in space can now be seen. And it looks like a doughnut.

To take a picture of a black hole, rather than simply simulating it digitally as was previously done, is a true scientific feat, and all credit is due to the photographic apparatus known as the Event Horizon Telescope (EHT). Although called a "telescope," the EHT is actually a well-choreographed ensemble of instruments, mechanisms, and computational techniques of detection, observation, and visualization, none of which "sees" anything the way that our naked eye or a mechanical camera does. Comprising seven units of antennas positioned around the world and geosynchronized accordingly, the EHT forms one giant lens (or ear) the size of Earth to collect radio signals emitted by the black hole at the center of the galaxy M87 as it sucks everything floating

Figure 3. First-ever image of a black hole. Credit: Event Horizon Telescope (NASA, JPL.gov).

nearby into its sublime abyss. All the signals received by the antennas are sent back to earth, readied soon after as numerical data to be processed and developed by scientists (who, by the way, might know little about astrophysics), ultimately producing the image that is shown in figure 3. A doughnut is seen—a black hole trans*formed.*

Devouring all, a black hole obscures itself perfectly. What happens in it stays in it, for nothing, not even light, escapes its gravitational pull, as scientists tell us. Giving off nothing because it gives nothing away, it is darker than a black night, holing up beyond the horizon of any event, including non-events. "The darkness of a black hole is *absolutely empty,*" as Benjamin Bratton observes.[18] So what makes figure 3 fascinating and "significant is that it *signifies true nothingness.*"[19] Although a true nothingness, a black hole can nonetheless be captured by the EHT and made visible *hic et nunc,* that is, as a "bright ring formed as light bends in the intense gravity" found only in the heavens. As in magic, but without deception, it is *there,* and we can see it *through* the EHT. What is supposed to be visually impossible and physically absent is made possible and absently present through technological ingenuity. The "bright ring" brought to us by NASA gives an all-devouring hole in darkness a visible figure whose ostension evidences the triumph of modern arts, sciences, and engineering.

Whether fascinated by figure 3 or not, one would be hard pressed to shut one's eye to the fact that the image of a black hole as seen on our screen exists nowhere except in the visual field opened up by the technical ensemble of cosmic tracking, recording, and imaging, for which the EHT acts as the sentry. In capturing the black hole in galaxy M87, multiple instruments and apparatuses, both soft and hard, work together to seek what they are designed to see and look at. Communicating with one another in a manner that no scientist or technician alone can fully understand, these seeing devices in conjunction create a vision out of the blue, as it were, giving viewers a visual composite that looks real and believable precisely because they are *already* positioned in the science-based theater of detection, observation, and image-making and firmly believe that sciences and technologies do not lie, even if the theories and techniques at work are well beyond their comprehension.

Taken by the EHT of a black hole in outer space, figure 3 is the "first-ever" picture of something that modern physics says is invisible.

It is an *image* of a black hole, not the black hole itself. However, rather than (or more than) a credible picture of something supposedly invisible, it is, in fact, a *re*presentation, a veritable visual laboriously synthesized out of the gravitational forces at work in space by a remote sensing body, of which the EHT functions like the eye. A product of digital mimicry, it is, in a word, a simulacrum that, as a copy of a copy, can claim a physical referent or origin precisely because it is spectral. Yet more than a specter conjured up digitally, it is also a technical object, an artifact that, as remarked above, stands at the end of a long array of electronic and computational tools and toolmaking and exists only in that ensemble that establishes and maintains its reality. As in magic, where image or thought is equated with reality and reality with image or thought, a miracle (mirari/miraculum) takes place— something to look at and wonder about—one staged skillfully by a techno-corpus of television, a carved figure, as it were, that, relying exclusively on sensing remotely, capitalizes on the value of shade, shadow, and light to give two-dimensional evidence to a figure that in itself is without outline and solidity. Brought near by the wonderous television, it can justifiably be called *archeiropoietic* in that it is made entirely digitally yet without our digits ever touching, grasping, or molding it. Taken of auras and cosmic waves, this photograph-like entity, as pointed out earlier, is the outcome of a technological and engineering feat that, upon showing itself as something to be seen, is transformed apace into an epistemological, even ontological, miracle that can happen only in the technosemiotic milieu circumscribing it. In that milieu, a black hole, never of our visible reality, is made to show itself and, showing itself in this way, attests to its existence and objectivity. *It* is out there, and we can see it *now*, though not directly. The black hole, say the scientists, is invisible, but it is not really unseeable. It is a "seen invisible."

To say that figure 3 is a technical object is to say that, before all else, it is a theoretical object. This means, first, that the referent of figure 3, a black hole at the center of galaxy M87, must be seen in theory *before* it can be found out there and, consequently, be captured, and properly imaged by the sensing apparatuses at work and, second, that a tracking device, such as the EHT, can succeed in "locking on" and "seeing" a black hole in the dark only because it is designed to seek it on the basis of the very theories that foresee the black hole's existence, tracks down its location, and describes what it may look like in the first place. Before the scientists and the public come around to look at it on their screen, there has to be a prior look, a look *qua theatrum*, which sets the stage for making visible the supposedly invisible black hole in a carefully choreographed "play of the apparent with the inapparent," which, as choreographed in this case, is but "a play of the apparent in its apparition."[20] To put it simply, the EHT can take a picture of a black hole because it first "ex-pects" (or "looks out") to see it, and it looks out for it because it is predicted to exist and is to appear in the manner and location as predicted. Without this expectation, without the foresight that a target can be found and aimed at, the EHT would not know where to look as it turns skyward, would not know what to "collect," that is, would not know what counts as signals, as opposed to meaningless noise, while being all ears to the cosmic cacophony.

Through a picture taken of a dark hole in the heavens, we come to see science and technology at play in the service of technology and science, as they partake of multinational Big Science projects, all in response to our fundamental "desire to see," which has as its pretext the no less fundamental "desire to show" that drives the scientists and engineers behind the project.[21] In this instance, the double desires of seeing and of showing can be seen to find a moment of arrest in the function that an image can perform, an quasi-epistemic function that, aided by the latest of all visual technologies, creates what could be called "perceptual realism" held dear by the general public precisely because it already believes in it. In this theater where something supposedly invisible takes the stage, not only is seeing believing and believing seeing, but "fact and truth are also exchangeable" (*Verum et factum convertum*), if only because, when the distinction between seeing and showing is rendered null, *verum ipsum factum* (truth lies in having produced the fact). Understood in this way, seeing figure 3 is tantamount to *having a vision*. It is to take as fact an artifact produced by means largely beyond one's grasp. It is to take as real and factual an image that is entirely technosemiotic in nature—an image to which no naked eyes or any "mechanical eye" correspond. This image, like any image, "is neither a mere logical object nor a real entity; it is something that lives ('a life') . . . in the medium of its own knowability."[22] In fact, were one to embark on an intergalactic safari, stop by M87, and look in the direction indicated by the space travel guidebook, it is doubtful that one would see anything that looks like the orange doughnut shown in figure 3.

An image is a shaped thing, its shape drawn by our desire to see and to see it as drawn.[23] Expertly drawn and skillfully presented, figure 3 makes appear what is thought to remain out of sight. To appear is to come forward, and to come forward implies veiling or concealment, for something can come forward only if it were hiding somehow somewhere. "The only things that appear," writes Georges Didi-Huberman, "are those which are first able to dissimulate themselves. Things already grasped in their aspect or peacefully resembling themselves never appear. They are apparent . . . but only apparent: they will never be given as *appearing*."[24] If a shape appears, if something invisible is made to appear as an image, there must be an *opening* that gives it access to the here and now, but, at the same time, it also suggests the contrary that the here and now is a realm of dissemblance.[25] "Appearing," Didi-Huberman goes on to say, "is destined to be something like dissimulation."[26] Every image, we could say, contains the seed of its own disappearance, its own dissimulation; it *is* its own erasure but also possible return. Herein lies the paradox of appearing: something appears only to the extent that it also disappears, receding or retreating into its own fading away so as to betray itself as an apparition. What takes place here is not a matter of camouflage, of a figure blending or merging into the background that both hides and sustains it, but rather of *dis-paring*, of something being so strictly disparate that we are ever dis-prepared to see it. The apparent appears, but in appearing it separates and un-compares. The apparent is the other of what it appears to reveal.

Seeing a picture of a black hole is interesting, no less so in learning how the image is made. However, if a black hole dissimulates itself when made to appear, that is, if it must forfeit its true face before it can take the shape given to it, then what is truly interesting about figure 3 is not so much the wonderful "procedures that produce it"— its shape and colors that, as we learn later on, are deliberately chosen among many possible ones by the scientists for their dramatic effects— as the fact that the image may force us to reflect on how insignificant (or significant), powerful (or powerless) we are in the cosmic scheme of things.[27] If the orange doughnut in figure 3 is in fact of a size larger than our galaxy, how infinitesimally small we the viewers must be, in spite of (or in light of) EHT's stunning magnifying power and the astronomical capacity of data processing involved in imaging figure 3.

Comprising multiple antennas scattered around the world, ETH turns planet Earth itself into a sensing, almost sentient body with sharp eyesight. When viewed from deep space, this sensing orb looks hardly different from any of the innumerable oculi dotting the infinite darkness. There are countless eyes in the sky, extra ones farther away. They look at us and we at them as well. In this exchange of gazes, what is hidden and what is shared, what unfurls and what is kept inside? "The desire to attach sight, however processed, to the phenomenon of the black hole is enormously compelling," says Peter Galison in an interview about the EHT.[28] So we looked into space and made an image of the so-called unseeable. Yet an image is but an image; it only appears and appears to work. When it works, it gives only an appearance, giving, that is, not what it appears to reveal but only what we think appears in it. Perhaps, after all, what meets our desire to see and to show lies only in the eyes of the beholder.

Dark and far away, a black hole is a crack in being. It is a hole in the whole, marking the limit of our universe, whose frontier is as much inside as ahead. As twentieth-century structuralism, among other methods of interpretation, has taught us, without a hole in it, the whole would not hold.[29] Looking at the photograph in figure 3, we may be awed, fascinated, or perplexed; more than that, we may experience a sense of relief, knowing that the whole universe, though dark, invisible, and unknown for the most part, is not likely to disappear and the blue sky not likely to fall.

SEEING WHAT?

I look. I look because I cannot find . . . I do not find, or find too much.

—Jacques-Alain Miller, "This Side of the Unconscious"

The painting carries presence, to the point of bearing absence . . . to direct visibility.

—Jean-Luc Marion, *In Excess*

The motivation and objective behind the scientists working in concert to bring home figure 3 are considerable and laudable. Not to be overshadowed in this respect is the keen interest in modern sciences shown decades earlier by artists who were curious about and intent upon exploring the mystery of space and time revealed by the findings of the twentieth-century physical sciences and beyond. Under the name of Dimensionism, a modern art movement "in the age of Einstein" founded by the Hungarian poet Charles Tamko Sirató in the 1920s, a group of artists—including Marcel Duchamp, Alexander Calder, Hans Arp, Robert Delaunay, Francis Picabia, Wassily Kandinsky, László Moholy-Nagy, to name but the better known—responded heartily to, in the words of Sirató, "the European spirit's new conceptions of space-time (promulgated most particularly by Einstein's theories) and the recent technical givens of our age."[30]

Scientifically minded, Dimensionist artists incorporated into their practice many of the discoveries of the hard sciences of the time, liberating the aesthetic one step further from its classical confines already shaken by such modern "isms" as Cubism, Surrealism, and Futurism. Einsteinian physics, non-Euclidean geometry, modern biological sciences, and the "crafty devices," such as microscope, telescope, and the like—all these offer a fertile source of inspiration for nonrepresentational art, making available a powerful means by which to question everything that we had accepted as realities of the universe.[31] Indeed,

Figure 4. Helen Lundeberg (American, 1908–1999), *Self-Portrait* 1944, Oil on Masonite 40–69 cm (15 3/4 x 27 3/16 in.). Collection Zimmerli Art Museum at Rutgers University, gift of the Lorser Feitelson and Helen Lundeberg Feitelson Arts Foundation 82.059.002. Photo by Peter Jacobs.

following Sirató's formula "N+1," according to which each medium should move up a dimension—with literature spreading to the plane, painting expanding to three-dimensional space, and sculpture vaporizing "rigid matters" and shattering "all the old limits and boundaries of the arts"—art practices will broaden themselves to symbolize Albert Einstein and Hermann Minkowski's fourth dimension of space time, unified in short order into one "Cosmic Art," which would no longer be viewed passively but has to be experienced with all the five senses.[32]

Although later than the first Dimensionists in exploring the "cosmic space" with paint and brush, Southern Californian artist Helen Lundeberg, who studied astronomy and zoology in her youth, was struck no less than her predecessors by the new conceptions of space and time and the generative forces of nature unraveled by the twentieth century natural sciences. Her 1937 painting *Microcosm and Macrocosm*, for example, shows the artist musing over globular forms that, observable simultaneously at both cosmic and microbial levels, reveal an interconnected vision of the universe, the smallest elements of which mirror the structure of the whole in a state of constant change driven by invisible dynamics that can be analyzed, measured, and modeled in purely logical, theoretical terms. In another work, *Self-Portrait*, dated 1944 (see figure 4), we see Lundeberg depicting herself plucking space and time in front of a canvas, while turning away from it to look at the viewer, who, as both she and we the viewers know well, exists far outside the picture frame. Painted in the American post-Surrealist style for which she is known, *Self-Portrait* is an unmistakable testament to Lundeberg's relentless quest for knowledge and undiminishing love of nature—not just about plants and animals but also about planets beyond our own Earth—betokening in her unique "subjective-classical" manner the idea that important motifs of nature's mystery recur without fail in arts irrespective of time and place.

Like many other paintings by Lundeberg in the period before she turned to the abstract in the early 1960s, *Self-Portrait* intimates a story. But it is not certain exactly what story is being told. What is clear when we look at *Self-Portrait*, however, is that with well-turned figures cast in lights and shadows and sky-colored in painterly harmony, it gives viewers the impression of catching itself in a moment of suspension. Akin to a snapshot, *Self-Portrait* is a painting of a painter in action, a still image taken of a painter at work by the painter herself, by her painting herself painting. It is at this moment of arrest or hesitation that as the viewer could easily ascertain, the self-portrayed artist, with both hands still occupied, turns away from within the painting and looks to the space outside it, to a virtual space where we the viewers (and Lundeberg the artist herself) are found. *Self-Portrait*, we could say, is a self-portrait of an act that paints it. Captured on canvas here is a veritable "decisive moment" of *painting* as such, an instance frozen in time when someone recognizable and internal to the frame is caught turning sideways to stare at and, in so doing, make intimate what lies outside the painted scene.[33] It is this "outward" look, a pregnant glance arising from within the painting to the outside and directed at what is present only in absence, that makes this moment *de-cisive* by occasioning an instance of *di-vision*, where the gaze of the viewer, of the painter in the painting, and of Lundeberg herself cross one another in an imaginary encounter. And it is through this virtual encounter, depicted, as the painting's title indicates, by the artist herself in an imaginary exchange of gazes, that the painting can be seen to reflect back on itself and, thanks to the simultaneity of looking and of being looked at in a mode of self-questioning, be viewed as commenting on the painting's very expression and intended purpose. Indeed, meeting the gaze of the viewer, which is also her own in this imaginary encounter, Lundeberg is shown to stare inquisitively as much at herself as at anyone looking at her—as if asking "just because we experience space and time in one way, it does not mean that is how it is. . . . So how could it really look like?"[34]

In an article written in 1935 for the Danish periodical *Konkretion*, Vasily Kandinsky, a longtime supporter of Sirató, describes what he calls the "inner gaze" that pierces the appearance of things to capture the secret forms of nature: "I call this experience of the 'secret soul' of all things which we see with the unaided eye, in the microscope or through the telescope, the 'inner gaze.' This gaze penetrates the outer shell, through the outward 'form,' to the interior of things, and allows us to experience the inner 'pulsation' of things with all our senses."[35] Though no less experimental and scientific in spirit and practice, Lundeberg is far less confident than Kandinsky in the ability of forms and colors to register the "inner pulsation" behind things and sensible phenomena. For the artist behind and within *Self-Portrait*, there is always something disappointing in painting, something that falls short of fulfilling the charge assigned by sciences to the new art. Despite the best intentions and efforts, painting, reliant as it is on form and color pertaining to surfaces and outward forms, would never be able to raise itself beyond figuration to reach what lies beyond appearance and experience. Indeed, when we look at *Self-Portrait*, we face the painter's inquisitive gaze and soon realize, as we try to figure out what she is trying to convey, that she has been waiting for us to see her in this way. But we are also unmistakably spurred to ask whether it is ever possible for us, through painting alone, to penetrate the "outer shell" of things to perceive directly their "secret soul," a soul so *secret*—namely, so set apart—as to be invisible. A gesture of doubt, arguably Cartesian, exfoliates from Lundeberg's self-portrait, silently taking apart that in which it also takes part. So, fittingly, no surprise . . . she looks at us . . . as if asking:

> Could you show me dear?
> Something I'm not seeing.
> Something infinitely interesting.[36]

A painting is a painting is a painting, and a self-portrait is a self-portrait is a self-portrait, but the mystery that *Self-Portrait* seeks to unravel remains in the air, kept unsolved in the virtual exchange of gazes staged by a self-portrait.

Like any allegorical text, *Self-Portrait* imparts a double message. On the one hand, it says that art in the age of Einstein should lead culture toward fuller enlightenment by helping the public visualize the hidden structure of our universe; on the other hand, it also makes a gesture, through a mixture of irony and reflexivity, that this reality behind phenomena cannot be transliterated by form and color, to which painting must submit. It is true, and Lundeberg undoubtedly recognizes it well, that concepts and thinking try not to go against things, and images and paintings want to go toward things. Yet things themselves might not accept the images inspired by thinking and concepts. At issue here is not merely that painting is always inadequate to reality or things as they are but whether painting may be (or may harbor) the very contradiction of painting itself, that it may let itself in to represent what it also acknowledges to be beyond representation, even to being contrary to what is painted or paintable.[37] Bearing in mind Lundeberg's self-questioning stare in *Self-Portrait*, let us recall another work by her, *The Veil*, completed four years later (see figure 5). Reflecting a sense of calm and order characteristic of Lundeberg's "Subjective Classism" period, *The Veil* shows an outsized hand—Lundeberg's own—dropping into the frame from one knows not where, through the upper right corner, to raise a drape that presumably hung over the entire scene before the hand pulls it aside.[38] Lifted by an intruding hand from nowhere, the drape, upon which a sunny world unfolds, slices half-diagonally through the canvas, revealing an uninhabited landscape in two slightly mismatched halves: their contrast in light and darkness speaks aloud the existence of a previously unseen reality behind the sunlit appearance, a hidden reality that would not come into view until the curtain is parted.

Through the image of a hand parting a veil, an image as lively or stale as the common expression "lifting the veil" in suggesting an "uncovering" or "discovery," *The Veil* goes further than *Self-Portrait* in questioning painting's ability to reach reality behind appearance, betokening in fine painterly fashion a painter's ever-thwarted attempt to expose what is hidden or concealed. The image of a curtain being pulled aside by a hand is a vivid gesture of unveiling, but the prominence of

Figure 5. Helen Lundeberg, *The Veil*, 1947, Macfarlane Collection.

an intruding hand (which appears to descend from heaven, but, as noted above, is in fact the painter's own and is therefore painting and is painted by itself) also works to belie painting's very declared purpose by the unapologetic suggestion that another hand, another intruder, may drop in to unveil another buried landscape whose exposure only leads to further (possibly endless) veiling and unveiling. Through this unveiling that veils only to unveil and, therefore, veil again, *The Veil* turns itself inside out to become an instance of knowledge. In this instance, and by showing failure to be constitutive of its performance, it also appears as a text, the reading of which leads no more to any conclusive close than to a clear distinction between legibility and non-knowledge. *The Veil* (and *Self-Portrait* as well, though to a lesser extent and in a less pronounced manner) are both paintings and texts, forms of presence playing and being played on two registers at once.

If *The Veil* is about painting's possible efficacy in unveiling, the announcement of this possibility is at once iterated as a repetition of this possibility, which, as a possibility, also entails that it be impossible precisely because it only repeats and repeats as mere possibility. It is in this self-annulling possibility that we can discern the origin and cause of painting's survival, an endless success sustained by its self-generated and generative failure. And it is in this success through failure—a failure that never fails—that one can find the reason why painting, however electrified by as rigorous a science as modern physics and yet easily seen to negate itself on its own, promises merely what it promises and, remaining a promise throughout, never delivers what is promised.[39] *The Veil* recalls the question raised by *Self-Portrait* painted ten years earlier. Instead of giving an answer, however, it affords a promise that painting is poised to give, but it is a promise that remains always to come (*a-venir*) (i.e., without arrival), thanks to which painting lives on, and painters are guaranteed a future.[40]

Things do not insist that they be painted, but painters cannot resist painting things. The desire to paint the "fourth dimension" or "the 'inner' pulsation of things" shares the scientists' desire to see wildlife as they see themselves and to see the black hole and take a picture of it. But what painters can do, as is the case with wildlife photographers and astrophysicists, is constrained by what the medium in use permits and makes possible. Like the veil in *The Veil*, painting unveils as much as it conceals and, regardless of its "break through the canvas," creates distance and separation as it also makes proximate.[41] Featuring a hand lifting a veil, *The Veil* allegorizes painting's power of unveiling, but this power is immediately counteracted by the presence of a hand, the painter's own, that clues one in on it as a lack of power. If *The Veil* shows painting's power of unveiling, it is a power that painting purports to have but does not. Whatever else it does, painting shows *seeing* as such before the image it is shows up, for to see is to be attracted by what meets the eye before one realizes what the eye has met. And to paint is to suffer—to undergo, that is, to go under—what first attracts but may also repel the gaze, while transcribing or memorializing the suffering. To look at a painting, then, is akin to becoming *via sympathia* the painter who, bolstered by creativity and artistry, manages to survive the "tortured paths leading the eye into the interior form which it is quickly expelled."[42] In all these instances, the eye sees beyond what is present, which is to say, one ends up un-seeing what is manifestly visible. To see, as remarked earlier, is at once to unsee and vice versa. Moreover, inasmuch as to see is to un-see, every image seen hides another one, which, containing the seed of its own disappearance, leads to another yet to be seen, and so on. Understood in this way, every image is an image of images and every painting, which begins and survives as an image, carries within itself other paintings. Like the Leibnizian paradise wherein every individual reflects all others in optimal harmony, the visible world, too, is a vibrating web of fluttering veils, each of which is an image that veils and unveils in turn as it flutters.[43] It is in this world that seeing eyes reach out and touch things, and painting takes place as a witness to its own (in)visibility, always and already under the silence of not-knowing for sure what attracts it to begin with.

We look at and see many things, but they might not be the things we look for or would like to see. And it is often the case that we do not know exactly what we are looking for while searching doggedly for it. Indeed, rarely can we foresee what attracts our attention and overtakes us until we can shake the fascination. Moreover, it is proven that a picture can *portray* what we witness—say, a car accident—better than words; images are not words, but a "painted image," remarks Meyer Shapiro, "has its *words to say*," and some images speaker louder than others.[44] Further still, not only do we see images and speak about them, but images also see and speak back to us.

Since seeing seems to have a will of its own and images work in their own productive ways, it makes sense to ask what it is that we see when something is seen. More precisely, what do we see or want to see when we look at a painting? Recall the story of a famous art theft. On the morning of August 21, 1911, Vincenzo Peruggia, an unassuming house painter employed by the Louvre, walked out of the museum with the *Mona Lisa* tucked in his smock.[45] The news of the heist shook the world, and the Louvre was soon overrun with visitors crowding in front of the empty space on the wall where the kidnapped lady had been displayed days earlier. Three weeks after the theft, Franz Kafka and his friend Max Brod arrived in Paris and joined the queues at the entrance to the Louvre. What did Kafka and Brod, along with the enthusiastic crowds beside them, expected to discover? What did they see or want to see when they looked at the bare wall? Unlike the art media events at which crowds flock to the gallery to see the masterpieces, Kafka and Brod were clearly not drawn to the Louvre by the famous painting, as they already knew it had been stolen. Other possible motives aside, it was actually the empty spot on the wall, a void made visible by the vanished *Mona Lisa*, that drove Kafka and Brod to the Louvre. They had gone to Paris, literally, for "nothing." "It was less a case of going to see a work of art because it was there, than, on the contrary, because it wasn't there."[46] What fascinated Kafka and Brod, and their fellow museum visitors as well, was actually an alluring absence, an image no longer visible but, perhaps precisely for that reason, fascinating and irresistible. To see, it seems, is to (want to) see the invisible, the no-longer visible. After all, we want to see what others want to see, and we see what we think others see. For Kafka and Brod, but also the crowd at the Louvre, they saw what they went to the museum to see.

After the *Mona Lisa* was found and returned to the Louvre, it was suggested, in reaction to skeptics who questioned the authenticity of the item retrieved, that the painting be displayed facing the wall, for the crack on the back of the panel proved its authenticity.[47] This suggestion—aside from the possibility that a physical mark on the work can be forged or its absence explained away in some plausible way—brings home the fact that what is important for an image to be an object of gaze is not so much the image itself but that there is something to take its place beforehand, that *it*, its face unseen notwithstanding, is there to fill in the blank. A void must be present beforehand, and it must be filled or satisfied because it is a void and is felt as a void—a hole in a whole, as described earlier—around which seeing brings about what is seen according to its own operation. As something that stands in for a prior absence, painting ought to be seen, as Shapiro puts it, "*not* as a surface on which colors are laid out, but as a *void* where colors appear and where one hesitates to *know* if they really do '*find a foothold on the surface.*"[48] If painting constructs forms in colors, its creation comes from there being formless space that awaits it, an absence of form and color, upon which the painted image floats as if in search of a home.

After it disappeared from the museum, the *Mona Lisa* was held in Peruggia's Paris apartment until it was discovered by the police two years later. In his interview with the police after his arrest, Peruggia claimed that he had stolen the painting in order to return it to its native Italy. To him, the *Mona Lisa* was a "lost object" and, like every missing object, it had to be returned to its proper place—a place it deserved but did not have. Thanks to the publicity about the theft ever since it happened, the *Mona Lisa* has become the most famous art object in history. Millions of people visit the Louvre every year to see the "real thing" hanging on the wall. But few of them realize that the real thing on display in the dimly lit special viewing room was once a missing item, an object that had to vanish in order to become the object that it is now.

For decades, the *Mona Lisa* has been protected from harm by a bulletproof glass enclosure, upon which glares and reflections blur the image for which the half-length painting is named. Staring through the glassy surface to make out the smiling face, viewers end up looking as much at themselves as at the face that is no less recognizable to them than their own. Because their own reflection is competing for attention with the image that is supposed to be the focus, what viewers end up looking at is not merely "an object of curiosity, or one of pure pleasure," but rather "an anchoring point or *vanishing* point, in all senses of that latter term, i.e., as the vanishing of lines in their more or less fixed convergence, but also with the self's own vanishing, its escape into hiding, as the subject works to cover its tracks."[49] There is a look for a look, into which the look takes its place and becomes a gaze. Like Leonardo da Vinci, who looks at the face he is painting, and like Lisa del Giocondo looking back at the painter, the viewer also gazes at an ever-receding point, a veritable "crack in being," which organizes the visible and, in this gaze, sees the *Mona Lisa* one is looking for, at the same time turning it into an image—one's very own—that begs for a better vision. To see is not just to look, which pertains to the visible, behind which the invisible endures and looks back. Rather, it is to fall into a crack in the field of vision and, through this crack, to let fall an image that is yet to be. In this falling, in an instant, darkness diminishes and, with the light and the shadows it affords, seeing begins to thrive beyond its own operation. We then begin to see the things that we do, even with eyes closed.

To see a rabbit in profile is to un-see a duck that is also there; to see like a lion is to see what it sees as we humans do (not as it sees it), and to see a black hole is to see a digitally manufactured picture that, without being told so by trustworthy sources, could be or resemble anything. Between the desire to see and the possibility that it will not be satisfied is the certainty of our always seeing something, behind which lies something else that we may or may not look at. To see is not simply to look. It is to see the invisible—at least, for now.

Briankle G. Chang is professor of communication at the University of Massachusetts, Amherst. He is the author of *Deconstructing Communication: Subject, Representation, and Economies of Exchange* (1996) and coeditor of *Philosophy of Communication* (2010). His recent publications include "Seeing Goddess in Typhoon," in *differences* (2018) and translations of Marie-José Mondzain that appeared in *Inter-Asia Cultural Studies* (2021) and *Journal of Communication Inquiry* (2022).

Notes

1. The issue of "aspect-seeing" is addressed by Wittgenstein, where he says, "I contemplate a face, and then suddenly notice its likeness to another. I *see* that it has not changed; and yet I see it differently. I call this experience "noticing an aspect." The concomitant sudden experience of "noticing an aspect" is called "aspect-dawning" (193c).

2. Wittgenstein underlines the importance of distinguishing between "'continuous seeing' of an aspect and the sudden 'dawning' of an aspect" (194–95). That one sees either this or that in aspect-seeing is also seen at work in what is called the "gaze." As that which first opens the visible, the gaze is what the subject can never see in his or her field of vision. When one looks at oneself in a mirror or at

one's own passport photo, for instance, one sees oneself as either seeing or seen but never as both at the same time.

3. See Cavell, 369.

4. As can be easily seen, the rabbit/duck drawing is much more complicated than Cavell's comment about it suggests. For an illuminating discussion from a perspective that questions the "univocity of sight" assumed by the usual readings of the drawing, see Paul North (2021, 112–23). A similar point is made by Pop when he observes that "far from visual context guiding what we see, we approach duck-rabbit with a *parti pris* (Wittgenstein! aspects! social construction of knowledge!)," and he goes on to state "if the image of the duck-rabbit is indifferent between its two interpretations, nothing can prevent a well-informed viewer from grasping the dilemma by the horns and seeing the two together: a rabbit and a duck joined at the eye. It is a biological improbability, but not logical impossibility nor any other kind" (205).

5. Nancy, 3; emphasis added.

6. Nancy, 3.

7. See Mondzain, 483–86.

8. We may recall here the "split" between eye and gaze, made famous by Lacan. An organ of vision, the eye can never be more than an eye-object in that one can only see the eyes of another individual or creature or those of one's own only in a mirror. As a result, "I cannot ever see myself from the place where I gaze, since I could do so only on the condition of seeing myself 'before' myself. In this sense, the eye actually is a separated organ—namely, my own lost, objectivized gaze" (Borch-Jacobsen, 235).

9. I should note that by the invisible, I don't mean absence. The laptop that was stolen or lost is no longer on my desk. It was seen but now absent. It is not invisible. See, for example, Farennikova.

10. See Caro.

11. See Melin et al.

12. This was already discussed in writings by critics in the nineteenth century. Heinrich Wölfflin, for example, saw in photography the idea expressed earlier by Adolf von Hildebrand: "there will always be *one* view that presents and unites the . . . figure as a coherent surface impression" (258; emphasis added).

13. See De Meyer, 470.

14. Although in need of being properly "anchored" by words that help determine how they are to be interpreted, images are generally thought to be stronger in terms of the evidentiary force they carry than words. With this in mind, it may nonetheless be helpful to recall here Ludwig Wittgenstein's remarks that "even if a lion can talk, we would not comprehend (*verstehen*) what it says" (223). We would not be able to understand a lion when he speaks because, quite simply, we are not lions. We do not live like them, do not share their point of view, and have no direct access as to how they feel, think, or confer among themselves and still less about how they think and talk about zebras or us humans. In other words, since lions relate to the world differently than we do—since, that is, we don't share their

"form of life"—we would not be able to understand lion talk, even if it speaks perfect English. For instance, recalling a day in the African grassland when he saw a wildlife photographer wandering around, a lion can tell us that he believes that the photographer was watching zebras, and he can also tell us that he could see the photographer watching himself while seeing himself being watched. Moreover, upon being shown the photos in figure 2, he could even say, "Oh, yes, I see this zebra at twelve o'clock, and this is how it appeared to me yesterday when I was out hunting." And so on. But we still would not be able to comprehend what he means, if only because the words he uses, such as "yes," "see," "twelve o'clock," and the rest, might not mean the same thing as we understand and use them. Indeed, the sense and meaning of a lion's "yes" or "no," "sunny" or "rainy" are internal to a lion's world, one which we can observe and participate in our own fashion but never live it as the lion lives and experiences it.

15. See Mondzain, 484.

16. See NASA Jet Propulsion Laboratory; emphasis added.

17. NASA Jet Propulsion Laboratory; emphasis added.

18. See Bratton; emphasis added.

19. See Bratton; emphasis added. And "the darkness of a black hole is absolutely empty, so part of what makes this image significant is that it *signifies* true nothingness"; emphasis added.

20. See Marion (1998, 59).

21. It is worth pointing out here that the desire to see is not a simple obverse of the desire to show. Indeed, "inventions born of a *desire to see*," as Mondzain (2019, 221) wisely observes, "should not be confused with scenes motivated by the *desire to show*. A nonenigmatic display can harbor no invisibility other than that of the procedures that produce it."

22. See Agamben, 83.

23. See Luke.

24. Didi-Huberman, 1.

25. Didi-Huberman, 1.

26. Didi-Huberman, 1.

27. See Weisberger.

28. See, for example, Galison, 74.

29. Take phonology à la Roman Jakobson, for a quick example. Without the zero phoneme, the phonemic binaries, such as p/b, k/g, t/d, etc., in English, would not form a structure and would not be able to account for all the meaningful sounds produced and producible in that language. See also the "empty square" discussed by Gilles Deleuze (1990, 66–81; 2004, 170–92, 305–8). In addition, see Chang (1999).

30. Sirató, 170; see also Henderson.

31. Sirató, 176; see also McGivern.

32. See McGivern.

33. Henri Cartier-Bresson's "decisive moment" is widely celebrated as an accurate reflection of photo-journalistic excellence, but it tends to give too much credit to the agency of the photographer. For a discussion on this, see Chang (2018).

34. See McGivern.

35. Vasily Kandinsky, quoted in Düchting (2017, 45); the original source is Düchting (1999, 80).

36. Lyrics by Brandon Boyd (Incubus).

37. For an example, one can point to *The Fourth Dimension*, the 1938 painting by Patrick J. Sullivan. As is well-known by schoolchildren, the fourth dimension propounded by Einsteinian physics, though mathematically fathomable, is not a perceptual object. Like space and time, it cannot be represented. Looking at *The Fourth Dimension*, one is likely to be touched by its pensive beauty, but it cannot be how the fourth dimension actually looks.

38. In an interview, Lundeberg speaks about using her own hand in *The Veil*; the hand, she says, "is a useful introduction of something human. I used my own hands because I was the most convenient model." See Stein, 15. Recall that the use of a disembodied hand was widely used for visionary and often erotic effects by Surrealists and photographers at the time as a substitute for a portrait of an individual; see, for example, Hoving.

39. For a discussion on "promise" as a performative act intended here, see Hamacher; see also Chang (2005).

40. On the relation of promise to gift and future, see Chang (2005).

41. To liberate painting from its two-dimensional medium is one of Dimensionism's express aims. As Mario Nissim, one of the first signatories to the "Dimensionist Manifesto," says, "Painting? The plan is dead. Today objects wish to *break through the canvas*. Every day, then, painting pursues its attempt at liberation: this is how it declares itself true to its tradition" (173; emphasis added).

42. See Einstein, 154.

43. See, for example, Chang (2018).

44. See Damisch and Shapiro, 62.

45. See Leader.

46. Leader, 3.

47. Leader, 174.

48. Damisch and Shapiro, 62; the first two emphases added.

49. Damisch, 151.

Works Cited

Agamben, Giorgio. 2011. *Nudities*. Translated by David Kishik and Stefan Pedatella. Stanford: Stanford University Press.

Borch-Jacobsen, Mikkel. 1991. *Lacan: The Absolute Master*. Translated by Douglas Brick. Stanford: Stanford University Press.

Boyd, Brandon (Incubus). "Echo." *Morning View*. Malibu, CA: Epic Records, 2001.

Bratton, Benjamin H. 2019. "Excerpt: 'The Terraforming.'" *Strelka Mag*. September 18, 2019. https://strelkamag.com/en/article/excerpt-bratton-the-terraforming (accessed May 17, 2020).

Caro, Tim. 2016. *Zebra Stripes*. Chicago: University of Chicago Press.

Cavell, Stanley. 1979. *The Claim of Reason: Wittgenstein, Skepticism, Morality, and Tragedy*. Oxford: Oxford University Press.

Chang, Briankle G. 1999. "Deleuze, Monet, and Being Repetitive." *Cultural Critique* 41:184–217.

———. 2005. "Of Giving Memory," *differences* 16, no. 2:116–37.

———. 2018. "Seeing Goddess in Typhoons." *differences* 29, no. 3:1–32.

Damisch, Hubert. 2019. "Staking the Subject: The Self's Own Gamble with Art." Edited by Hubert Damisch and Meyer Shapiro. Special Issue. *October* 167: 149–70. https://doi.org/10.1162/octo_a_00340.

Damisch, Hubert, and Meyer Shapiro, eds. 2019. "Letters, 1972–1973." Special Issue. *October* 167:25–123. https://doi.org/10.1162/octo_a_00337.

Deleuze, Gilles. 1990. *Logic of Sense*. New York: Columbia University Press.

———. 2004. "How Do We Recognize Structuralism?" In *Desert Islands and Other Texts, 1953–1974*, edited by David Lapoujade, 170–92. Translated by Mike Taominia. Los Angeles: Semiotext(e).

De Meyer, Thibault. 2018. "A Leibnizian Fieldwork: Zebra Stripes and the Monadology." *Parallax* 24, no. 4:466–79.

Didi-Huberman, Georges. 1989. "The Paradox of the Phasmid," 1–4. Translated by Alisa Hartz. http://www.usc.edu/dept/comp-lit/tympanum.html (accessed December 21, 2019).

Düchting, Hajo. 1999. *Wassily Kandinsky 1866–1944, Revolution de Malerei*. Cologne: Taschen Verlag.

———. 2017. *Vasily Kandinsky*. Munich: Hirmer Verlag Gmbh.

Einstein, Carl. 2004. "Critical Dictionary: "Nightingale" The Etchings of Hercules Seghers." *October* 107 (Winter): 151–57. https://www.jstor.org/stable/3397599.

Farennikova, Anna. 2013. "Seeing Absence," *Philosophical Studies* 166, no. 3:429–54.

Galison, Peter, with Elizabeth Kessler. 2019. "To See the Unseeable." *Aperture* (Winter 2019): 73–76. https://galison.scholar.harvard.edu/files/andrewhsmith/files/aperture_237_galison.pdf (accessed May 18, 2020).

Hamacher, Werner. 2001. "Lingua Amissa: The Messianism of Commodity-Language and Derrida's *Specter of Marx*." In *Futures, of Jacques Derrida*, edited by Richard Rand, 130–78. Stanford: Stanford University Press.

Henderson, Linda Dalrymple. 2013. *The Fourth Dimension and Non-Euclidean Geometry in Modern Art*. Cambridge, Mass.: MIT Press.

Hildebrand, Adolf von. 1994. "The Problem of Form in the Fine Arts." In *Empathy, Form, and Space: Problems in German Aesthetics, 1873–1893*," edited and translated by Harry Francis Mallgrave and Eleftherious Ikonomous, 222–79. Santa Monica, Calif.: Getty Center for the History of Art and the Humanities.

Hoving, Kirsten A. 2004. "'Blond Hands over the Magic Fountain': Photography in Surrealism's Uneasy Grip." In *Speaking with Hands: Photographs from the Buhl Collection*, edited by Jennifer Blessing, 93–113. New York: Guggenheim Museum.

Leader, Darian. 2004. *Stealing the Mona Lisa*. Washington, DC: Shoemaker & Hoard.

Luke, Megan R. 2019. "A Picture is a Shaped Thing." *October* 168 (Spring): 148–65.

Marion, Jean-Luc. 1998. *Reduction and Givenness: Investigations of Husserl, Heidegger, and Phenomenology.* Translated by Thomas A. Carlson. Evanston, IL: Northwestern University Press.

———. 2002. *In Excess: Studies of Saturated Phenomena.* Translated by Roby Horner and Vincent Berraud. New York: Fordham University Press.

McGivern, Hannah. 2018. "When the Avant-Garde Met E=MC2: The Story Behind Dimensionism." *Art Newspaper.* November 7. http://www.theartnewspaper.com/preview/when-the-avant-garde-met-e-mc2 (accessed May 18, 2020).

Melin, Amanda D., Donald W. Kline, Chihiro Hiramatsu, and Tim Caro. 2016. "Zebra Stripes through the Eyes of Their Predators, Zebras, and Humans." *PLoS One* 11, no. 1 (January 22). https://doi.org/10.1371/journal.pone.0145679.

Mondzain, Marie-José. 2019. "An Interview with Marie-José Mondzain: What Is an Image?" Trans. Briankle G. Chang. *Inter-Asia Cultural Studies* 20, no. 3:483–86.

Nancy, Jean-Luc. 2013. *The Pleasure in Drawing.* Translated by Philip Armstrong. New York: Fordham University Press.

NASA Jet Propulsion Laboratory. "How Scientists Captured the First Image of a Black Hole." *NASA Education News.* April 19, 2019. https://www.jpl.nasa.gov/edu/news/2019/4/19/how-scientists-captured-the-first-image-of-a-black-hole/ (accessed May 17, 2020).

Nissim, Mario. 2019. "The Deminsionist Manifesto." In *Dimensionism: Modern Art in the Age of Einstein.* Edited by Vanja M. Molloy, 167–246. Cambridge, Mass.: MIT Press.

North, Paul. 2021. *The Bizarre-Privileged Items in the Universe: The Logic of Likeness.* New York: Zone Books.

Pop, Andrei. 2019. *A Forest of Symbols: Art, Science, and Truth in the Long Nineteenth Century.* New York: Zone Books.

Sirató, Charles Tamkó. 2019. "The Dimensionist Manifesto." In *Dimensionism: Modern Art in the Age of Einstein,* edited by Vanja M. Molloy, 167–246. Cambridge, Mass.: MIT Press.

Stein, Donna. 2006. "The Art of Helen Lundeberg: Illuminating Portraits." *Woman's Art Journal* 27, no. 1:10–16. https://www.jstor.org/stable/i20358062.

Weisberger, Mindy. 2019. "Why Is the First-Ever Black Hole Picture an Orange Ring?" *Live Science.* April 10. https://www.livescience.com/65199-why-black-hole-orange.html (accessed February 29, 2020).

Wittgenstein, Ludwig. 1952. *Philosophical Investigations.* Translated by G. E. M. Anscombe. Oxford: Blackwell.

TECHNOLOGICAL CATASTROPHE AND THE ROBOTS OF NAM JUNE PAIK

G Douglas Barrett

INTRODUCTION

Robots are at once emblems of the posthuman while often designated as technological replacements for an activity—labor—that is said
to mark humans as unique. In this article, I argue that, rather than
any positive distinguishing feature, the difference between human
labor and its robotic simulation lies in the human capacity to refuse
it. To make this argument, I examine Korean American artist and
composer Nam June Paik's *Robot K-456* (1964)—an anthropomorphic
robot sculpture that both performed and *refused* to perform experimental music—in light of cybernetic robots since the Second World
War. In addition to these robots, Paik's work relates to their precedents in eighteenth-century musical automata, which, as incipient post-
humans, had already challenged boundaries between humans and
machines. Ultimately, I contend that Paik's robot affirms a capacity for
self-negation as uniquely human by failing at radical refusal—by failing at its own self-destruction during an event Paik staged in 1982.
Yet before analyzing that performance, *K-456*'s final appearance, let us
begin with its first.

    K-456 first appeared before an audience at the Second Annual
New York Avant Garde Festival at Judson Hall on August 30, 1964.
Before he arrived in New York earlier that year, Paik had assembled
the life-sized robot with one of his brothers along with the help of
the Japanese electrical engineer Shuya Abe while in Tokyo. In transit
and in transition, *K-456* had foam breasts that could rotate and a penis
made of sandpaper and flint, which Paik had removed before the two
traveled to New York. The robot's exposed "skeleton" stands at about
six feet and consists of aluminum frame profiles of various lengths

Cultural Critique 118—Winter 2023—Copyright 2023 Regents of the University of Minnesota that are bolted together and, in the case of the arms, head, and torso, attached to servo motors that allow a limited range of motion when engaged via Paik's twenty-channel radio controller. During the robot's various public appearances, which continued intermittently for almost twenty years, Paik used between one and four small control boxes adapted from model airplane remotes. Each control box has an antenna and several individual knobs and switches for executing a variety of actions from a distance, including a slow walking motion using a set of four wheels attached to the bottom of each of its legs. Footage of Paik in Berlin in 1965 shows him crouched on the street carefully alternating between two of the remotes to produce the robot's measured stride[1]— robots appear to replace some forms of labor and generate others.

Nevertheless, it was with this shambling pace that *Robot K-456* first greeted its audience at Judson Hall for the premiere of Paik's *Robot Opera* (1964), a title used to refer to the robot's solo act as well as a number of subsequent collaborative performances with the cellist and performance artist Charlotte Moorman. Moorman, who had organized the festival, invited Paik to participate after learning that he was integral to Karlheinz Stockhausen's *Originale* (1964), which they, along with several other artists and musicians, performed on the latter five of the festival's ten days. *Robot Opera* was programmed on the first five days, starting off each concert after composer James Tenney's magnetic tape realization of the initial half of Fluxus artist George Brecht's *Entrance Music/Exit Music* (1964), which consisted of a three-minute crossfade between white noise and a pure sine tone. The lights gradually dimmed as *K-456*, controlled by Paik in the wings, took the stage (Rothfuss, 92). It walked around, moved its limbs, bowed, and twirled its breasts.[2] It also played John F. Kennedy's inaugural "ask not" speech using a small tape recorder held in the robot's left foot wired to a four-inch speaker in its head (Kerner, 15). Afterward, *K-456* greeted visitors and passersby in front of Judson Hall; it then took to the streets and squares of New York (Fifty-Seventh, Park Avenue, Washington Square), where, in an homage to the French inventor Jacques de Vaucanson's digesting duck automaton of 1739, it left trails of defecation in the form of dried beans.

An artistic commentary conceived during the cold war cybernetic era, *K-456* also refers to musical, cultural, and technological developments dating back to the eighteenth century, which played a significant role in humanism's construction of the human. In addition to Vaucanson's defecating duck automaton, Paik's title, *Robot K-456*, is a play on the *Köchelverzeichnis*, or "K-system" of naming used to catalogue the works of Mozart; in this case "K. 456" refers to Mozart's *Piano Concerto No. 18* in B-flat major of 1784. Such music, and its technological mediation in the form of self-playing musical automata, was integral to the early modern negotiation of the boundary between humans and machines. Just as materialist philosophers began to conceive of humans and animals in mechanical terms—and hence to imagine their ability to be simulated in automata—musical pedagogy insisted that performers, through the use of expressivity in realizing works like Mozart's *Piano Concerto*, avoid appearing too rigid or machine-like. Despite being remembered mostly for his video work, Paik's formal music training (he wrote a thesis on Arnold Schoenberg at the University of Tokyo and studied music history at the University of Munich) suggests that his use of such references was self-conscious. Along similar lines, *Robot Opera*'s deflationary humor resonates with experimental music practices of the 1960s, especially those emerging from or influenced by Fluxus (which Paik joined at the invitation of George Maciunas, starting in 1960), but it also derives from *opera buffa*, the eighteenth-century genre that made use of comedy and gag.[3]

Such references that simultaneously straddle eighteenth- and twentieth-century musical, cultural, and technological discourses are as important to an analysis of *K-456*, I think, as are the specifics of its performances. Although its use of recorded speech draws on a technology in existence since the nineteenth century, the issuers of those speeches, including the (at that time) recently assassinated JFK and then-mayor elect of New York, John Lindsay, were of contemporary relevance. And while *Robot Opera* made reference to the prominence (and duration) of high nineteenth-century opera—Wagner is too long. Money is too short, read a flyer for the work—it also compared opera buffa to contemporary soap opera, a genre Paik refers to as "cheap."[4] Concerning its physical construction, *K-456* was not cheap, but it wasn't exactly state of the art either.[5] Paik didn't, for instance, provide his robot with the kind of photoelectric sensors that would allow it to roam semiautonomously like those included in the British cybernetician W. Grey Walter's famous tortoises of the 1940s. In this sense, despite Paik's references to contemporary cybernetics, his robot resembles more the automata of the late eighteenth century, which did *not* simulate sensory processes, than those of the twentieth.[6] What to make of *K-456*'s spinning breasts, then, a feature of *Robot Opera* that invites comparisons perhaps as much to the history of Pygmalionism as to more recent discussions of sex robots? The gesture was conspicuous enough to appear in virtually all of the festival reviews at the time. Crossing Fluxus and experimentalism with the genre of burlesque, the *New York Times* compared *K-456*'s display to the striptease performer Carrie Finnell, whose act had also featured breast spinning (Ericson).[7]

If sex work seems like an unlikely context for analyzing *Robot Opera*, then perhaps that is due to the contradictory view of robots as both embodiments of and ostensible replacements for labor more broadly. Paik's work from the 1960s exhibits a sustained interest in erotics and sexuality, including for instance his musical striptease *Sonata for Adults Only* (1965). That work consists of a marked-up copy of the prelude to Bach's third cello suite in C Major that asks the musician to pause every three measures and remove an article of clothing; Paik proposed the performance to Moorman during their first meeting in New York as part of what would become an ongoing artistic partnership, and they toured with it together in 1965 (Stern; see Piekut, 160–62). A consideration of these performances as forms of sexualized labor is complicated, not only by the multiple (and at times ambiguous) musical/artistic roles that Paik and Moorman inhabited (performer, composer, collaborator, concert organizer) but also by the questionable and at times sexist attitude Paik expressed toward Moorman and toward women in general, alongside Moorman's reciprocal racialization and objectification of Paik as an Asian diasporic subject (Margaret Rhee, 29). In an undated letter to Gordon Mumma (likely written around 1966), for instance, Paik attempts to describe Moorman's uniqueness: "Pretty girl, who is ready to strip, cannot play cello. [A]nd young and pretty cellist will never strip" (qtd. in Piekut, 161). *Robot Opera* nevertheless transposes these performances' sexualized spectacle into robotics. The systems art theorist Jack Burnham compares Paik's robot to Marcel Duchamp's *The Bride Stripped Bare by Her Bachelors, Even (The Large Glass)* (1915–1923), writing that the robot is "'stripped bare' of everything but her skeletal and aluminum components" (351). Whether in the context of collaborating with humans or with machines, a question of agency appears: who (or what) is being exploited (or exposed), and who/what is doing the exploiting?[8]

In this sense, robotics discourse complicates the thing/human distinction, which *K-456* extends to the figure of the artist. As Paik would have it, the robot's bean defecation action represented the technological recuperation of his own artistic labor. His 1962 work *Simple* also called for excreting beans, for instance, by throwing them into an audience.[9] Through a different conflation between human and mechanical subjects, Paik's *K-456* may have also been playing off of existing racial stereotypes, especially in the West, of Asians as "robotic," or akin to a thing. Moorman recalls her response in conversation with Stockhausen to his insisting that Paik was central to a performance of *Originale*: "You have to have Paik," pleaded Stockhausen. To which Moorman responded, "What's a paik? It turns out it's a human being. Nam June Paik." Reflecting further on their first conversation, furthermore, Moorman refers to Paik as an "Oriental man," a phrase that similarly conflates thing and human (Margaret Rhee, 295).[10] Paik apparently saw robots as a technological extension of slavery's original conflation of thing and human, an idea already imbricated in the etymological origins of "robot" as the Czech *rabota*, or forced labor, found as early as Karel Čapek's 1920 play *Rossum's Universal Robots* (*R.U.R.*); incidentally, the play also involves robots refusing to work (a refusal some of its characters attribute to illness).[11] In Paik's (1965) utopian vision, the robotic overtaking of human labor would lead to lives of pure leisure.[12] Short of such a fantasy, though, robotics often heralds a *dys*topian counterpart, as seen in Čapek's fictional imaginary, but also in real economic inequality and unemployment. Robotics discourse is posthuman, then, in its technological marginalization of the human but also through its continuation of the machine–human boundary refiguring that emerged as early as the musical and nonmusical automata of the eighteenth century.

This article analyzes Paik's *Robot K-456* in the context of postwar cybernetics, while it grounds Paik's robotics work in a longer history of musical automata, or the kinds of self-playing musical robots that emerged in the late eighteenth century. These "Enlightenment androids" (Voskuhl) established a link between music, machines, and humanism's original construction of the human. Paik's *K-456* points to these eighteenth-century automata and related musical artifacts through specific signifiers as well as through the robot's construction: Paik's reluctance to model sensory organs, *K-456*'s lack of sensors or feedback mechanisms, and its consequent reliance on human assistance make the robot, functionally speaking, closer to its Enlightenment-era ancestors than its cybernetic contemporaries. What *K-456* shares with cybernetic robotics is an interest in *simulating* the human, loosely in terms of its skeletal anatomy or its ability to "speak" certain phrases but more importantly in its capacity to perform and, apparently, to resist performance. Simulation, in N. Katherine Hayles's periodization, belongs to the final phase of cybernetics, "virtuality," in which the posthuman appears as the technological decentering of the human (234). In the historian Jessica Riskin's analysis, simulation refers to an experimental process set in motion in order to discover the properties of a natural subject. Such simulation appears as early as Vaucanson's eighteenth-century musical automata, which played a significant role in negotiating the boundaries between humans, animals, and machines.[13] The Enlightenment had given birth to the human alongside its posthuman twin: the musical automaton.

As much as historical musical automata are central to *K-456* and its meanings, Paik used his robot to engage with cultural and technological themes of his day, including cybernetics. Paik conceived of cybernetics, in his reading of Norbert Wiener, as a kind of "interscience" comparable to Dick Higgin's intermedia and the boundary crossings of the postwar arts, of which *K-456* was exemplary (1967, 7). Paik links Wiener's cybernetics, which itself challenged human, animal, and machine boundaries, to Marshall McLuhan's understanding of media and machines as human "extensions" (1967, 7–8; McLuhan, 43). Relatedly, Paik's robot also extended the artist's own cultural and technological speculations. In addition to his vision of a fully automated robot economy (cited in Herzogenrath, 21), Paik considered "cybernated art" as a kind of homeopathic treatment for what he called "cybernated life," a state that reciprocally called for moments of shock and catharsis (1966, 24). Paik's robotics work therefore thematizes not only the posthuman birth of the human but also its technological crisis, even its imminent death. Following an exhibition of *K-456* in 1982 at the Whitney Museum in New York, and Paik's staged collision between the robot and a car on Madison Avenue, the artist prophesied that *K-456* represented the "catastrophe of technology in the twenty-first century" (qtd. in Hanhardt). Challenging the modernist investment in technological mastery—in addition to "human[izing] technology," Paik also sought to make it "ridiculous" (qtd. in Youngblood, 306)[14]—his eschatological vision turns on the figures of disaster and failure. *K-456*'s ultimate failure to self-destruct, its unfulfilled refusal, as noted, serves in my analysis as an affirmation of the uniquely human capacity for labor's refusal, its self-negation. In addition to an analysis of *K-456*, this article considers Paik's project in light of a contemporary posthuman era of global economic crisis catalyzed by automation and robotics. How are we to understand robots in cultural and economic terms? In order to analyze Paik's *K-456* and its simultaneous resonances with cybernetics and historical musical automata, we must first articulate the contemporary figure of the robot, particularly as it relates to political economy and labor.

WHAT IS A ROBOT? TOWARD A ROBOT LABOR THEORY OF VALUE

Paik suggests that *K-456* speaks to the common understanding of robots as technological replacements for human labor. "[G]enerally people say that robots are created to decrease people's work," he explains, "but my robot is there to increase the work for people because we need five people to make it move for ten minutes" (in Sharp, 14). Strictly speaking, robots do not actually labor, nor do they produce value. Yet one way to understand them is through the observation that they simulate labor processes, which they appear to replace and to embody. Such an apparent replacement of labor does not necessarily produce gains for the human worker but rather results under capitalism in the generation of surplus value (Marx 2005; 2019). Like any other kind of machine, robots rearrange the labor time of an already stratified population of human workers, whose labor, once relieved from roboticized tasks, is assigned—in typically unequal distributions of race, ethnicity, gender, sexuality, ability, and class—to other, yet-to-be automated processes. How, then, do robots embody labor?

First, the robot literally takes the form of a biomorphic body, as in its resemblance to an animal or, in specifically anthropomorphic variants, a human. For many critics of political economy, Karl Marx included, animals are excluded from the category of value-producing labor, since virtually all productive uses of animals, not unlike machines, require some form of human input or control. In resembling non-human animals, such devices might be described then as "biomorphi-cally regressive"—think of how the popular domestic cleaning robot Roomba resembles, not unlike one of Walter's tortoises, a shell-covered reptile.[15] Nevertheless an understanding of such machines as robots captures their value as the transformation of labor (the work it takes to design, execute, and manufacture the device) into labor-saving machin-ery: domestic cleaning robots apparently require less work than vacu-uming. In this second sense, the robot also embodies labor in that it *stores* it as the objectified or "dead" labor that went into their produc-tion in the first place—whether that consists of research, development, manufacturing, or the programming of other robots. We can under-stand robots, then, as biomorphic simulation as objectified labor in the form of machinery.[16] Since we understand labor as social, in that it requires and creates human relations, we can add, following Matteo Pasquinelli, that roboticization is *sociomorphic*.

Robots thus simulate the *form* of labor while they remain, as non-laboring machinery, strictly external to it. Robots often execute work-like tasks that might otherwise be assigned to or taken up by humans, including historically nonwaged forms such as housework or repro-ductive labor. Paik's *Family of Robot* series, which consists of TV and radio sets arranged to resemble members of an extended family, alludes for instance to the way telecommunications devices are sometimes used to supplement or even replace care labor.[17] The contention that robots do not labor and thus don't produce value may nevertheless seem provocative in the context of cybernetics, whose principal theo-rists including Wiener and John von Neuman saw the potential for feedback and self-replicating systems to radically undermine the notion that machines produce value only at the hands of humans. Further-more, technologies such as AI and brain emulation may eventually not only challenge the human–machine distinction but also suggest that software versions of us might be capable of "experiencing" exploita-tion not unlike their fleshy counterparts. Prior to such a future sce-nario, the ability to mathematically model virtually any finite decision procedure—and hence any determinate work process—was proven as early as the 1930s in the universal Turing machine. If every labor process can, at least in theory, be simulated computationally and exe-cuted by robots, then what is it that makes human labor unique? For one cannot point to any positively unique feature of labor since, as Catherine Malabou has argued, even the brain's supposed "plasticity," its potential for creative adaptation and malleability, can be modeled in silicon.

Although there may be no positive distinction between robotic and human labor, there is perhaps a *negative* one, in the historically specific ability for humans to refuse it. Indeed, this formal freedom to opt out of work constitutes one of the basic conditions of liberal market human-ism: the ability to sell one's labor on the free market—or not. Such a freedom is fundamental, under liberal humanism, to the very way we understand ourselves *as* humans. On the one hand, its absence would reduce everyone, including what Alexander G. Weheliye describes as the "heteromasculine, white, propertied, and liberal subject" (135) to nonhuman slaves. This "freedom" of the free labor market is of course only formal in that, as liberal subjects, there is no actual choice, if one expects to survive in a capitalist society, but to sell one's labor. Its transformation into concrete freedom, on the other hand, may even-tually be the result of a radical political formation beyond capitalism, or indeed it could accompany a significant mutation of the biotech-nological coordinates of the human beyond its current frame of refer-ence: the posthuman. What gives human labor its value, then, is not its inability to be simulated in the form of robotics, on which there seems to be no actual limit, but rather its constitutive negativity. Such a capacity can already be seen in René Descartes's conception of the human soul as capable of intervening upon and interrupting our other-wise mechanical bodies (Descartes, 185; Bates, 63). Yet what makes human labor human, as George Caffentzis argues, is not its "non-mechanizability" but rather its "self-negating capacity" (162; emphasis removed): its very ability to refuse to be. Doubtless capitalism distrib-utes the consequences of and stakes for labor's refusal unequally across divisions of race, ethnicity, gender, sexuality, ability, and class. At the same time, labor's political negation in the form of strikes, revolts, and revolutions—and, perhaps by extension, of failure, catastrophe, and disaster—has been integral to the history of capital.

This speaks, conversely, to the paradox of a robot strike, an im-plausibility seemingly not beyond the imagination of cyberneticians and, at least programmatically, within the scope of Paik's project of making technology "ridiculous" ("Nam June Paik"). Consider K-456's frequent malfunctions. Following its appearance in *Robot Opera* during the Second Annual New York Avant Garde Festival, for instance, *K-456* was supposed to play percussion alongside Moorman in Stockhausen's *Plus-Minus* (1963). But it broke down at the last minute. The reasons reviewers gave were a "nervous short circuit" (Kerner, 15) and "stage fright" (Bowers, 173): facetious of course yet revealing perhaps in their hyperbolic rendering of an all-too-human alibi for the robot's apparent refusal to perform. This article concludes with a reading of *K-456*'s final performance, *First Accident of the Twenty-first Century* (1982), in which Paik staged its collision with a car on Madison Avenue. Such an event has precedents in cybernetics. For instance, Claude Shannon's own foray into artistic production suggests a similar aporia of the labor-refusing robot. Conceived together with Shannon's colleague, the AI engineer Marvin Minsky, the *Ultimate Machine* (1952) consisted of a small wooden casket with a single switch on it. When a viewer flips the switch, the casket lid rises, and out of it comes a hand that turns the switch back off. Is Shannon's robot committing suicide or going on strike? In her wonderful book entitled *The Freudian Robot: Digital Media and the Future of the Unconscious* (2010), the media theorist Lydia H. Liu interprets Shannon's gesture as a kind of robot manifestation of the Freudian death drive, particularly given the relationship between cybernetics and psychoanalysis since as early as Joseph Weizenbaum's famous AI therapist of 1964, ELIZA (and considering applications of Freud's notion of the uncanny to robotics studies, including interpretations of Masahiro Mori's highly popularized "uncanny valley").[18] But such a project can also be read, despite Shannon's own hesitations around the application of his information theory to fields outside of communications, in light of the intimate connection between cybernetics and economics (to which Shannon himself nonetheless contributed), alongside shifting relationships between machines and labor (Mirowsky, 373).[19]

In this complex historical negotiation between humans and robots, automation and cybernetics exert similar forces on labor's composition, yet labor as negation plays a role as well. For instance, the first industrial robot arm, known as the Unimate and developed in the late 1950s (just a few years before Paik created *K-456*), did not result in

automobile workers losing their jobs immediately. In the decades following its introduction, strikes, absenteeism, and sabotage led to the
arm's slow adoption by auto manufacturers. But robotics would eventually lead to the wholesale transformation of the auto industry and
indeed to the larger changes in labor that we now associate with post-
Fordism. This included mass layoffs and a significant reduction in
the workforce in favor of small groups operating several machines at
once—an average of five, initially, at Toyota (Dyer-Witheford, 50)—
incidentally, the same number Paik notes were required to operate
K-456 (Paik qtd. in Sharp, 14).[20] But it also included the redefinition
of the worker: rather than simply an obedient hand operating on an
assembly line, the exemplary post-Fordist worker became an "active
participant" in more open-ended production processes. An ambiva-
lence is already at play: on the one hand, this new, "flexible" worker
of the just-in-time auto plant gives up the job security of the previous
generation (Dyer-Witheford, 50). And, in the process, many traditional
forms of labor would consequently become degraded or "deskilled"
in favor of service and clerical work (see Braverman).[21] On the other,
through the introduction of industrial robots like the Unimate, each
worker's tasks came to demand more unscripted "creativity" and to
point toward a cognitive laborer expected to be, in some sense, less
robotic.

Rather than participating directly in such processes, *K-456* addresses
cybernetic robots through fantasy by creating a series of connections
and disconnections with what Jennifer Rhee calls a "robotic imaginary." Paik did not use just-in-time work processes, for instance, nor
did he create *K-456* in a robot factory (although starting in the 1980s
he produced his work in a factory in Cincinnati).[22] *K-456* contained
servomotors not unlike those found in the Unimate arm, yet rather
than a single appendage, Paik's robot simulated all four. The Unimate's
functional hand is versatile enough to pick up objects such as auto
parts and to operate welding guns (Brooks, 114). *K-456*'s arms move
at the shoulders and wrists, but its hands appear to be mostly for
show: the left hand consists of a large, cartoonish cloth glove; on the
right is what appears to be a retooled pair of wire clippers at times
covered with a similar glove. The Unimate can be programmed and
reprogrammed on the fly, allowing for changes in performance; for auto
plants this represented a paradigm shift away from single-purpose

machines and toward meeting the demand for rapid adjustments to new car models and variants (Dyer-Witheford, 51). Similarly, Paik reused *K-456* in multiple performances, including his work and that of other composers.

Yet Paik's robot relates to its cybernetic contemporaries more through hyperbole than through homology. *K-456* contained a ten-channel data recorder that could, at least in theory, be used to capture the robot's movements sent via its remotes and then replay them at a later time. Although there are no references to the data recorder's use in performance, it appeared in the work's official title: *Robot K-456 with 20-Channel Radio Control and 10-Channel Data Recorder.*[23] Like the Unimate arm, *K-456* was apparently capable of storing a series of maneuvers that could allow Paik to command a performance in his absence. Yet unlike the Unimate, *K-456*'s data recorder appears to have offered no practical benefits to the robot's actual performances. *K-456* departs further from self-governing cybernetic robots in its lack of feedback mechanisms, including sensors and limit switches, that would allow it to operate autonomously or even semiautonomously. Moreover, *K-456*'s reliance on the remote control compounds the robot's necessity for multiple assistants; rather than decreasing labor, his robot counterproductively increases it. By contrast, the Unimate sought to minimize certain forms of labor by maximizing automation—an aspiration evident perhaps in the name of its parent company, Unimation: a portmanteau that combines "universal" and "automation."

It would not be for a few decades, yet still during Paik's lifetime (he died in 2006), that the cybernetic dream of a fully automated robot factory would, to some extent, be realized. Apparently Fanuc, a Japanese company that builds robots that assemble cars, has been running an automated factory supposedly without any on-site human presence for over twenty years (Null and Caulfield; cited in Dyer-Witheford, 56). Such a facility is referred to as a "lights out" factory because they have no need to supply human occupants with the means to view their surroundings. "Not only is it lights-out," claims Fanuc vice president Gary Zywiol, "we turn off the air conditioning and heat too" (qtd. in Null and Caulfield). By 1948, Wiener had already imagined the "automatic factory and the assembly line without human agents." And, not unlike Čapek, he compares such a scenario to slavery in a formulation that, despite its progressive appearance, risks catachresis if we accept the incommensurability between human labor and its machinic equivalent: "Such mechanical labor has most of the economic properties of slave labor, although unlike slave labor, it does not involve the direct demoralizing effects of human cruelty" (40). In his 1965 poem "Pensée" (which contains a reference to Wiener's "control and communication"), Paik expresses a similar interest though he lacks Wiener's inhibitions: "leisure for the leisure's [sic] sake / not as vacation for more work . . . / cultured idleness à la slave owner / of Greece, but with robot-slave . . ."[24] As with robots, lights out factories have yet to eliminate the need for workers. Fanuc employs nearly fifty-five hundred across the United States, Japan, and Europe.

The point isn't to find the human component of robotics and automation but rather to better refine our distinctions between robotics, automation, and labor. Human labor can be defined, again, not through any positive difference with its roboticized or automated equivalent but rather through its self-negating capacity, its ability to choose not to be. What distinguishes robotics from automation is that robots are based on biomorphic simulation, which is further differentiated from the mere representation of life in whatever form or medium. At a minimum, a robot models some part of the *functionality* of a biological organism, from individual organs to body parts or even a complete humanoid. Paik takes some liberties with the human form in *K-456*. Its gangly, exaggerated appearance is perceived as comic by most viewers. As noted, the robot's legs are capable of producing bipedal motion yet use abnormally large "feet," each fitted with four wheels. Such a design derives from Paik's interest in radio-controlled airplanes and remote-controlled cars, which he discovered while in Cologne before he left for Japan in 1963; once in Japan, he adapted the remote controllers in constructing *K-456* with Abe.[25]

Through this wheeled solution to ambulatory motion, *K-456* invites other comparisons to robots of the era. The Stanford Cart was a four-wheeled "robot car," for instance, created in the computer scientist John McCarthy's Stanford Artificial Intelligence Laboratory (SAIL) around the same time Paik erected his robot (Brooks, 25). Described as a precursor to today's self-driving cars, the Stanford Cart was similar to Paik's robot in that it incorporated a radio controller, yet different in that it roamed autonomously.[26] While a cart with four wheels seems an unlikely source of anthropomorphism, the thinking was that it simulated the way animals navigate their surroundings using sensory data. *K-456* again had no sensors, but according to one viewer it could "simulate most human actions"[27] and as noted could, theoretically, be preprogrammed to move without continuous human control. The Stanford Cart's breakthrough was its shift away from a computer vision-based approach—which was slow and computationally expensive but provided a complete map of its surroundings—and toward a more "embodied" design capable of "sensing" what was in front of it. This was not altogether unlike Walter's use of photoelectric sensors in his tortoises. The Polish artist Edward Ihnatowicz's *The Senster* (1969–1970) uses sensors and microphones to detect quiet sounds, toward which it then cranes its long necklike appendage, as though listening. Paik's robot "spoke" but did not listen.

Receptive sense modeling was novel for cybernetic robots, yet the broader paradigm of biomorphic simulation stretches back to the eighteenth century. The robotics expert Rodney Brooks describes the shift to sensory simulation, for instance, in the Stanford Cart and in Walter's tortoises, as producing a "situated" robot that "does not deal with abstract descriptions, but through its sensors with the here and now of the world, which directly influences the behavior of the creature" (51–52). Rather than the AI-based approaches of his colleagues that used a virtual, software model of the world—imagine a primitive version of Google Maps running on a 1960s mainframe—Brooks equipped his robots with "senses" that respond spontaneously to their surroundings. Such responsive behavior, as opposed to being processed through a "computational homunculus," emerges out of an interaction between the machine's body and its environment. Beyond a machine used merely to execute tasks, such an embodied robot "experiences the world," Brooks contends, "directly through the influence of the world on that body" (50, 52).

But how can "experience" be attributed to robots if we understand them as machinery? What kind of metaphysics would support such a view? To answer that, we have to trace a longer history of robotics that accounts for biomorphic simulation and its supporting ideologies as early as the eighteenth century. For the origins of artificial life and AI can be found not only in these various proto-robots, or automata, of which Vaucanson's defecating duck was exemplary, but we should also consider materialist philosophies contending that life itself is mechanical. It is in this nexus that we find, for instance, in one of the earliest French materialists of the Enlightenment, Julien Offray de La Mettrie, humanism's own *Machine Man*: a posthuman avant la lettre.

ALREADY POSTHUMAN? POSTHUMAN AUTOMATA AND THE ROBOT ORIGINS OF THE HUMAN

More than two centuries before the contemporary posthuman, a similar figure had already taken shape in the philosophy and artisanal practices of eighteenth-century Europe. This figure, elaborated through musical and nonmusical automata and accompanying materialist philosophies, was "posthuman" because it contributed to a complex renegotiation of the boundary between humans, animals, and machines. Doubtless this version of the posthuman is far removed from the later instantiation of it that Hayles locates in the Macy Cybernetics conferences of the 1940s and 1950s, but it nevertheless foreshadows the posthuman conceived as the human's technological decentering. As such, these *posthuman automata*, rather than simply rendering inanimate objects as living, embodied the contradictory belief that animal life was at once reducible to mechanism while mechanism remained unable to explain the basis of human consciousness (Riskin, 602).[28] I call these posthuman automata in order to expand the historical purview of the posthuman while also relativizing the latter term's claims to novelty. Indeed, posthuman automata like Vaucanson's defecating duck can be understood as important precursors to contemporary robots and AI. Riskin goes as far as to claim that, despite significant changes in technology and science between the eighteenth century and the present, we still live in the "age of Vaucanson" (612). Since the emergence of the human of humanism, we've lived alongside its robotic doubling in posthuman automata.

In addition to the duck automaton to which Paik's *K-456* alludes, Vaucanson created two other automata that were similar yet anthropomorphic in appearance and musical in their actions: a flautist and a pipe and tabor drum player. Rather than a music box whose outward appearance only represented a musician, remarkably, each of these androids actually played its instrument, a first in the case of the flautist. Automata date back to antiquity, yet this principle of bio-morphic simulation represented a novel invention for the automata of the eighteenth century. These musical automata further represented a shift in music-technological mediation from the score's prescriptive function to physically simulating the *causes* of musical sound. With the advent of recording technology, this paradigm would shift again to include the capture, storage, and replaying of acoustic *effects*. In this sense, *K-456* joins together, anachronistically, all three phases of musical mediation (scores, musical automata, and recordings) in a robot that, like Vaucanson's pipe and tabor player, was a percussionist, but in Paik's case "read" from scores (for instance, in its planned but failed 1964 performance of Stockhausen's *Plus-Minus*) and played speech recordings in the place of a voice.

K-456 signals the broader legacy of Vaucanson, while Paik further references music technologies of the era. Few commentators have interpreted the name Paik gave *K-456*—aside from the general reference to Mozart—despite the historical relevance such music has to the human–machine boundary that Paik engages. Mozart's K. 456 may have been written for Maria Theresa von Paradis, a renowned Austrian pianist and composer who was blind and used one of Wolfgang von Kempelen's printing machines for the visually impaired to write letters and typeset her scores.[29] This, coupled with the fact that Mozart himself went temporarily blind from smallpox as a child, may have been a reason Paik refrained from using cameras or light sensors in *K-456*; in the place of eyes, Paik attached two small motorized propellers. Further related to robotics, Mozart also composed works for mechanical instruments. The composer describes, for instance, his F Minor Fantasie, K. 608 (1791), as "an organ piece for a clock," a work commissioned by the Austrian Count Franz Deym to play on the hour, every hour via an automatic musical clock on display in a Viennese *Kunstkabinett*. According to Annette Richards, such works demonstrated for audiences that it was possible for the "mechanical to supersede the human" (383).

Such a musical fascination with mechanism also anticipates advents in computer music to which Paik was an early contributor. In 1967 and 1968, Paik was a resident artist at Bell Laboratories working with the programmer and artist A. Michael Noll and under the invitation of computer music pioneer Max Mathews. During this time Paik created a handful of works using computer code as their source or means including the concrete poem *Confused Rain*; a film consisting of rotating numbers and flashing dots, *Digital Experiment at Bell Labs* (both 1967); and *Etude 1* (1967–1968), likely a result of his attempt to compose the first "computer-opera in music history."[30] Shortly after his stay at Bell Labs, Paik described his use of permutation sets (i.e., ordered combinations of a certain number of elements) in a manner that resembles some of the earliest automatic compositions. Paik explained that a computer program he created can write all of the haikus possible in Japanese, a finite number given the language's 111 syllables and the seventeen allowed in the poetic form: "When I let the computer write out all these possibilities, which is pretty easy, thereafter no one *can* write any more Haiku poems" (Paik qtd. in Yalkut, 50; emphasis in original).[31] Like Mozart's *Musikalisches Würfelspiel* (Musical dice game), K. 516f (1787), which allows "the composition of as many waltzes as one desires with two dice, without understanding anything about music or composition," such work deskills composition.

In addition to political-economic implications, posthuman automata had a profound influence on philosophical conceptions of the human. All three of Vaucanson's automata were precursors to the inventor's automatic loom of 1747, which led to the wholesale deskilling of weaving (Riskin, 628). Although it did not simulate animal biology, the automatic loom was similar to automata in that it illustrated that tasks once thought of as uniquely human—whether playing music or weaving fabrics—could be done by a machine. As such, posthuman automata tested the hypothesis that life itself was mechanical, ultimately reducible to a complex system of clockwork: a machine man. "The human body," de La Mettrie writes along these lines, "is a machine that winds itself up, a living picture of perpetual motion" (7). Descartes is known for contending that the human body is an automaton, and de La Mettrie's title, *Machine Man*, is a reference to this hypothesis (Thomson, xvi). Yet distinct from his interpretation in de La Mettrie, Descartes offers a concept of the human that breaks with pure mechanism.

In addition to his references to eighteenth-century automata, Paik's robots also refer to Enlightenment philosophy (including that of the seventeenth century). His work *Descartes in Easter Island* (1993), for instance, consists of a robot head composed of laser discs, circuit boards, video screens, and speakers (Silver). The very notion of the Cartesian mind-body split is already, in some sense, robotic. If the mind is truly separate from the body, then the body is simply incidental; it can be replaced by any number of prostheses corresponding to organs, body parts, and, potentially, up to a full mechanical body. Cyberneticians Wiener, Shannon, and McCarthy acknowledged Descartes as an early theorist of automata. Yet despite his conception of the human *body* as mechanical, Descartes identifies the soul as ultimately unsimulatable, irrecuperable in automata (Bates, 46). For Descartes, "The soul intervenes on behalf of the organism," according to historian David Bates, "by forcing the automaton to act against its own automaticity" (46; emphasis removed). Is it possible, then, that Paik's *K-456* stages a similar kind of interruption of its own automaticity? We've considered how *K-456*'s various performative refusals, its breakdowns and bouts of "stage fright" (Bowers, 173), parallel the human capacity for self-negation in the form of strikes, sabotage, staged accidents, and even suicide. In light of this intersection, we turn now to Paik's staged collision between *K-456* and an automobile, which the artist likened to technological catastrophe.

ROBOT K-456 AND THE CATASTROPHE OF TECHNOLOGY

Robot K-456's final performance, *First Accident of the Twenty-First Century*, occurred as part of Paik's retrospective at the Whitney Museum of American Art organized in 1982 by the curator John G. Hanhardt. On June 22 at 11 a.m., Paik removed the robot from its display on the fourth floor of the museum, which at the time was located on Madison Avenue on the Upper East Side of Manhattan. Paik placed *K-456* on the sidewalk and stood behind the electronic creature while operating his radio controller. As spectators and a TV crew looked on, *K-456* began to move with the same shambling stride of its first appearance nearly twenty years prior. The robot moved north on Madison, stopping first in front of the Whitney to "eat" a hot dog purchased from a stand, then continued until it reached the crosswalk at Seventy-Fifth Street. *K-456* waited for the light and, as impatient commuters honked, crossed the busy intersection. The robot then traversed Madison but roughly halfway across was struck from behind by a white Volkswagen turning from Seventy-Fifth Street.[32] The robot's initial encounter with the car, which was driven by the artist William Anastasi, left the figure standing. But then the robot's metallic frame jolted forward again, and after further thrusts of the automobile's bumper, *K-456* fell on its face, its backside lodged underneath the vehicle's front end (Paik et al.). A group of onlookers approached Paik's life-sized creature, dragged it back onto the sidewalk, and later hoisted it onto a "stretcher" (Herzogenrath, 24; Jennifer Rhee, 60). During an interview with a TV reporter on the scene following the incident, Paik prophesied that the event represented the "catastrophe of technology in the twenty-first century. And we are learning how to cope with it" (qtd. in Hanhardt).

Paik's *First Accident of the Twenty-First Century* expresses two antithetical conjectures—that the robot is autonomous and that it is unfree—which both challenge and affirm distinctions between the human and its machinic equivalent. As anthropomorphic simulation, Paik's robot *takes the form* of the human's capacity for self-negation, its radical potential for refusal. *K-456*'s accident might be thought of as the result of carelessness or neglect. As suggested, it can also be read as rendering the paradoxical gesture of a robot suicide not unlike the "robot strike" found in Shannon's *Ultimate Machine*. Through its display of vulnerability during the collision, *K-456* simulates the human susceptibility to harm and, in perhaps the robot's only foray into sense modeling, a sensitivity to touch. In addition to its appetite, Paik attributes other features to the robot that "humanize technology" (qtd. in Youngblood, 306). As the recipient of faux medical attention, *K-456* functions, according to Jennifer Rhee, as a kind of technological "surrogate" for care labor (60).[33] Speaking to an on-site TV reporter, Paik suggested in his typical deadpan manner that *K-456* had health issues commonly associated with aging, which may have contributed to its impeded movement: "This robot is almost twenty years old, and [it's] got arthritis." Robots apparently age more quickly than humans, although Paik noted that *K-456* "has not yet [had a] bar mitzvah" (Paik et al.). Even religious ceremony is not beyond the robot's refusal— which speaks to ways, beyond labor, that robotic simulation can be understood as *sociomorphic*.

At the same time, *First Accident* stages the robot's attempt to escape from captivity. Such a reading is complicated by the fact that Paik's robot, while in some ways lifelike, seems far from autonomous. *K-456*'s autonomy is undermined, that is, by the knowledge that the robot acts not on its own volition but according to the will of another. *K-456* is both "humanized" and tethered to Paik's control, rendered in this sense as subhuman. As the news anchor noted following the event, "On Madison Avenue today, a speeding car struck a pedestrian stepping off the curb. But [it] was no normal pedestrian. It was a remote-controlled robot" (Paik et al.). Recalling Čapek's *R.U.R.*, but also Wiener's fully automated factory and Paik's poem "Pensée," *K-456* appears as no more than a slave under Paik's control. As noted, in "Pensée," Paik compares robotics to slavery ("slave owner / of Greece, but with robot-slave"), and he goes further to comment on and artistic medium and property ("Painting is the private property . . . / Music is the public common good . . ."); race, global economics, and class. Paik continues, tentatively foreshadowing perhaps *K-456*'s attempted suicide: "Kill Paik's Art?" "Kill the Robot Opera?"

Paik's staged collision between robot and automobile invites, as suggested, a longer view of such intersections between humans and robots. According to Wulf Herzogenrath, Paik became interested in constructing an anthropomorphic robot after learning that the brain began to grow after early humans ceased moving around on all fours and as a result had to operate two newly freed hands (cited in Herzogenrath, 21). The biotechnological legacy of this story of human ambulation returns in the postwar automobile industry through the Unimate arm. That invention not only transformed the manufacturing of cars but brought about a major change in the structure of labor. Paik's *K-456*, as noted, shares features with the post-Fordist factory automation the arm helped to bring about, while another origin of the robot is remote-controlled toy cars (19). Following his performance in front of the Whitney, Paik's interest in cars appeared as a leitmotif in *Electronic Superhighway* (1995) and, in a work that recapitulates *K-456*'s links between eighteenth-century music and twentieth-century technoculture, *32 Cars for the 20th Century Play Mozart's Requiem Quietly* (1997). *First Accident* uses these technological themes of the twentieth century as a basis to speculate about their catastrophic development in the twenty-first.

What is the catastrophe of technology in the twenty-first century? Paik prophesied that "in the next century New York will be filled with robots, so we have to teach robots how to avoid cars" (qtd. in Werner,

40). There's of course no way to know what the remainder of the twenty-first century will bring. Data suggest that automation and robotics have already contributed to unemployment in the transportation industry. Paik's literal collision between automobile and robotics in the late twentieth century anticipates perhaps the figurative one in the twenty-first. Specifically, autonomous vehicles are projected to significantly transform the U.S. economy in the coming decades. Paik of course had no knowledge of the emergence of contemporary self-driving vehicles, let alone any anticipated political-economic consequences. But he was likely aware of McCarthy and SAIL's attempts to create a "robot car" around the same time the artist created *K-456*. And Paik did not speculate on the consequences of autonomous vehicles, yet he expressed a professional interest in economics and computing, writing of his potential for a "Copernic[an] discovery" in line with Marx or Keynes (Paik, n.d., letter to Cage). Weary of catastrophe, Paik also saw in technology utopian potential. In an undated letter to Cage written following Paik's stay at the art and technology commune Pulsa, he attempted to describe a life that "would be more relevant in the decentralized, post-industrial, jobless-oriented future [of] communal living" (Paik, n.d.. letter to Cage).[34] One can only speculate whether robotics and automation will lead to such a future or to its dystopian reflection.

The catastrophe of technology, in this sense—and in conclusion—is not limited to the twentieth or twenty-first century but applies to a longer history of robotics and automation. This history is underpinned by ideological supporters and artistic and philosophical detractors alike. From de La Mettrie's machine man of the Enlightenment to Brooks's robotic "experience," such mechanistic views of the human encounter our capacity for self-interruption articulated as early as Descartes. Music, from Vaucanson and Mozart to Paik and Moorman, plays a central role in this negotiation, not because it announces a romantic core of the human ultimately irrecuperable by technological simulation. Rather, the experiments of eighteenth-century posthuman automata link perhaps unexpectedly to postwar experimental music through Paik's confrontation with robotics and cybernetics. It is in this context that Paik's robot seems to parody the project of artificial life as found in cybernetics but also stretching back to posthuman Enlightenment automata. As opposed to Eduardo Kac's reading of *K-456* as a "caricature of humanity" (78), I interpret Paik's work as a critique of robotics as technological catastrophe. There may be no positive limit to the kinds of things, including various forms of labor, that robotics and automation are capable of doing. But by failing to achieve the human's purely negative difference from the mechanical as radical refusal, Paik's robot demonstrates that such a capacity for self-negation might be the human's last determining attribute.

G Douglas Barrett works on postwar experimental music and related art movements. He is currently assistant professor in the Media Arts Department at New Jersey City University.

Notes

1. "There's a Message in There Somewhere" British news program. The performance the news report documents was part of the *24 Stunden* event held at Galerie Parnass, Wuppertal, Germany, June 5–6, 1965.

2. Several accounts of the event indicate that both breasts twirled (e.g., Ericson, 20), whereas Benjamin Piekut interprets *New York Times* music critic Raymon Ericson's comment, which was written after the festival's opening night, as suggesting that only the left breast rotated (Piekut, 159). If this was, in fact, a variation, it's possible that it was either intentional or produced as a result of one of *K-456*'s frequent malfunctions. During the same festival *K-456* was supposed to perform alongside Moorman in Stockhausen's *Plus-Minus* (1963), but broke down due to a "nervous short circuit" (Kerner, 15). Another reviewer called it "stage fright" (Bowers, 173).

3. Sophie Landres analyzes *Robot Opera* in the context of *opera buffa* (19).

4. Undated flyer for *Robot Opera*; punctuation added, capitalization removed (Nam June Paik Archive). Reprinted in Chiu and Yun, 63.

5. Although the robot's ad hoc appearance implied for some that the artist had "made it for next to nothing" (*Electronic Design* 14, no. 1 [1966], reproduced in Hoggett), it was valuable enough that Paik considered selling it for parts in order to pay for several months of living expenses in New York. In an undated letter to John Cage (ca. 1970), Paik listed the total cost to make *K-456* as $2,400, which would be equal to roughly $18,300 today.

6. Although the robotics enthusiast Reuben Hoggett does not detect any sensors or limit switches in photographic documentation of the 1964 version of *K-456*, Jack Burnham lists unspecified "sensory devices" in his account of Paik's robot (351).

7. Hoggett includes an image with a caption that refers to *K-456* as a "radio-controlled belly dancer."

8. On the question of Moorman's agency in performing Cage, see Piekut, 140–76.

9. See Landres, 18. See also Paik's *Listening to Music through the Mouth* (1963); cited in Rothfuss, 84–85.

10. Paik created *K-456* prior to his arrival in the United States, yet its references to eighteenth-century automata can nonetheless be interpreted as pointing to a biological, gendered, and ethnic "otherness" of these devices that resonates with the treatment he experienced while in America. Specifically, Vaucanson's duck was one of several automata that resembled animals; other automata like the harpsichord player by the French clockmaker Jaquet-Droz possessed exaggerated feminine features and behavior; and one of the most notorious automata of this era was Wolfgang von Kempelen's chess player of 1770, widely known as the Turk. On Vaucanson's duck and the Turk, see Riskin. On the Jaquet-Droz automaton, see Voskuhl. I thank one of the anonymous *Cultural Critique* reviewers for their suggestions pertaining to this interpretation.

11. See Jennifer Rhee's instructive analysis of Čapek's *R.U.R.* (17–24).

12. See also Herzogenrath, 21.

13. Riskin is careful to note that her use of "simulation" is based on its twentieth-century meaning as an "experimental model from which one can discover properties of the natural subject" (605 n.4).

14. "[T]he real issue implied in 'Art and Technology' is not to make another scientific toy, but how to humanize the technology and the electronic medium" (Paik qtd. in Youngblood, 306). See also Paik in "Nam June Paik: Edited for Television."

15. Rodney Brooks's genealogy links Walter's tortoises with the Roomba, a product of iRobot, the company Brooks cofounded in 1990 with two other members of the MIT Artificial Intelligence Lab (17–21, 34 n.1).

16. Some robots appear more biomorphic than others, and so my use of the term is to be expansive. Many industrial robots such as the Unimate arm discussed below simulate only a single body part. For others, bodily resemblance is latent, vestigial, or, as with the Stanford Cart, relates to their sensing and / or navigational abilities. Software "bots" lack physical embodiment altogether, yet they may be understood as biomorphic with respect to the mind. Other machines appear to straddle distinctions between nonbiomorphic automation and robotics. Vaucanson's loom, also discussed below, while not a robot, used the same mechanical design the inventor later used in his proto-robotic musical automata. Relatedly, Jean-Claude Beaune locates an incipient biomorphism already at play in automation, claiming that "before thinking of automating manual labor, one must conceive of mechanically representing the limbs of man" (257; translated and cited in Riskin, 623 n.54).

17. Jennifer Rhee analyzes *K-456* in terms of care labor (58–60).

18. Liu, 139–42. Note, however, that Mori's text does not explicitly engage with Freud's notion of the uncanny. For a reading that relates Mori to the establishing of boundary conditions of the human, see Jennifer Rhee, 13–17.

19. Mirowski cites evidence that Shannon encouraged the scientist John Larry Kelly Jr. in his application of information theory to economics (373).

20. Wulf Herzogenrath claims that four were necessary to operate *K-456* (21).

21. On deskilling in an art-historical context, see Roberts.

22. See Hölling, 39–40. Relatedly, Hölling suggests that later in his career Paik's role in his artistic process had become increasingly that of a "manager and designer" (37).

23. See, for example, Burnham, 351; or Jennifer Rhee, 58.

24. Kalindi Vora and Neda Atanasoski locate a related symmetry between slavery and roboticization as a form of "surrogacy" inherent to liberal humanism that includes "the body of the enslaved standing in for the master, the vanishing of native bodies necessary for colonial expansion, as well as invisibilized labor including indenture, immigration, and outsourcing" (6).

25. See "Art and the Future: Extract of Douglas Davis interview with Nam June Paik" (reproduced in Hoggett); and Herzogenrath, 19.

26. See Lester Earnest's genealogy linking the Stanford Cart to self-driving cars.

27. *Electronic Design* 14, no. 1, reproduced in Hoggett.

28. An analysis of these automata as living dolls and machines appears in Wood.

29. There is some disagreement about whether or not Mozart wrote K. 456 for Maria Theresa von Paradis (see Ullrich; Maunder). On the flute solo, see Ward, 303.

30. Paik in Application to Rockefeller Grant, 1967; cited in Kaizen, 231.

31. Paik's computer-generated Haiku emerges from the same place, and around the same time, as Alison Knowles's *House of Dust* (1967), a similarly composed permutation poem that was engineered by fellow Bell Labs resident and computer music composer James Tenney.

32. A scrap of Whitney Museum letterhead labeled "file: ROBOT" contains the performance's time and date ("6/22/82 11:00 AM") and the fourfold order of events (capitalization removed):

Robot stops & eats hot dog
Robot waits for light, crosses 75th Street. Cars honk.
Robot turns to cross Madison
Robot struck by car from rear.

Corresponding numbers appear next to locations on a map sketched to show the order of events. The document was likely authored earlier in the month of June 1982.

33. For an extended treatment of technological surrogacy, see Vora and Atanasoski.

34. On the Pulsa commune, see McKee.

Works Cited

Bates, David. 2013. "Cartesian Robotics." *Representations* 124, no. 1 (Fall): 43–68.

Beaune, Jean-Claude. 1980. *L'Automate et ses mobiles*. Paris: Flammarion.

Bowers, Faubion. 1964. "A Feast of Astonishment," *The Nation*, September 28, 1964, 172–75.

Braverman, Harry. 1998. *Labor and Monopoly Capital: The Degradation of Work in the Twentieth Century*. New York: Monthly Review Press.

Brooks, Rodney. 2003. *Flesh and Machines: How Robots Will Change Us*. New York: Vintage Books.

Burnham, Jack. 1968. *Beyond Modern Sculpture: The Effects of Science and Technology on the Sculpture of the Century*. New York: George Braziller.

Caffentzis, George. 2013. "Why Machines Cannot Create Value: Marx's Theory of Machines." In *In Letters of Blood and Fire: Work, Machines, and the Crisis of Capitalism*. Oakland, Calif.: PM Press, 139–63.

Chiu, Melissa, and Michelle Yun, eds. 2014. *Nam June Paik: Becoming Robot*. New York: Asia Society Museum.

Descartes, René. 1983. *Traité de l'homme*. In *Oeuvres de Descartes*. Edited by Charles Adam and Paul Tannery. 11 vols. Paris.

Dyer-Witheford, Nick. 2015. *Cyber-Proletariat: Global Labour in the Digital Vortex*. London: Pluto Press.

Earnest, Lester. 2018. "Stanford Cart: How a Moon Rover Project was Blocked by a Politician but Got Kicked by Football into a Self-Driving Vehicle," March 11, 2018, https://web.stanford.edu/~learnest/sail/cart.html.

Ericson, Raymon. 1964. "Avant-Garde Music. Festival Opens." *New York Times*, August 31, 1964.

"file: ROBOT." Box 0109–111, Folder 35. Nam June Paik 1982. April 30–October 24 81.0. Whitney Museum of American Art. Frances Mulhall Achilles Library and Archives, New York.

Hanhardt, John. 2006. "Chance in a Lifetime." *ArtForum*, April 2006. https://www.artforum.com/print/200604/nam-june-paik-10623.

Hayles, N. Katherine. 1999. *How We Became Posthuman: Virtual Bodies in Cybernetics, Literature, and Informatics*. Chicago: University of Chicago Press.

Herzogenrath, Wulf. 1988. *Nam June Paik Video Works 1963–88*. Hayward Gallery.

Hölling, Hanna. 2017. *Paik's Virtual Archive: Time, Change, and Materiality in Media Art*. Berkeley: University of California Press.

Hoggett, Reuben. 2010. "1964—Robot K-456—Nam June Paik (Korean) & Shuya Abe (Japanese)—cyberneticzoo.com." September 1, 2010. http://cybernetic zoo.com/robots-in-art/1964-robot-k-456-nam-june-paik-korean-shuya-abe -japanese/ (accessed June 17, 2019).

Kac, Eduardo. 2001. "The Origin and Development of Robotic Art." *Convergence: The International Journal of Research into New Media Technologies* 7, no. 1 (2001): 76–86.

Kaizen, William. 2012. "Computer Participator: Situating Nam June Paik's Work in Computing." In *Mainframe Experimentalism*, edited by Hannah Higgins and Douglas Kahn, 229–39. Berkeley: University of California Press.

Kerner, Leighton. 1964. "Buzz, Buzz." *Village Voice*, September 3, 1964.

La Mettrie, Julien Offray de. 1996. *Machine Man and Other Writings*. Translated and edited by Ann Thomson. Cambridge: University of Cambridge Press.

Landres, Sophie. 2018. "The First Non-Human Action Artist: Charlotte Moorman and Nam June Paik in *Robot Opera*." *Performing Arts Journal* 118:11–25.

Malabou, Catherine. 2019. *Morphing Intelligence: From IQ Measurement to Artificial Brains*. New York: Columbia University Press.

Marx, Karl. 2005. "The Fragment on Machines." In *Grundrisse: Foundations of the Critique of Political Economy*, 670–712. New York: Penguin.

———. 2019. "Machinery and Modern Industry." In *Capital: Volume I*, 405–556. New York: Dover.

Maunder, Richard, 1991. "J. C. Bach and the Early Piano in London." *Journal of the Royal Musical Association* 116, no. 2:201–10.

McKee, Yates. 2008. "The Public Sensoriums of Pulsa: Cybernetic Abstraction and the Biopolitics of Urban Survival." *Art Journal* 67, no. 3 (Fall): 46–67.

McLuhan, Marshall. 1994. *Understanding Media: The Extensions of Man*. Cambridge, Mass.: MIT Press.

Mirowski, Philip. 2001. *Machine Dreams: Economics Becomes a Cyborg Science*. Cambridge: Cambridge University Press.

Mori, Masahiro. 2012. "The Uncanny Valley." Translated by Karl F. MacDorman and Norri Kageki, *IEEE Robotics and Automation Magazine* 19, no. 2:98–100.

"Nam June Paik: Edited for Television." 1975. Interview with Calvin Tompkins. Hosted by Russell Connor. New York: WNET/Thirteen.

Null, Christopher, and Brian Caulfield. 2003. "Fade to Black: The 1980s Vision of 'Lights-Out' Manufacturing, Where Robots Do All the Work, Is a Dream no More." *Fortune*, June 1, 2003. http://archive.fortune.com/magazines/business2/business2_archive/2003/06/01/343371/.

Paik, Nam June. 1965. "Pensée (1965)." In *Treffpunkt Parnass: Wuppertal 1949–1965*, 286–89. Cologne: Rheinland-Verlag.

———. 1967. "Norbert Wiener and Marshall McLuhan." *The ICA Bulletin*. Bulletin of the Institute of Contemporary Art, London. no. 172/3: 7–9.

———. n.d. Flyer for *Robot Opera*. Smithsonian American Art Museum, Nam June Paik Archive. Box 19, Folder 11.

———. n.d. Letter to John Cage, likely written around 1967. John Cage Collection, Series II: Notations Project, Subseries 2: Correspondence, Box 10. Folder 6: Nam June Paik, Northwestern Archival and Manuscript Collections.

Paik, Nam June, with Betsy Connors and Paul Garrin. 1989. *Living with the Living Theatre*. Video. Coproduction of WGBH New Television Workshop, Electronic Arts Intermix.

Pasquinelli, Matteo. 2016. "Abnormal Encephalization in the Age of Machine Learning." *e-flux* 75 (September 2016). https://www.e-flux.com/journal/75/67133/abnormal-encephalization-in-the-age-of-machine-learning/.

Piekut, Benjamin. 2011. *Experimentalism Otherwise: The New York Avant-Garde and Its Limits*. Berkeley: University of California Press.

Rhee, Jennifer. 2018. *The Robotic Imaginary: The Human and the Price of Dehumanized Labor*. Minneapolis: University of Minnesota Press.

Rhee, Margaret. 2015. "Racial Recalibration: Nam June Paik's *K-456*." *Asian Diasporic Visual Cultures and the Americas* 1:285–309.

Richards, Annette. 1999. "Automatic Genius: Mozart and the Mechanical Sublime." *Music & Letters* 80, no. 3 (August): 366–89.

Riskin, Jessica. 2003. "The Defecating Duck, or, the Ambiguous Origins of Artificial Life." *Critical Inquiry* 29, no. 4 (Summer): 599–633.

Roberts, John. 2007. *The Intangibilities of Form: Skill and Deskilling in Art After the Readymade.* New York: Verso.

Rothfuss, Joan. 2014. *The Topless Cellist: The Improbable Life of Charlotte Moorman.* Cambridge, Mass.: MIT Press.

Sharp, Willoughby. 1982. "Artificial Metabolism: An Interview with Nam June Paik." *Video* 80, no. 4 (Spring/Summer): 14–17.

Silver, Kenneth. 1993. "Nam June Paik: Video's Body." *Art in America* (November).

Stern, Fred. 1980. "Charlotte Moorman and the New York Avant Garde." December 14, 2006. YouTube video, https://www.youtube.com/watch?v=wiEJdOlgcDE.

"There's a Message in There Somewhere." 1954. June 24, 1954. http://www.movietone.com/N_search.cfm?ActionFlag=back2ResultsView&start=1&pageStart=1&totalRecords=1&V_DateType=1&V_DECADE=1929&V_FromYear=19 (accessed June 11, 2019).

Thomson, Ann. 1996. Introduction to *Machine Man and Other Writings.* Edited and translated by Ann Thomson. Cambridge: University of Cambridge Press.

Ullrich, Hermann. 1946. "Maria Theresia Paradis and Mozart." *Music & Letters* 27, no. 4 (October): 224–33.

Vora, Kalindi, and Neda Atanasoski. 2019. *Surrogate Humanity: Race, Robots, and the Politics of Technological Futures.* Durham: Duke University Press.

Voskuhl, Adelheid. 2013. *Androids in the Enlightenment: Mechanics, Artisans, and Cultures of the Self.* Chicago: University of Chicago Press.

Walter, W. Grey. 1950. "An Imitation of Life." *Scientific American* (May): 42–45.

Ward, Martha Kingdon. 1954. "Mozart and the Flute." *Music & Letters* 35, no. 4 (October): 294–308.

Weheliye, Alexander G. 2014. *Habeas Viscus: Racializing Assemblages, Biopolitics, and Black Feminist Theories of the Human.* Durham: Duke University Press.

Werner, Laurie. 1986. "Nam June Paik—Laureates." *Northwest Orient* (June): 36–40.

Wiener, Norbert. 2019 (1948). *Cybernetics: Or Control and Communication in the Animal and the Machine.* Cambridge, Mass.: MIT Press.

Wood, Gaby. 2002. *Living Dolls: A Magical History of the Quest for Mechanical Life.* London: Faber and Faber.

Yalkut, Jud. 1968. "Art and Technology of Nam June Paik." *Arts Magazine* (April): 50–51.

Youngblood, Gene. 1970. *Expanded Cinema.* New York: E. P. Dutton.

EMBRYONIC CITIZENSHIP
DISIDENTIFICATIONS OF ASIAN RACIALIZED SETTLERHOOD

Jennifer F. Wang

In their 2007 survey of second-generation racial minorities in Canada, "Racial Inequality, Social Cohesion and Policy Issues in Canada," Jeffrey Reitz and Rupa Banerjee provide a finding that, at first glance, may appear unsurprising but ultimately overturns conventional assumptions concerning citizenship. Studying factors that indicate social integration, such as strength of interpersonal relations, overall life satisfaction, and civic participation, Reitz and Banerjee conclude that relative to the first generation of immigrants (that is, their parents), second-generation Canadian-born racial minorities consistently scored more negatively on indicators of social integration (31, 33–34). Put another way, for racialized minority immigrants, the *more* extensive and familiar one's experience with Canadian society is, the *less*, in fact, one feels one belongs to it.

As Reitz and Banerjee suggest, these results upend the conventional account of citizenship and belonging that are premised on long-term embedded factors, such as education and employment experiences, since there tend to be more opportunities across the board for the second generation compared to their first-generation parents (15). Yet "despite improvement in the economic circumstances of immigrants as they adjust to Canadian society and labour markets and the generally more positive employment experiences of the second generation, a racial gap in *perception of discrimination* is notable among immigrants with longer experience in Canada. This gap is even greater among the children of immigrants" (Reitz and Banerjee, 9; my emphasis). The noted discrepancy at play here exists precisely in the intangible realm of perception and feeling. For although the second generation may possess increased access to the economic, legal, and political guarantees of citizenship—as measured through education and employment—they *perceive* and *feel* themselves to be "lesser" citizens.

In her analysis of this survey, Lily Cho points out that "in placing vulnerability alongside discrimination in their research, Reitz and Banerjee suggest that the less concrete, more ambiguous experiences of exclusion—those that reside in feeling something even if one cannot prove it—are just as crucial to understanding racism and access to full citizenship as those of discrimination" (109). Ultimately, for Cho, "The Reitz and Banerjee report suggests that there is a relationship between feeling and citizenship . . . [t]hat is, it marks an inverse relationship between feeling and citizenship: feeling is connected to citizenship, and the greater the racialized subject's claim may seem to be to Canadian citizenship, the more she will feel alienated from it" (109). Building on Cho's insights, I take up this emergence of—to slightly append her description—what I name "perverse feelings" toward citizenship in order to illuminate a twofold conundrum in the context of Asian North American racial formation: first, the contradiction between race and citizenship and, second, the contradiction between racialization and settler colonialism.[1]

Situated within the historical context of Asian American racial formation, such perverse feelings would hardly be surprising. As Lisa Lowe explains in her foundational study *Immigrant Acts*, citizenship has functioned as a "'technology' of racialization and gendering" (11) for Asian Americans. Beginning in the nineteenth century, immigration exclusion laws have served to define the American citizen over and against the Asian immigrant, such that Asian immigrants are cast "both as persons and populations to be integrated into the national political sphere and as the contradictory, confusing, unintelligible elements to be marginalized and returned to their alien origins" (4). As Lowe elaborates, the historical origins of this recursive contradiction by which Asian American subjects are construed as "perpetual foreigners" arises out of an *economic* contradiction, one between capital's need for a steady supply of "cheap labour" and the state's imperative to reserve capital accumulation for a "unified" (that is, racially homogenous, white) citizenry (13). It was by excluding and disenfranchising different waves of Asian immigrant groups (Chinese, Indian, Japanese, Filipinx, etc.) at multiple historical junctures that the state was able to resolve this contradiction between the economic drives of capitalism and the political imperatives of the nation-state.[2]

Read through this lens, we might therefore understand the perverse feelings of second-generation Asian North American subjects as the irreducibly material trace or residue of this foundational history of Asian racialization, as one that—constituted through the regulations of immigration, naturalization, and citizenship—cast the Asian American political subject in "'alien-ated' relation to the category of citizenship" (12). As David Leiwei Li points out, "Although the law necessarily ensures the contractual terms of citizenship in abstraction . . . it [cannot] undo the historically saturated epistemological structures and structures of feeling, which continue to undermine the claims of Asian American subjectivity" (11). Thus, the antithetical relation between the Asian racialized subject's affective versus legal statuses functions as a critical reminder that these histories of racialization continue to haunt and determine the material conditions of Asian Americans in the present, even beyond the lifting of legal restrictions and putative inclusion within the nation-state.

If Asian racialized perverse feelings signal the enduring racializing effects and technology of citizenship, then they also serve to illuminate yet another predicament in Asian North American formation. To return to Reitz and Banerjee's survey, it is notable (though perhaps not so surprising) that the "control group" to which they compare racialized minorities' broader social integration within Canadian society consists of white, European-descended Canadians (10). While it is understandable that the survey requires such a comparative move in order to highlight "deviation" (and deviance) from the normative structures of "integration," it nonetheless raises questions about the unspoken or implicit colonial presumptions that might possibly undergird these second-generation racialized minorities' perceived claims to and lack of national belonging. Who is, by default, constructed as the consummate model citizen, whose feelings and citizenship are "properly" aligned, in these articulations of affect and perception? What does "true" belonging in, identification with, or claiming of the nation-state entail? Such slippages belie how the hegemony of the settler state can be reproduced even—and perhaps, especially—in the very moment of its contestation.

In this way, the perverse feelings of citizenship are also the effect of *and* enact what Quynh Nhu Le terms "settler racial hegemonies," which describe the "uneven incorporation of Indigenous and non-Native racialized communities' social, cultural, and political articulations into the imperatives of the settler state, thus reinscribing the territorial claims and telos of the settler nation" (4). Le supplements the Gramscian notion of hegemony—premised on the logic of consent—by probing the "formation of liberatory dissent. That is, how consent to the settler state can be enacted through actions that are seen as a refusal of or counteraction against settler and racial power," such that "the liberatory demands (or resistance) of one racialized/colonized community can hinge on the very logics that dominate the other" (4). In the context of Asian North American citizenship, critiques of racial exclusion and demands for national inclusion can serve to bolster the "territorial claims and telos" of the settler colonial state as the guarantor of legal and political rights. Taken together, perverse feelings shed light on this historically constituted impasse in Asian North American racial formation, wherein the very apparatus of racialization (citizenship) is precisely that which ensures the reproduction of settler colonialism.

In this essay, I am interested in tracking this dense nexus of Asian North American racialization, citizenship, and settler colonialism through the work of literary representation. Traditionally, literature has performed an integral function in resolving the contradictions of citizenship through the nineteenth-century form of the bildungsroman, in which the narrative of youthful education allegorizes national development. In *The Theory of the Novel,* Lukács describes the aim of the bildungsroman as "the reconciliation of the problematic individual, guided by his lived experience of the ideal, with concrete social reality" (132). Drawing out the submerged role of the national form in the works of Lukács and Franco Moretti, Jed Esty argues that for the realist bildungsroman, "The crucial symbolic function of nationhood . . . gives a finished form to modern societies in the same way that adulthood gives a finished form to the modern subject" (4). Put another way, the transition by which youth progresses into adulthood serves to resolve the contradiction between individual particularity and national identification. Thus, the developmental narrative smooths over ruptures in the process of social and national integration such that the story of growing up into adulthood is one of becoming a citizen.

If the traditional bildungsroman plays such a crucial role in the construction of proper citizenship, then how might the racial and colonial ruptures of Asian American citizenship—that is, its perverse feelings—be mediated through literary form?[3] What narrative modes of development are specific to the doubled contradiction that Asian racialization poses to citizenship and settler colonialism? Conversely, what insights into the latter might be gained by tracking the work that the former performs? Tracing the imperial and colonial imaginaries that underpin modernist developmental arcs, Esty identifies the tropes of "arrested development" and "unseasonable youth" as serving to "expose[. . .] and disrupt[. . .] the inherited conventions of the bildungsroman in order to criticize bourgeois values and to reinvent the biographical novel, but also to explore the contradictions inherent in mainstream developmental discourses of self, nation, and empire" (3). In a similar vein, I turn my attention to the racially and sexually demarcated allegorical figure of the Asian North American child-citizen in order to home in on the temporal registers of how this minor character grows up. It is my contention that doing so will reveal much about how the double bind of Asian racialized citizenship and settlerhood comes to be mediated and resolved. More specifically, I will illuminate how the developmental arc of the Asian North American child is profoundly asynchronous, one through which the Asian American subject is racialized, in part, through a liminal position of premature adulthood and prolonged childhood. Taking as my case study the 2001 novel *The Kappa Child* by Hiromi Goto, I read its articulation of embryological development as a feminist and queer critique of Darwinian theories of evolution, which also seeks to provide a (new) materialist account of Asian racialized asynchronous development. I argue that ultimately such an account mediates the Asian North American subject's uneven disidentification with the settler colonial logics of racialized settlerhood, one structured through a simultaneous desire for *and* disavowal of the violent erasures of Indigenous presence within settler-state formations.

In so doing, the critical interventions of my analysis are, broadly, twofold. First, building on recent work in childhood studies that approach "the child as a means of thinking in new ways about the adult self and the social, civic, and erotic elements that comprise it" (Levander and Singley, 3), I focus on the distinctive features of an Asian American racialized childhood and its temporal specificity.[4] While others have examined particular aspects of the Asian American child—such as "intergenerational conflict" with its parents (Wong; Li; Ninh), its participation in the "family business" (Glen; Miri Song;

Park), its consumption practices (Ho), its inhumanity (Chang), its play (Fickle), its gendering (Reddy; Tran), and its queering (Min Song; Sohn)—I propose that childhood itself is not merely epiphenomenal to but rather comprises a constitutive site of Asian racialization as such.[5] Robin Bernstein has observed that "racial binarism—understanding race in terms of white and nonwhite, or a 'black and white' polarization that erases nonblack people of color—gained legibility through nineteenth-century childhood" (8). From this, I propose that if childhood plays an instrumental role in obscuring divergent racializations, then it also poses a special relevance and resonance for conceiving of Asian racialization in particular. Whether in the context of a Black/white racial binary or, more recently, Native/settler colonial binary, Asian North American racial formation has been theorized as a triangulation that disrupts such binaries.[6] Thus, in returning to an incipient site at which racial and colonial binaries are reinforced, childhood offers up a generative means for limning the distinctly triangulated form of Asian racialization.

To be clear, then, my aim is not merely to claim visibility for the Asian American child-citizen by way of elucidating the distinctions, significant as they may be, between the "universal" (white) child-citizen and its racialized counterpart. Rather (and this brings me to my second main intervention), I hope that parsing the figure and figurations of the Asian racialized child-citizen will serve to illuminate the multiple— and, at times, competing—colonialisms between Asian racialization and Indigeneity that undergird the formation of settler racial citizenship. In this sense, then, my essay also responds to recent calls in the scholarship of Asian North American and transpacific studies to attend to the place of settler colonialism within Asian diasporic formations. The contributors to "Settler Colonial Studies, Asian Diasporic Questions" (2019) articulate this critical work and its stakes as such:

[T]here has been a decisive shift toward interrogating the role Asian communities play in extending or disrupting the structural dynamics of colonial dispossession, displacement, and disposal that are imposed on Indigenous populations in the Americas, Australasia, Africa, Asia, and the Pacific Islands. This shift represents a critical reorientation that requires that we grapple with the complex interplay of race and Indigeneity, compelling us to challenge Asian settler mythologies—particularly those that celebrate early Asian labor migrants as "pioneers," while ignoring their complicity with colonial expansion and the genocidal elimination of Native peoples and cultures. (Day et al., 2)

Following from this, it is my contention that childhood is a breeding ground for Asian racialization (as triangulated through racial and settler colonial binaries) and that the trope of the child-citizen can be deployed precisely in service of such "settler mythologies." Thus, this essay wagers that what is needed is a study of the Asian North American child that both enacts and repudiates settler colonial eliminations of Indigenous presence within settler-state formations; such a study will have much to tell us about the distinctly ambivalent logics of Asian racialization consolidated through the technologies of citizenship.

GROWING PAINS: THE CHILD-CITIZEN AND ITS RACIAL ALLEGORIES

As a shorthand for the allegorical work that children and childhood are put to use for in the service of national identification, I examine a figure that I term the "child-citizen." Theorists of affect and citizenship have long identified children as an apposite repository for fantasies of ideal national identity and belonging.[7] Diagnosing the cultural persistence with which the American national subject is figured as childlike or attributed with childish qualities as "infantile citizenship," Lauren Berlant points out that "the nation's value is figured not on behalf of an actually existing and laboring adult, but of a future American, both incipient and pre-historical: especially invested with this hope are the American fetus and the American child" (6). What lends the child-citizen its allegorical credence—its capacity to figure the idealized imaginaries and investments of citizenship—is the sanctity of growing up. As Lee Edelman has convinced us, children are synonymous with futurity: "We are no more able to conceive of a politics without a fantasy of the future than we are able to conceive of a future without the figure of the Child. That figural Child alone embodies the citizen as an ideal, entitled to claim full rights to its future share in the nation's good, though always at the cost of limiting the rights 'real' citizens are allowed" (11). Essential to the Child's figural capacity to displace the "actual" rights of citizenship by its promissory ideal, is its "freedom to develop undisturbed . . . uncompromised by any possible access to what is painted as alien desire" (21). Thus, even as, according to Edelman, the Child "must never grow up" (21) in order for the fantasy to be sustained, the future is always invoked and marshalled as that which must be preserved in the name of this minor figure's "proper" development (so that it can grow up at all).

As a number of queer theorists have noted, the future tends to go belly-up when the queerness of children is revealed. In the case of the queer child, who does not remain "innocent of sexual desires and intentions" (Bruhm and Hurley, ix), their development, unlike Edelman's Child, is not "relentlessly figured as vertical movement upward toward full stature, marriage, work, reproduction, and the loss of childishness" (Stockton, 4). Instead, they "delay" temporally sideways and backward into alternate, even "utopian," orders of activation, desire, and relation (Stockton; Muñoz 2009). Working backward from a queer critique of Edelman's Child, we can grasp the hegemonic function of the child-citizen as twofold. First, the child-citizen, in order to be determined a child—that is, distinguished from adulthood—must yet still grow "up." Second, the neat chronological ordering of its growth and maturation—what Elizabeth Freeman terms "chrononormativity"— is precisely what lends this figure its allegorical power, what imbues it with the capacity to call forth the very future into which it can and will seamlessly extend.[8]

If the child-citizen's development has much to tell us about the normative orders and ordering of citizenship, then what of those children who are not children and, therefore, do not get to grow up in uninterrupted ways, if at all? What forms of national belonging and identification do they embody, if any? Robin Bernstein has persuasively argued that children are defined as such through innocence but that the latter is exclusively reserved for white children. Conversely, as many have noted with devastating clarity that "Black children are still denied consideration as children" (Fielder). While others have shed crucial light on the myriad ways in which Black children are "de-childed" (Bernstein, 54), that is, evacuated of childhood—through racialized innocence (Bernstein), legacies of enslavement (Abdur-Rahman, 116), policing and incarceration (Fielder), "premature knowledge" of sexual violence (Wright)—I build on these insights to probe how the operating logic of the child-citizen drastically short-circuits in the face of Black racial difference.[9] If "Black childhood" as such constitutes, as some have put it, an "ontological negation" (Teshome and Yang, 162), then the clear temporal demarcation between childhood and adulthood—integral to the figural logic of the child-citizen—does not hold.

As Teshome and Yang point out, the very concept of "growing up," "fall[s] apart anagrammatically for black children . . . when there is no being/becoming and there is no growing up. There is only transitioning from meager to harvestable . . . adult" (165). This use of an *economic* ("meager" to "harvestable") "grammar of suffering" predicated on accumulation and fungibility (Wilderson, 28) to characterize the un-distinction between childhood and adulthood figures the structural position of Blackness within the national order as "foundational" but "unthought" (Hartman and Wilderson, 184–85). More specifically, in attending to the roles of (white) affect and sentiment in displacing (Black) civil and political rights in nineteenth-century constructions of citizenship, Saidiya Hartman argues, "The affiliation of happiness and subjugation and prosperity and exclusion gave shape to a social body identifiable by isolated and stigmatized internal aliens and the illusory integrity of the dominant race. Basically, the wholeness of the social body was made possible by the banishment and abjection of blacks, the isolation of dangerous elements from the rest of the population, and the containment of contagion" (199). That national identification is fomented by conjoining (white) happiness and (Black) subjugation and (white) prosperity and (Black) exclusion illuminates the role of constitutive negation (banishment and abjection) that Blackness plays in the circuits of citizenship. Put together, then, the figural Black un-child—who does not grow up so much as transition into degrees of accumulation and fungibility—limns the foundational occlusions by which national identification is facilitated and made possible through the economic, political, and affective negations of Blackness.

Turning now to take up the categorical contradictions of Asian American childhood, I bring together the insights of Lisa Sun-Hee Park and erin Khuê Ninh. In her ethnographic study *Consuming Citizenship*, Park notes that for Asian American children raised in immigrant entrepreneurial households, the demarcation between family and work is often blurred, and thus, "the usual division 'childhood' and 'adulthood' is not applicable" (65). On the one hand, when these immigrant children "help out" the family business by performing labor—

usually unremunerated (Park, 74)—they take on the adult roles, responsibilities, and tasks of an employee or worker (66). On the other hand, in navigating back and forth between fulfilling the duties of worker *and* family member, Asian American children of immigrant entrepreneurs often retain their familial role of being treated like a child by their parents, even after becoming adults (67). Thus, as Park argues, "More so than role reversal, role conflict, or status inconsistency, the concepts *premature adulthood* and *prolonged childhood* best describe the complexity of the lived experiences of entrepreneurial children" (66). In naming the experiences of "children who grow up too fast and, as young adults, never age" (Park, 65), premature adulthood and prolonged childhood are two sides of the same coin, one ultimately rooted in being "out of synch with the larger, socially determined concept of adulthood and childhood" (66). Although Park's study is limited to Asian American children of immigrant entrepreneurs and small family business owners, I contend that her insights of premature adulthood and prolonged childhood can be categorically extended to second-generation Asian American development.

It is no coincidence that immigrant entrepreneurship has come to epitomize Asian American identity in the post-1965 era. The source of this ideological conflation arises out of the historical production of Asian American subjects as model minorities through the Immigration and Nationality Act of 1965. Heralded as a liberalizing corrective to former immigration restrictions, the Immigration and Nationality Act of 1965 abolished racially exclusionary "national origin" quotas and ushered in the largest wave of Asian immigration to the United States to date. However, the 1965 Immigration Act resulted in more rather than less legal specifications by establishing a preference system that targeted skilled professional and technical labor as well as family reunification. In doing so, the 1965 Immigration Act drastically altered the socioeconomic landscape of Asian America, producing a severe bifurcation in the demographics of post-1965 immigrants along classed and ethnic lines: including, on the one hand, a skilled professional-managerial sector (such as doctors, scientists, engineers, computer programmers, etc.), and on the other, an underclass of low-wage service workers and laborers. Such employment and family-based immigration preferences served to constitute middle-class Asian American family formations that reinforced the pernicious model minority myth

(Shelley Lee, 241–42), which casts Asian Americans as exceptionally capable of achieving ethnic assimilation and socioeconomic upward mobility in the face of structural barriers.[10]

At the same time, however, a number of structural conditions have served to funnel Asian immigrants and Asian Americans, particularly those in the working class, into higher rates of entrepreneurship than the general U.S. population (236). These include exploitative working conditions, racism and racial discrimination within professions, language barriers, nontransferable education and skills, and the fact that the 1965 Immigration Act favored "investor immigrants" who brought start-up capital with them, whether in modest or large sums (236). Thus, the economic organization of Asian immigrants into family entrepreneurship and small businesses has been structurally conditioned by immigration law. In turn, this historical production has given rise to the stereotypical image of the resourceful and self-reliant immigrant entrepreneur as the consummate model minority, who, through sheer hard work, overcomes adversity in order to achieve the American Dream. Extending even further this metonymical chain by which Asian American subjects are rendered model minority entrepreneurs, scholars have suggested that as a result of post-1965 policies of Asian migration and racialization, the Asian immigrant family has been transformed into a (re)productive site of human capital.[11] In this vein, erin Ninh has persuasively illustrated how the Asian American nuclear unit, as "a special form of capitalist enterprise" (2), engages in family as a business; in short, is in and of itself a small family business. In Ninh's account, the Asian American immigrant nuclear family constitutes "a production unit—a sort of cottage industry, for a particular brand of good, capitalist subject" (2), that is, the model minority. If such is the case, if the Asian immigrant household can be viewed as an entrepreneurial unit of sorts—one employed in the particular business of producing model minorities—then all second-generation Asian American children categorically experience premature adulthood and prolonged childhood.[12]

Indeed, reinforcing this idea, a number of the experiences described by Park's subjects resonate with and apply to all children of Asian immigrants, not only those operating family businesses. For example, Park points out, "In entrepreneurial households . . . as much as parents try, financial security, discrimination, and family stability are worries shared by both adults and children" (66), serving to prematurely age these children whose juvenile status does not afford them the unburdened inner life of a "carefree childhood" (Park, 70). However, financial security, discrimination, and family stability are threats that not only Asian entrepreneurs or small business owners face but ones that the majority of working-class Asian immigrant households share to one degree or another. Thus, premature exposure to these worries is an experience that resonates across second-generation children raised in such households. In addition, Park observes that among the "adult" roles performed by entrepreneurial children working at the family business are those of "problem-solver," "cultural mediator," and "translator." Once again, second-generation children of working-class Asian immigrant households generally have firsthand experience in variously occupying each one of these roles throughout their childhood because immigrant parents face extensive linguistic and cultural barriers in navigating the bureaucratic and legal infrastructures of North American social life, especially when they lack the financial resources to outsource these necessities. The adult tasks that some of Park's subjects describe performing for their parents, such as effectively communicating with the plumber or speaking to credit card and utilities companies over the phone (79–80), extends to all Asian American children of immigrant parents, and in particular, those from working-class households.

Put together, I propose that the post-1965 model minoritization—as a historically situated form of racialization—of Asian American childhood has produced a distinctly asynchronous temporality of development, one characterized as simultaneously premature and prolonged. If such is the case, what might such asynchronous trajectories reveal about Asian North American negotiations of the contradictions of citizenship? Neither the teleological reproduction of national belonging nor its ontological negation, the asynchronicity of Asian racialized childhood, I suggest, mediates a distinct relationship to national identification. To discern the precise nature of this figuration and relation, I turn now to Hiromi Goto's novel *The Kappa Child*. First, I begin by tracking how it deploys the tropes of asynchronous development in order to register the historical shifts in Asian North American racial formation. At the same time, however, it aims toward a materialist revision of these tropes by excavating an alternative account of embryological development, one that emphasizes the generative potential in the discontinuities of and disruptions to teleological evolution. Next, I argue that this materially specific character of Asian racialized childhood's asynchronicity—its simultaneous bifurcation and liminality—figures the disidentificatory position that it holds to consolidations of national belonging. It is a disidentification that both approximates and disavows settler colonial eliminations of Indigeneity, one that reveals the racialized contradictions of citizenship and settlerhood embodied by Asian North Americans.

"NOT GROWING, BUT SPLITTING": NEW MATTERS OF DEVELOPMENT

The Kappa Child, the second novel (2001) published by Japanese Canadian author Hiromi Goto, constitutes a fitting site for probing my interest in the figure of the child-citizen for a number of reasons, as we will come to see.[13] As signaled by its title, it is a novel entirely preoccupied with children and childhood as well as the broader apparatuses through which they take form, that is, circuits of reproduction, birth, genealogy, and kinship. Briefly summarized, the novel centers on its unnamed narrator, a gender-nonconforming Japanese Canadian lesbian, who is impregnated by a mythical creature of Japanese origin (known as a "kappa") during the last lunar eclipse of the twentieth century. The diegetic plot follows the narrator trying to make sense of and adjusting to her fantastical pregnancy—the symptoms of which include an intense craving for Japanese cucumbers and embodied communications (inconvenient kicks and jabs) from the unborn but migratory fetus (who refuses to remain confined to her uterus)—while navigating her job as a professional shopping cart collector as well as her relationships with her estranged family and close friends (a lesbian couple who suspect her pregnancy to be psychosomatic). However, interspersed throughout the narrative present are the narrator's flashbacks to her childhood familial migration from British Columbia to the barren Albertan prairie farm on which her father stubbornly tries to cultivate Japanese rice. The longer her pregnancy "progresses," the more the narrator is involuntarily plunged into the memories of her childhood past, described as the sudden onset of "memory cramps" that leave her "reeling in the aftermath of delayed emotions" (233). Extra-diegetically, punctuating the narrator's plotting of her pregnancy and childhood remembrances, are also brief episodes of first-person narration, given presumably by the unborn kappa-hybrid fetus itself, which detail its embryological passage into being.

If one were to get lost in the speculative or fantastical elements of the novel, one might miss just how much of it is suffused by trauma.[14] As Nancy Kang astutely points out, despite the fact that the narrator spends much of her time grappling with the extensive domestic, physical, and psychological abuse committed by her father during her early years, "critical responses to The Kappa Child have avoided deep engagement with this subject" (26). However, it is precisely the traumatic nature of her difficult childhood that her impossible pregnancy and its symptomatic "memory cramps" recursively return her to with such relentless and compulsive force. In the narrator's remembrances of these childhood years, we can discern the characteristics of premature adulthood that mark the experiences of Asian American immigrant children. For example, from the early age of ten, the narrator and her sisters are consigned into the "family business" by performing hard, physical labor to help realize her father's "futile dream" (Goto, 192) of growing Japanese rice in the Albertan prairies. She vividly recalls the grueling work of heaving slabs of sandstone "onto the flatbed that never seemed to fill. The bend of back, childish muscles straining into cramps" (181). As the narrator intimates, such duress took an untimely toll not only on her physical development—as expressed in the "straining" and "cramping" of childish bodies unsuited to adult-ranged motions that leave her with "prematurely well-developed forearms" (200)—but also psychological state.

Beyond their economic contributions to the household in the form of agricultural labor, the narrator and her sisters also perform the roles of cultural mediators and translators between their parents and white mainstream Canadian society. When the family first arrives in rural Alberta from British Columbia, the narrator's mother becomes too overwhelmed to leave the motel room in which they are staying. The narrator explains, "Okasan refused to leave the room and Slither and I made dashing runs to the Lucky Dollar for eggs and apples. PG sent to the motel man for more toilet paper" (110). Thus, rather than performing the parental role during a time of instability and transition,

Okasan appears to be more of the vulnerable child, attended to by her own children who must translate her needs linguistically (and otherwise) to the outside public, demonstrating the reversal of "child" and "adult" roles in the narrator's household. In reflecting on the psychological toll of her childhood years, the narrator muses, "A child isn't born bitter. I point no fingers as to who tainted the clean, pure pool of my childhood. . . . Knowing that being grown up was no swell place to be means that you are grown up enough to notice. And you can't go back from there" (13). This paradox, by which a child's anticipatory knowledge of adulthood's hardships already renders her an adult, signals the premature aging characteristic of Asian American childhood.

Conversely, even as the narrator and her sisters display the "premature adulthood" identified by Lisa Park, they simultaneously remain suspended in a stage of "prolonged childhood." For example, when they return to their childhood home for a holiday visit during Easter, they slip back into ingrained patterns of tiptoeing around their father. During a moment of bickering, the narrator and her sisters hear from the other room "the snap of a newspaper being straightened, loud and sudden, like the pop of a gun. We jump, then we are still" (24). Even as adults, then, the sisters revert back to their childish deference to their father's displeasure. Indeed, the rest of their visit is punctuated by the all-too-familiar kind of domestic violence that permeated the narrator's childhood. As the narrator observes, "My sisters and I are all physically grown but people would be hard-pressed to describe us as adults in the house of our parents. Every time we come home, we slip into our childhood roles. No one is exempt. Until death do us part" (28). However, the durational extension of the narrator and her sisters' childhood habitus does not end at the threshold of their parents' house, for the narrator describes the trauma of childhood domestic violence as "the baggage of our lives together. Even when we live apart. Baggage carried, with nowhere to check it in" (192). The ongoing quality of this trauma's "baggage" and its constant intrusion into her adult present manifest as an agonizing sense of childhood's demonic reach for the narrator. As she notes, "I've always hoped that childhood could be a book, a sequence of pages that I could flip through, or close. . . . But, of course not. Childhood isn't a book and it doesn't end. My childhood spills into my adult life despite all my attempts at otherwise and the saturation of the past with the present is an ongoing story" (215). In Goto's revision of Park's thesis, it is the traumas induced by premature aging—"spilling" into and "saturating" adult life—that, in turn, render childhood traumatically interminable. Thus, the asynchronicity of Asian North American childhood is a condition of trauma, both its symptom and cause.

The narrator's melancholic suspension between her adult present and childhood flashbacks positions her in precisely the asynchronous, liminal state of simultaneously premature adulthood and prolonged childhood endemic to the model minoritization of Asian racialized childhood. Thus, Asian North American childhood, while diverging from the ontological negation of Black childhood, remains hopelessly out of joint. In this way, it bears temporal kinship with queer childhood, as previously discussed. However, even as the two overlap—as in the case of the Asian Canadian *and* lesbian narrator—the distinctions between them are worth parsing. While sharing in the perverse disruption of a linear and vertical telos of development, *The Kappa Child* posits Asian racialized asynchronous maturation through a distinct model of temporal disjuncture, one that is specifically and materially articulated through its critical interrogation of Darwinian notions of evolutionary development. Such an account is directly narrated for us from the first-person perspective of its eponymous character, the unborn fetal "kappa child" residing inside the narrator, and formally demarcated in italicized passages that episodically punctuate the "main" text.

Through a feminist and queer reckoning with and revisioning of Darwinian evolution, the kappa child narrativizes the process of its own embryological growth through an emphasis on degeneration rather than preservation, bifurcation rather than proliferation, and potentiality rather than succession.[15] To begin with, at its conception, the kappa child ponders, "*And how I feel! The perpetual sense of potential, vibrant and meticulous. How can the infinitely possible be compared to terminal growth? Degeneration? . . . It's a bad sign, don't you think? How we develop, not by growing, but by splitting*" (18; my emphasis). In a subsequent passage, the kappa child further emphasizes the process of bifurcation: "*At least I do trust, until the time of the splitting. When something whole is made to fracture in order to grow*" (30; my emphasis). In this juxtaposition between potential (infinite) and growth (terminal), the latter comes to be experienced, paradoxically, as "degeneration."

Such an account of "growth," as its very obverse, aligns with Darwin's account in which accumulation and attrition are more counterposed than interlocked. As Elizabeth Grosz points out in *The Nick of Time*, "Darwin describes natural selection as a 'principle of preservation,' but this preservation is quite ambiguous and multilayered" (47). In point of fact, the "positive productivity" (47) of preservation, simultaneously, in Darwin's own words, "entails extinction" (qtd. in Grosz, 47). Such a contradiction, as expressed by the kappa child, by which progressive proliferation can produce its own reversal, is extended by revealing an emphasis on bifurcation and splitting intrinsic to the Darwinian narrative of exponential development that underpins evolution.

In *On the Origin of Species*, Darwin's account of natural selection is one that prioritizes increase—both in individual variations and species population—as a measure of evolutionary "success," for the former results in the latter. As he writes, "The truth of the principle, that the greatest amount of life can be supported by great diversification of structure, is seen under many circumstances" (87). In order to produce more and more variation, and thus life, "natural selection is daily and hourly scrutinizing . . . every variation, even the slightest; rejecting that which is bad, preserving and adding up all that is good; silently and insensibly working, whenever and wherever opportunity offers, at the improvement of each organic being in relation to its organic and inorganic conditions of life" (66). Darwin's characterization of the evolutionary project is a synthetic one, in a doubled sense, which views the work of natural selection as an automatized—even "algorithmic" (Grosz, 48)—process that coalesces variations (subtracting the bad and adding up the good) to their natural environment ("conditions of life") for the purposes of proliferating ever-increasing diversifications of life. In this account, then, growth is based on exponential processes of configuration, cumulation, and synthesis.

In contradistinction, the kappa child's insistence on development through "splitting" and growth through "fracture" defamiliarizes Darwin's evolutionary account by reaffirming the obscured dimensions of bifurcation and divergence from it. To explain how variation is continuously generated and successfully reproduced (through the numerical maximization of offspring), Darwin introduces the process of sexual selection—which he takes care to distinguish as separate from the "struggle for existence" that animates natural selection (68)—as one that relies on the essential bifurcation or "splitting" of all species forms into two irreducibly distinct categories. As Grosz aptly observes, however, in Darwin's work, the role of sexual selection constitutes a kind of Derridean supplement to natural selection, for the former, in "amplifying" (70) and "inflecting" the latter often serves to, at the same time, "compromise" it (66). Thus, although (sexual) bifurcation plays an indispensable role in the process of natural selection, it tends to get submerged as a "secondary," complementary characteristic within an evolutionary account that prioritizes synthesis and accretion in service of an ever-increasing telos. In foregrounding sexual bifurcation—splitting and fracture—as, in fact, essential to the principles of gain and increase (in variation and species life), the kappa child signals the "queerness" of Asian racialized growth, in that it is less cumulative than proceeding through its own attenuation.

The shift in emphases from preservation to degeneration and from continuity to fracture, as articulated by the kappa child, holds crucial implications for disrupting the temporal tenets of a Darwinian evolutionary account that hews to a teleological narrative of progress. For Darwin, the result of survival through proliferation is that species life proceeds in a relentlessly forward-marching, unilateral direction, for "evolution never reverses itself: it never goes from more to less developed, from more differentiated to less differentiated" (Grosz, 67). Grosz glosses this temporal dynamic of growth through the concept of "self-overcoming," which she defines as the essential work of natural selection, for "it provokes life, inciting the living to transform themselves, to become something other than what they once were" (64). In addition, she further elaborates, "self-overcoming . . . is the most basic characteristic of life, this self-overcoming attesting to the irreducible investment of life in the movement of time, its enmeshment and organization according to the forward direction of time" (64). Refuting precisely such a linear model of self-overcoming, through which life develops by constantly transforming itself forward, the kappa child describes its embryological development as one that instead draws on a reservoir of infinite potentiality.

As the kappa child describes: "*Beneath the skin itself, my cells resound. There is a memory of the body, memory held within ancient cells, always ever-present. My cells tell me what has passed and what may pass before"* (Goto, 105; my emphasis). Then, in a subsequent passage: *"I see with kappa eyes what will come to pass in times long forgotten. I see with kappa eyes what has never come to pass. The forwardbackward spiral which collapses in the ever-present"* (150; my emphasis). The kappa child's narration of the "memory" of a body contained within developmental (and yet ancient) cells disrupts the neat chronology of evolutionary progression. In this case, it is a future transformation (the body), which has *already* been manifested, that "resounds" to haunt (as "memory") and condition its "less developed" and "less differentiated" form (the cellular). Thus, rather than a telos of self-overcoming by which the latent is superseded by what it manifests into, the kappa child's development traverses a logic of radical potentiality, one in which the latent retains its latency even "after" manifesting into something else. As Grosz argues, the "un-selected" of natural selection comprises:

> The evolutionary residue, those that leave no trace, no progeny . . . remain the undeveloped, the latent, the recessive, a virtual forever unactualized. . . . These residues of selection cannot be simply conceived, in Hegelian terms, as that which is overcome or sublated, the negative that is transcended in a movement of the positive; they are not dialectical remnants but virtualities that remain unactualized, potentials unexpressed, forces redirected in their trajectory. (50)

Does the kappa child not constitute precisely such "evolutionary residue"? In its development qua bifurcation, the kappa child encapsulates the process whereby becoming (selected) "splits" from its potential (un-selected). However, the latter (undifferentiated cells) is not simply "sublated" or "transcended" but remain latent virtualities "forever unactualized," located within both the "before" and "after" of its manifestation (the body). As self-narrated, the kappa child's temporally advanced ("ancient") cells retain the (un-differentiated and undeveloped) potential for a fully formed body they have already once become. In turn, entirely dissociated from the linear and teleological thrust of becoming *into*, the kappa child remains suspended ("ever-present") in a "forwardbackward spiral" (*"what has passed"* rebounding back into *"what may pass"*; *"what will come to pass in times long forgotten"*; and *"what has never come to pass"*), perpetually advancing forward in a backward motion and regressing in order to "grow up."

DISIDENTIFICATIONS OF ASIAN SETTLERHOOD

As the embryological development of *The Kappa Child*'s eponymous character reveals, the "out of synch" disjointed Asian North American not-quite-child resolutely does not grow up. Instead, she bifurcates—splitting in two (or more) parts. In so doing, Asian racialized development disrupts the linear telos of succession in favor of radical potentiality, such that childhood is, on the one hand, simultaneously haunted by what it has already become (prematurely aged) and yet, on the other, constitutes a latent "residue" that resists sublation to remain unactualized and redirected in its trajectory (interminably prolonged). In turn, such an asynchronous developmental model premised on bifurcation and simultaneity, as embodied by the Asian North American child-citizen, is one that figures a temporally specific position to the mediations by which national identification and incorporation are fulfilled. The inextricable relation between the traumatic condition of "growing up" (or rather, the lack of a childhood) and fantasies of national belonging is made explicit by the reigning conceit through which the narrator articulates the melancholic remembrances of her childhood.

In her reflections, the narrator repeatedly references the immensely popular children's book *Little House on the Prairie* by Laura Ingalls Wilder as a kind of cipher by which she translates and adapts her own family's migration.[16] As she excitedly exclaims to her sisters after the family first arrives to their Albertan farm, "The Ingalls family were from the east so they went west. We're from British Columbia, so we were in the west, but we moved east to get to the same place, funny, huh?" (Goto, 42). The narrator extends this comparison between the Ingalls family's journey to the prairies (of Kansas) and their relocation to the same (in Alberta) in order to claim the pioneer identity for her and her family. While reading aloud from the book, she informs her sisters, "It's about being pioneers. See, we're like that right now, get it?" (43). It is no coincidence that *Little House on the Prairie*—and its iconic status as a frontier myth for national identity—functions as the dominant symbolic vehicle through which the narrator gives shape to her own childhood and development.

In *Little House, Long Shadow*, Anita Fellman points out that the perennial themes of every book in the Little House series—"the training of children to hard work and deferred gratification, obedience to parents, the close-knit quality of the family, appreciation for education and respect for teachers [. . .], and the clear gender division of labor between husband and wife—have appealed to people whose distress at the current state of the American family and discomfort with the values implicit in contemporary American culture have been escalating since the 1960s" (247). Therefore, as "a primer for traditional values such as religiosity, patriotism, and the traditional family" (Fellman, 246), the *Little House* books were in fact key to preparing the ground for and contributing to the acceptance of a post-1970s Reaganite conservatism that emphasized "the importance of the intact nuclear family in instilling values of hard work, conventional morality, clearly defined gender roles, patriotism, and religious values and observance" (235). In this way, we might consider Laura Ingalls Wilder the archetypal child-citizen, one whose upbringing—characterized by indomitable ingenuousness (read: racialized innocence) and unerring commitment to familial unity—mediates the trajectory by which she learns and internalizes national values, and in doing so, comes to figure and embody idealized citizenship in post-1970s Reaganite America.

If *Little House on the Prairie* functions as the yardstick by which the narrator measures her childhood, then, by the same token, the liminal condition of this childhood and the asynchronous forms of development it engenders are limned precisely by the fissures that open up between Laura Ingalls Wilder's romanticization of "pioneer life" (as nation building) and the lived reality of settlement experienced by the narrator and her family. For the narrator, the discrepancy between the former and latter is most epitomized through the question of Indigenous presence. As critics of *Little House on the Prairie* have pointed out, its "racist" representations of Native Americans (Heldrich, 99)—in particular, the Osage peoples, on whose unceded territory the Ingallses were illegally occupying—deployed images of the "noble savage" and "vanishing American" (Kaye, 126) in order to legitimize "not just the inevitability but the desirability of native dispossession and erasure as a means to facilitate frontier settlement" (Smulders, 200). The narrator's growing awareness of the settler colonial representational logics that structure and pervade her beloved book is first roused by the possibility that the "pioneer experience" might simply be a euphemism for "settlerhood," one simultaneously premised on the expropriation of Indigenous land and elimination of Indigenous presence.[17] When her family first arrives at their newly purchased homestead, the narrator ponders, "Strange how Pa [Ingalls] just parked their wagon anywhere he felt like and called that place his. Maybe Dad did the same thing. Maybe everyone did" (Goto, 45). The sense of doubt anaphorically conveyed in the "maybe" casts aspersion on the legitimacy of Pa Ingalls's territorial claim as a performative act.

The narrator's initial suspicion concerning the logics of land ownership—that it may not be as straightforward as "calling" it into truth—is further extended into a recognition of settler colonial violence. Later on, as they settle into their new home, the narrator considers, "Maybe Dad was just like Pa parking his wagon wherever he wanted. Maybe it was like Pa chopping down trees by the river. He didn't ask for anyone's permission. It wasn't stealing. No one called it that. I hoped" (129). Performing the same syntactic function as the previous "maybes," the tentative "I hoped" that the narrator appends to her disarticulation of Pa's actions from "stealing" serves to contest rather than confirm it. In addition, the conspicuous absence of a grammatical subject in her anxious proposition that "it wasn't stealing" raises the question of from and against whom would Pa be committing theft? As a number of scholars have pointed out, "the Ingallses were part of the mass of white . . . settlers who crowded illegally onto the Osage Diminished Reserve, gambling that they would be able to buy the land at bargain rates once the Indians were forced to move" (Fellman, 17). In defamiliarizing the experience of pioneering as one that, in fact, consists of unfounded claims to territorial ownership and theft of natural resources, the narrator posits it to be synonymous with settler colonial expropriation of Indigenous land.[18]

These violent contradictions of settler colonialism—by which (Indigenous) dispossession is transfigured into (settler) belonging and theft into ownership[19]—are thrown into sharpest relief for the narrator through her growing friendship with Gerald, her neighbor's son who is of Japanese Canadian and First Nations descent.[20] As she confesses, "I didn't not want to see a Laura Ingalls Indian, but then, I didn't want to see one either. When I met Janice and Gerald, I had to meet someone I'd never imagined. . . . When we station-wagoned our way to the prairies, moving east instead of the traditional west, I didn't really think about Indians, First Nations or otherwise. I didn't think" (Goto, 189). Here, the narrator acknowledges that the desire for "being pioneers" cultivated by *Little House on the Prairie* results in her "un-thinking" assimilation into and cooperation with a settler colonial logic that relies on the psychic and geographic disavowal of Indigeneity from the national landscape. Such a fantasy of seamless conquest, expro-priation, and belonging is ruptured, however, by the reinsertion of this previously elided Indigenous presence into the narrator's child-hood. As she comes to realize, "Gerald Nakamura Coming Singer was incomprehensible. In Laura Ingalls's book-world, Indians meant tee-pees on the prairies and that was that. Indians didn't equal someone who was both Blood and Japanese Canadian. Indians certainly never meant someone who lived next door on a chicken farm" (188). That the limits of representation in *Little House on the Prairie,* the irreconcil-able gulf between fact and fiction that opens up, are epitomized for the narrator by Gerald's embodied ("someone who was both Blood and Japanese Canadian") and proximate ("someone who lived next door") presence highlights the necessary function of Indigenous elimination and erasure to the settler colonial project.

The narrator's increasing recognition of and discomfort with how Laura Ingalls's idyllic pioneer myth condenses a settler colonial logic, which predicates settler belonging on Indigenous dispossession, inten-sifies into a fever pitch of symbolic renunciation when she burns her copy of *Little House on the Prairie* after she loses her friendship with Gerald, and he moves away. However, the book and character return to periodically haunt her throughout her adult life. For example, when the narrator learns of a new coworker named "Laura Ng," it causes her "eyes [to] pop wide. Stifle a guffaw" (223) at such a pun on an all-too-familiar name. In another instance, the narrator hallucinates Melissa Gilbert, the actress who plays Laura Ingalls in the television adaptation of the book series, speaking to her directly from within the screen and insisting that "they changed the books. . . . They got it all wrong" (252). Such recursive reminders of the original prototype's mediated refractions within the narrator's own life suggest the endur-ing hold of the former over the latter.

The narrator's ambivalent relationship to the settler colonial log-ics encoded by *Little House on the Prairie* and Laura Ingalls, as one char-acterized by simultaneous approximation and disavowal, recalls José Esteban Muñoz's theory of "disidentification." As a "survival strategy," disidentification is a "third mode of dealing with dominant ideology, one that neither opts to assimilate within such a structure nor strictly opposes it; rather, disidentification is a strategy that works on and against dominant ideology" (1999, 11). It does so by "scrambl[ing] and reconstruct[ing] the encoded message of a cultural text in a fashion that both exposes the encoded message's universalizing and exclusionary machinations and recircuits its workings to account for, include, and empower minority identities and identifications" (31). The narrator's persistent desire for and fantasies of the kind of idyllic pioneer experience proffered through *Little House on the Prairie* are distinctly disidentificatory because not only do they reveal the settler colonial logics animating it, but they also re-vision the implications of foregrounding Indigenous presence in its representations. In so doing, the narrator traces the contradictions of an Asian racialized national identification (signified through asynchronous childhood), as one premised on the simultaneous complicity with and interrogation of Indigenous erasure from the psychic and geographic landscapes of the settler colonial state.

In *Alien Capital*, Iyko Day deploys a similar framework to suggest that the landscape photography of Asian North American artists, as "parodic strategies of countermemory" (78), enact disidentification with the aestheticized beauty of iconic North American landscapes in order to reveal how Asian racialized bodies are perceived "as unnatural to the landscape as Indigenous peoples are natural" (112) under a system of settler colonial capitalism. As Day elaborates, the antinomy by which Asian racialized subjects are defined against the concrete and authentic dimension of nature in order to be aligned with the perverse and unnatural circuits of capitalist abstraction constitutes the settler colonial ideology of "romantic anticapitalism" that triangulates "Native, alien, and settler subject positions" (34). In an effort to complicate the traditional Native/settler binary that primarily characterizes settler colonialism through an opposition between settler and Indigenous populations in order to shed light on "the status or role that racialized migrants play within white settler colonialism" (19), Day theorizes the concept of the "heterogeneously racialized alien"—to which Asian North Americans belong—as a "unique innovation of settler colonialism," whose "exclusive and excludable" (24) surplus labor serves to produce and expand white property when mixed with expropriated Indigenous land (31).

Building on Day's crucial insights, I hope to provide an alternate avenue to consider the complexities and contradictions of Asian racialized settlerhood under settler colonial capitalism. As Malissa Phung explains, the very question as to whether Asian racialized (and other racial minority and migrant) subjects should be considered settlers at all can be a contentious one. On the one hand, while some contend that "the term *settler*, when applied to migrant, diasporic, and racialized minorities, reinforces power binaries, lacks historical specificity, confuses migration with colonialism, or fails to account for the involuntary conditions of migration," others hold "an unequivocal stance in assigning a settler colonial status to these migrant communities" (21). While it is beyond the scope of my essay to offer a firm stance on either side of this question, I hope, instead, to highlight precisely the dissonances, ambivalences, and ruptures opened up by placing the two terms, "Asian" and "settler," alongside *and* against one another. As I have been proposing, the disidentificatory routes of citizenship figured through asynchronous temporalities of childhood illuminate the Asian North American racialized subject's simultaneous identification with and disavowal of settler colonial erasures of Indigenous presence. However, as I have also suggested, such a bifurcated and liminal positioning is worth attending to precisely because it resists sublation into dialectical movements that might proffer unequivocal conclusions and instead may provide a means to dwell a while longer on other—as-of-yet unimagined—possibilities that may well arrive before their time.

Jennifer F. Wang is an assistant professor of English at Middlebury College. Her research is focused on post–Cold War racialization, financialization, and literary form in the contemporary novel. She teaches classes on twentieth-century and contemporary American literature and Asian American cultural studies.

Notes

1. Throughout the essay, I use the terms "Asian North American," "Asian American," and "Asian Canadian" interchangeably to refer to the process by which Asian diasporic formations are racialized in North America. While I heed Asian Canadian scholars who caution that enfolding "Asian Canadian" and "Asian

American" under the rubric of "Asian North American" runs the risk of eliding histories specific to each respective national context while reproducing "U.S. cultural imperialism" (Goellnicht, 21), I am also informed by Iyko Day's articulation of how the "corresponding features of Asian racialization in settler colonies" reveal settler colonialism as "a formation that is transnational but distinctively national" (17). Thus, my interchangeable use of the terms signals my foregrounding of settler colonial capitalism as the shared frame of reference for Asian diasporic formations across both Canada and the United States.

2. Although Lowe's account focuses on Asian migration to the United States, its theorization of citizenship and immigration as technologies of Asian racialization can be extended to the Canadian historical context as well. As Iyko Day helpfully explains: "The racialization of Asian Americans and Asian Canadians has unfolded as a parallel evolution of yellow peril to model minority—from immigration restriction and segregation, wartime internment of Japanese civilians, to the 1960s-era liberalization of immigration policy" (23).

3. For an account of how Asian American authors have remediated and revised the traditional bildungsroman form in order to address the historical and political conditions faced by Asian immigrants, please refer to Patricia P. Chu's work, *Assimilating Asians: Gendered Strategies of Authorship in Asian America.*

4. Levander and Singley cite the scholarship of Lauren Berlant, Roger Cox, Lee Edelman, James Kincaid, Michael Moon, Jacqueline Rose, Carolyn Steedman, and Michael Warner as belonging to this category (3). "Introduction: What Is the Now, Even of Then?" (2016) by Julian Gill-Peterson, Rebekah Sheldon, and Kathryn Bond Stockton, which is an intro to a special issue of *GLQ* on the intersection of queer and childhood studies in the twenty-first century, offers a helpful sketch of the current state of the field.

5. On the construction of Asian American childhood within specific literary genres, see Davis.

6. Claire Jean Kim has prominently formulated the "racial triangulation" of Asian Americans between Black and white racial positions—such that they are simultaneously "valorized" relative to the former while "civically ostracized" by the latter (107). More recently, Iyko Day theorizes Asian racialized subjects as forming the category of "alien labour" in "the triangulation of Native, alien, and settler positions" that "moves beyond a binary theory of settler colonialism" (19).

7. For example, see: Sánchez-Eppler; Levander; Singley.

8. In *Time Binds,* Elizabeth Freeman defines chrononormativity as "the use of time to organize individual human bodies toward maximum productivity" (3). Furthermore, "chrononormativity is a mode of implantation, a technique by which institutional forces come to seem like somatic facts" (3).

9. Emphasizing the role of literary genres in the construction of Black (un)childhood, Ebony Elizabeth Thomas points out, "Something about Black childhood confounds children's and young adult literature, which is why Black characters are often trapped in narratives about slavery, Civil Rights, ghetto survival, or survival in the White world. While historical fiction and contemporary realism

are important genres for Black childhood and teen life, Black children and adolescents are often missing from other kinds of stories" (55).

10. As many have pointed out, the model minority myth emerges out of the precise historical juncture that it did in order to serve specific ideological purposes. On the one hand, the myth is a Cold War product that serves to obscure U.S. empire and militarism as "the violent conditions of possibility for why it is that Asian Americans are here in the first place" (Jodi Kim, 12). The pernicious stereotype that Asian Americans are successfully assimilated implies that they have "recovered from histories of exclusion, internment, exploitation, and colonialism" and that these effects are not ongoing (Bascara, 4). On the other hand, the construction of the model minority myth in the midst of the civil rights movement functions to discipline other minorities, mainly Blacks and African Americans, by invalidating their grievances against structural racial inequalities and injustices as well as their struggles to transform them (Robert Lee). Ultimately, these model minority stereotypes give the lie to the U.S. nation-state's reputation as a postracial liberal meritocracy absolved of its violent and ongoing histories of imperialism, enslavement, colonialism, and militarism, where if one simply works hard enough, one will be rewarded with socioeconomic success.

11. See Koshy; Heran, 123–47.

12. Juliana Chang makes a similar claim in her study when she writes, "Along similar lines, *Inhuman Citizenship* considers how the children of Asian immigrants not only participate in family business but *are themselves* family business" (20). However, whereas Chang concludes that the "child of immigrants who . . . is thus rendered deviant in temporality, simultaneously over- and underdeveloped" becomes "foreclosed from normative citizenship and indeed normative humanity by this simultaneous excess and lack" (22), I suggest otherwise.

13. Goto's prolific body of work tends to feature young Asian protagonists navigating the experiences of growing as racial minorities, from her first novel *Chorus of Mushrooms* (1994) to her turn to the genres of children's literature (*The Water of Possibility*, 2002), young adult fiction (*Half World*, 2009; *Darkest Light*, 2012), and graphic novels (*Shadow Life*, 2021) in recent years. Thus, the figuration of the Asian racialized child-citizen threads across Goto's work, positioning her oeuvre as an especially relevant and fruitful site for its study. In addition, although it is beyond the scope of this current essay, I invite readers to draw connections between the insights I offer here to Larissa Lai's novel *Salt Fish Girl* (2002), which shares many thematic resonances with Goto's in its focus on reproduction, evolution, asynchronous development, and racialized settlerhood.

14. Much of the critical commentary on *The Kappa Child* emphasizes, understandably, the speculative and fantastical elements of the novel as a means for articulating the social experience of being an "other," such as that of "gendered Asianness" (Cuder-Domínguez, 116), alienation and displacement (Almeida, 48), or "queer racialized humanity" (Pearson, 190).

15. For a very helpful and comprehensive overview of the history of feminist scholarly engagement with Darwin's work, see Brilmyer.

16. Both Karin Beeler and Belén Martin-Lucas have written on how *The Kappa Child* remediates *Little House on the Prairie* in order to draw attention to the discontinuities between racialized migration and the "classic" pioneer narrative.

17. Patrick Wolfe has characterized settler colonialism as driven by the primary logic of (Indigenous) elimination because "settler colonialism seeks to replace the natives on their land rather than extract surplus value by mixing their labor with a colony's natural resources" (868), as is most often the case with franchise colonialism.

18. Glen Coulthard argues that in the context of settler colonies, "colonial domination continues to be structurally committed to maintain—through force, fraud, and more recently, so-called 'negotiations'—ongoing state access to the land and resources that contradictorily provide the material and spiritual sustenance of Indigenous societies on the one hand, and the foundation of colonial state-formation, settlement, and capitalist development on the other" (7).

19. Lorenzo Veracini terms this process "settler indigenisation," which is "driven by the crucial need to transform an historical tie ('we came here') into a natural one ('the land made us')" (21–22).

20. Kim gives a detailed and sustained treatment of the "friendship" between the narrator and Gerald, which the author suggests symbolizes "ongoing attempts at dialogue and companionship between Asian Canadian and First Nations communities" (300). My own analysis of the contradictions of Asian racialized settler-hood in the novel is aligned with Kim's penultimate conclusion that the relationship between these two characters "invites questions about how to reconcile the failed dreams of diaspora with the violences they have helped enact" (304).

Works Cited

Abdur-Rahman, Aliyyah I. 2012. *Against the Closet: Black Political Longing and the Erotics of Race*. Durham: Duke University Press.

Almeida, Sandra R. G. 2009. "Strangers in the Night: Hiromi Goto's Abject Bodies and Hopeful Monsters." *Contemporary Women's Writing* 3, no. 1 (June): 47–63.

Bascara, Victor. 2006. *Model-Minority Imperialism*. Minneapolis: University of Minnesota Press.

Beeler, Karin. 2008. "Japanese-Canadian Girl Meets Laura Ingalls: Re-Imagining the Canadian and American West(s) in Hiromi Goto's *The Kappa Child*." In *American and Canadian Literature and Culture: Across a Latitudinal Line*, edited by Klaus Martens and Paul Morris, 55–69. Saarbrücken: Amarant Presse.

Berlant, Lauren. 1997. *The Queen of America Goes to Washington City: Essays on Sex and Citizenship*. Durham: Duke University Press.

Bernstein, Robin. 2011. *Racial Innocence: Performing American Childhood from Slavery to Civil Rights*. New York: New York University Press.

Brilmyer, S. Pearl. 2017. "Darwinian Feminisms." In *Gender: Matter, Macmillan Interdisciplinary Handbooks*, edited by Stacy Alaimo, 19–34. New York: Macmillan Reference USA.

Bruhm, Steven, and Natasha Hurley, eds. 2004. *Curiouser: On the Queerness of Children.* Minneapolis: University of Minnesota Press.

Chang, Juliana. 2012. *Inhuman Citizenship: Traumatic Enjoyment and Asian American Literature.* Minneapolis: University of Minnesota Press.

Cho, Lily. 2011. "Affecting Citizenship: The Materiality of Melancholia." In *Narratives of Citizenship: Indigenous and Diasporic Peoples Unsettle the Nation-State,* edited by Aloys N. M. Fleischmann, Nancy Van Styvendale, and Cody McCarroll, 107–27. Edmonton: University of Alberta Press.

Chu, Patricia P. 2000. *Assimilating Asians: Gendered Strategies of Authorship in Asian America.* Durham: Duke University Press.

Coulthard, Glen Sean. 2014. *Red Skin, White Masks: Rejecting the Colonial Politics of Recognition.* Minneapolis: University of Minnesota Press.

Cuder-Domínguez, Pilar. 2008. "The Politics of Gender and Genre in Asian Canadian Women's Speculative Fiction: Hiromi Goto and Larissa Lai." In *Asian Canadian Writing Beyond Autoethnography,* edited by Eleanor Ty and Christl Verduyn, 115–31. Waterloo: Wilfrid Laurier University Press.

Darwin, Charles. 2008. *On the Origins of Species.* Edited by Gillian Beer. Oxford: Oxford University Press.

Davis, Rocío G. 2007. *Begin Here: Reading Asian North American Autobiographies of Childhood.* Honolulu: University of Hawai'i Press.

Day, Iyko. 2016. *Alien Capital: Asian Racialization and the Logic of Settler Colonial Capitalism.* Durham: Duke University Press.

Day, Iyko, Juliana Hu Pegues, Malissa Phung, Dean Itsuji Saranillio, and Danika Medak-Saltzman. 2019. "Settler Colonial Studies, Asian Diasporic Questions." *Verge: Studies in Global Asias* 5, no. 1 (Spring): 1–45.

Edelman, Lee. 2004. *No Future: Queer Theory and the Death Drive.* Durham: Duke University Press.

Esty, Jed. 2012. *Unseasonable Youth: Modernism, Colonialism, and the Fiction of Development.* Oxford: Oxford University Press.

Fellman, Anita Clair. 2008. *Little House, Long Shadow: Laura Ingalls Wilder's Impact on American Culture.* Columbia: University of Missouri Press.

Fickle, Tara. 2019. "Family Business: The Work of Asian American Child's Play." *Journal of Asian American Studies* 22, no. 2 (June): 159–83.

Fielder, Brigitte. 2019. "The Enslaved Child and the Carceral Child." In "Global Horror." *Post45 Contemporaries.* https://post45.org/2019/04/the-enslaved-child-and-the-carceral-child/.

Freeman, Elizabeth. 2010. *Time Binds: Queer Temporalities, Queer Histories.* Durham: Duke University Press.

Gill-Peterson, Julian, Rebekah Sheldon, and Kathryn Bond Stockton. 2016. "What Is the Now, Even of Then?" *GLQ: A Journal of Lesbian and Gay Studies* 22, no. 4:495–503.

Glen, Evelyn Nakano. 1983. "Split Household, Small Producer and Dual Wage Earner: An Analysis of Chinese-American Family Strategies." *Journal of Marriage and Family* 45, no. 1: 35–46.

Goellnicht, Donald C. 2000. "A Long Labour: The Protracted Birth of Asian Canadian Literature." *Essays on Canadian Writing* 72 (Winter): 1–41.

Goto, Hiromi. 2001. *The Kappa Child.* Calgary: Red Deer Press.

Grosz, Elizabeth. 2004. *The Nick of Time: Politics, Evolution, and the Untimely.* Durham: Duke University Press.

Hartman, Saidiya V. 1997. *Scenes of Subjection: Terror, Slavery, and Self-Making in Nineteenth-Century America.* New York: Oxford University Press.

Hartman, Saidiya V., and Frank B. Wilderson, III. "The Position of the Unthought: An Interview with Saidiya V. Hartman, Conducted by Frank B. Wilderson, III." *Qui Parle* 13, no. 2:183–201.

Heldrich, Philip. 2000. "'Going to Indian Territory': Attitudes toward Native Americans in *Little House on the Prairie.*" *Great Plains Quarterly* 20, no. 2 (Spring): 99–109.

Ho, Jennifer Ann. 2005. *Consumption and Identity in Asian American Coming-of-Age Novels.* New York: Routledge.

Jun, Helen Heran. 2011. "Asian Americans in the Age of Neoliberalism: Human Capital and Bad Choices in *a.k.a. Don Bonus* (1995) *and Better Luck Tomorrow* (2002)." *Race for Citizenship: Black Orientalism and Asian Uplift from Pre-Emancipation to Neoliberal America,* 123–47. New York: New York University Press.

Kang, Nancy. 2010. "Domestic Violence and Monstrosity in Hiromi Goto's *The Kappa Child.*" In *Transnationalism and the Asian American Heroine: Essays on Literature, Film, Myth and Media,* edited by Lan Dong, 26–45. Jefferson, N.C.: McFarland.

Kaye, Frances W. "Little Squatter on the Osage Diminished Reserve: Reading Laura Ingalls Wilder's Kansas Indians." *Great Plains Quarterly* 20, no. 2 (Spring): 123–40.

Kim, Christine. 2010. "Diasporic Violences, Uneasy Friendships, and *The Kappa Child.*" In *Troubling Tricksters: Revisioning Critical Conversations,* edited by Deanna Reder and Linda M. Morra, 289–305. Waterloo: Wilfrid Laurier University Press.

Kim, Claire Jean. 1999. "The Racial Triangulation of Asian Americans." *Politics & Society* 27, no. 1 (March): 105–38.

Kim, Jodi. 2010. *Ends of Empire: Asian American Critique and the Cold War.* Minneapolis: University of Minnesota Press.

Koshy, Susan. 2013. "Neoliberal Family Matters." *American Literary History* 25, no. 2 (Summer): 344–80.

Le, Quynh Nhu. 2019. *Unsettled Solidarities: Asian and Indigenous Cross-Representations in the Américas.* Philadelphia: Temple University Press.

Lee, Robert G. 1999. "The Cold War Origins of the Model Minority." *Orientals: Asian Americans in Popular Culture,* 145–79. Philadelphia: Temple University Press.

Lee, Shelley Sang-Hee. 2014. *A New History of Asian America.* New York: Routledge.

Levander, Caroline F., and Carol J. Singley, eds. 2003. *The American Child: A Cultural Studies Reader.* New Brunswick: Rutgers University Press.

Levander, Caroline. 2006. *Cradle of Liberty: Race, the Child, and National Belonging from Thomas Jefferson to W. E. B. Du Bois.* Durham: Duke University Press.

Li, David Leiwei. 2000. *Imagining the Nation: Asian American Literature and Cultural Consent.* Stanford: Stanford University Press.

Lowe, Lisa. 1996. *Immigrant Acts: On Asian American Cultural Politics.* Durham: Duke University Press.

Lukács, Georg. 1971. *The Theory of the Novel.* Translated by Anna Bostock. Cambridge, Mass.: MIT Press.

Martín-Lucas, Belén. 2011. "Burning Down the Little House on the Prairie: Asian Pioneers in Contemporary North America." *Atlantis: Journal of the Spanish Association of Anglo-American Studies* 33, no. 2 (December): 27–41.

Mathison, Ymitri, ed. 2018. *Growing Up Asian American in Young Adult Fiction.* Jackson: University Press of Mississippi.

Muñoz, José Esteban. 1999. *Disidentifications: Queers of Color and the Performance of Politics.* Minneapolis: University of Minnesota Press.

———. 2009. *Cruising Utopia: The Then and There of Queer Futurity.* New York: New York University Press.

Ninh, erin Khuê. 2011. *Ingratitude: The Debt-Bound Daughter in Asian American Literature.* New York: New York University Press.

Park, Lisa Sun-Hee. 2005. *Consuming Citizenship: Children of Asian Immigrant Entrepreneurs.* Stanford: Stanford University Press.

Pearson, Wendy Gay. 2019. "Cruising Canadian SF's Queer Futurity: Hiromi Goto's *The Kappa Child* and Larissa Lai's *Salt Fish Girl*." In *Canadian Science Fiction, Fantasy, and Horror: Bridging the Solitudes*, edited by Amy J. Ransom and Dominick Grace, 185–201. London: Palgrave Macmillan.

Phung, Malissa. 2019. "Indigenous and Asian Relation Making: Settler Colonial Studies, Asian Diasporic Questions." *Verge: Studies in Global Asias* 5, no. 1 (Spring): 18–29.

Reddy, Vanita. 2016. "Fashioning Diasporic Citizens in Literary Youth Cultures of Beauty and Fashion." *Fashioning Diaspora: Beauty, Femininity, and South Asian American Culture*, 101–38. Philadelphia: Temple University Press.

Reitz, Jeffrey G., and Rupa Banerjee. 2007. "Racial Inequality, Social Cohesion and Policy Issues in Canada." *Institute for Research on Public Policy.* January 11. https://on-irpp.org/2MoeSpk.

Sánchez-Eppler, Karen. 2005. *Dependent States: The Child's Part in Nineteenth-Century American Culture.* Chicago: University of Chicago Press.

Singley, Carol J. 2011. *Adopting America: Childhood, Kinship, and National Identity in Literature.* Oxford: Oxford University Press.

Smulders, Sharon. 2002. "'The Only Good Indian': History, Race, and Representation in Laura Ingalls Wilder's *Little House on the Prairie*." *Children's Literature Association Quarterly* 27, no. 4 (Winter): 191–202.

Sohn, Stephen Hong. 2014. "'Burning Hides What It Burns': Retrospective Narration and the Protoqueer Asian American Child in Alexander Chee's *Edinburgh*." *Journal of Asian American Studies* 17, no. 3 (October): 243–71.

Song, Min Hyoung. 2013. "Allegory and the Child in Jhumpa Lahiri's Fiction." *The Children of 1965: On Writing, and Not Writing, as an Asian American*, 152–78. Durham: Duke University Press.

Song, Miri. 1999. *Helping Out: Children's Labor in Ethnic Businesses*. Philadelphia: Temple University Press.

Stockton, Kathryn Bond. 2009. *The Queer Child, or Growing Sideways in the Twentieth Century*. Durham: Duke University Press.

Teshome, Tezeru, with K. Wayne Yang. 2018. "Not Child but Meager: Sexualization and Negation of Black Childhood." *Small Axe* 22, no. 3:160–70.

Thomas, Ebony Elizabeth. 2019. *The Dark Fantastic: Race and the Imagination from Harry Potter to the Hunger Games*. New York: New York University Press.

Tran, Sharon. 2018. "*Kawaii* Asian Girls Save the Day! Animating a Minor Politics of Care." *MELUS: The Society for the Study of Multi-Ethnic Literature of the United States* 43, no. 3 (Fall): 19–41.

Veracini, Lorenzo. 2010. *Settler Colonialism: A Theoretical Overview*. New York: Palgrave Macmillan.

Wilderson, Frank B., III. 2010. *Red, White & Black: Cinema and the Structure of U.S. Antagonisms*. Durham: Duke University Press.

Wolfe, Patrick. 2001. "Land, Labor, and Difference: Elementary Structures of Race." *The American Historical Review* 106, no. 3 (June): 866–905.

Wong, Sau-ling Cynthia. 1993. "Big Eaters, Treat Lovers, 'Food Prostitutes,' 'Food Pornographers,' and Doughnut Makers." *Reading Asian American Literature: From Necessity to Extravagance*, 18–76. Princeton: Princeton University Press.

Wright, Nazera Sadiq. 2016. *Black Girlhood in the Nineteenth Century*. Urbana: University of Illinois Press.

LOTUS FLOWER'S COLORS
INTERRACIAL AUTOEROTICISM AND *THE TOLL OF THE SEA*

Erin Nunoda

I don't suppose I'll ever marry. Whom could I marry? Not a man of your race,
for he would lose caste among his people and I among mine.

—Anna May Wong[1]

In this statement—conveyed with a combination of resolve and resignation to Helen Carlisle from *Motion Picture Magazine* in 1928, actor Anna May Wong suggests that her singlehood arises not from her own actions but from a condition of systemic isolation. The unspoken thesis of these three sentences is that the recalcitrance Wong begins with is only a single element in a larger relational puzzle, one that is inextricable from barriers placed upon interracial marriage.

Figure 1. Lotus Flower (Anna May Wong), *The Toll of the Sea* (1922).

Wong concludes by suggesting that legible, state-facilitated intimacy between her and a white man is a conceptual impossibility: one that is secured not just by contemporaneous miscegenation law but by an impression of lost status, one shared by both white and Chinese American communal standards. The negation of marital potential is taken to be self-evident: contrary to a vision of prepolitical romanticism, coupling in Wong's eyes is always accompanied by an awareness of inherited parameters.

At the same time, suggesting that Wong lacked agency in terms of her marriage prospects and that her lifelong uncoupled-ness was inseparable from structural racism are not especially novel observations. Moreover, presuming that the sentiments Wong expresses here could be amended by a recourse to intraracial marriage is also a flawed premise: it suggests that racial difference is always the site of subjugation and that racial belonging is not itself fostered in contradiction or loss.[2] In fact, Wong's collapse of interracial marriage into *marriage writ large* is telling for how she perceived her elision from Chinese and Chinese American life, how she understood her exoticized Asianness as both what made her stardom viable *and* what made her irreconcilable to either "authentic" diasporic existence or white assimilation. Wong's sexual isolation is therefore not just embodied by her alternately Orientalized and excluded figuration in 1920s Hollywood but also elaborated in her strained relationship with racialized community. The collision of these discourses is crystallized in the title of the interview, which collapses celibacy and Asian femininity in its own racist formulation of Wong's essentialized predicament: "Velly Muchee Lonely." As noted by Karen J. Leong, "The conspicuous absence of a publicized romance, a topic that immediately connoted a private life, became the core of Wong's public image" (Leong, 71). In this sense, even if the above quotation cannot be transparently attributed to Wong (or was invented entirely by Carlisle), it attests to a nonnegotiable barrier that was established at the core of Wong's stardom, one that painted her life as tragically isolated.

Yet, in absenting the potentiality of marriage, Wong also rejects a narrative of heterosexual love as the site of reconciliation and erasure of distinction. In her answer, the beginnings of a different formulation of both interracial intimacy and singleness are hesitantly visible: one that illustrates relationality not in the unification of couples but in the very fact of their institutional foreclosure. If the answer to "Whom could I marry?" is strongly implied to be *no one*, this obviously does not foreclose upon Wong's libidinal investments. Yet such a conclusion does defer these desires from the conjugal realm (married or otherwise partnered) to the illegitimately erotic. Although these pleasures need not be masturbatory, this article will suggest that autoeroticism is the (non)relationality most possible for doubly surveilled figures like Wong: alienated from marriage by racialization, alienated from promiscuous sex by gender, and, as I will later explore, simultaneously over- and undersexualized by the concatenation of both. While this article does not claim that the absence of marital obligation necessarily entails a complete lack of sexual partners (among others, Wong had rumored relationships with Tod Browning and Marlene Dietrich), it *does* propose that these conditions permit nonnormative flourishes to percolate underneath hetero-eroticism. In other words, in the voiding of consummative alternatives, a person necessarily takes up *herself* as an erotic object, transforming a scene of coupled prohibition into a speculative realm for both style and intimacy. As this article will explore through a series of aesthetic, historical, and queer theoretical optics, autoerotic flourishing is one of the unintended consequences of xenophobic miscegenation and immigration law: iterating not just a compensatory gesture in a desired partner's absence but a realm of (in)expression unto itself. This autoeroticism is continuously imbued with a recognition of racialized enclosure, with a melancholy that is stitched into any elaboration of delight. Autoeroticism is therefore not a vehicle for an emboldened selfhood or a healthy sexuality but may, instead, perform the opposite function: it acknowledges limitation and constantly reminds the practitioner of what is possible and what is not.

On this account, racialized autoeroticism also differs from the most (in)famous queer account of traceless self-love, Eve Sedgwick's "Jane Austen and the Masturbating Girl." In this article, Sedgwick is aware that masturbation has been easily displaced from a trope of degeneracy to one of entirely normative sexual teleology and that myths of self-destructive onanists do not carry much weight in a landscape where autoeroticism is ordinary and universalized. At the same time, her article traces how the fundamental closed loop of masturbation—its resistance to a procreative impulse or to the reproduction of identity—renders it amenable to antipropriety forms of temporality, to inchoate history, artistic flight, and even the rearrangement of relational strat-ification. "And in the context of hierarchically oppressive relations between genders and between sexualities, masturbation can seem to offer—not least as an analogy to writing—a reservoir of potentially utopian metaphors and energies for independence, self-possession, and a rapture that may owe relatively little to political or interpersonal abjection" (Sedgwick, 821). In the midst of the AIDS crisis, Sedgwick suggests that masturbation's revised status—no longer an execrated sexual form associated with immorality and solipsism—provides a modicum of hope for queer people to not just refute punitive medical-ization but also to foster relationalities grounded in ephemeral creativ-ity, rather than the ossified reduction of a homo/heterosexual binary.

There is much that I find compelling in this theoretical revision, especially Sedgwick's proposition that autoeroticism troubles contem-porary sexual categories, their accompanying historical legibility, and their continued, replicating relevance. Yet I also note an impression of doubt in the above paragraph that seems to undercut its boldest claims: not only the qualifiers on many of the verbs ("can seem," "potentially utopian," "may owe") but also in the argument itself, which is obvi-ously indebted to Foucault's suspicion of confessional sexuality but here places a great deal of faith in the mechanisms of empowering, actualized enunciation. In essence, I think that two crucial elements of autoeroticism are being neglected here, and I hope to draw out both in this article. Firstly, while Sedgwick rightly suggests that indictments of aesthetic or intellectual excess tend to be construed as "mental mas-turbation," in calling upon images of writing, she also imbues auto-erotic pleasure with an authorial capacity, an expression of selfhood that escapes extant social conditions rather than being defined by them. Therefore, masturbation becomes encased in a rhetoric of sublimity, somehow extending beyond historical capture or interpersonal rela-tions. It is also seemingly infused with a transcendent agency: sug-gesting new sexual forms that are electively chosen and remarkably frictionless. There is little space here for autoerotic lives that are pur-sued because no other option exists.

Secondly, while Sedgwick recognizes that the absolute alignment of masturbation and antinormativity is dubious, in illustrating this por-trait of autoeroticism as politically emancipatory—or at the very least, a site outside phobic pronouncements—she disavows some of the strange complicity of the form. This slippage is perhaps more effectively defined in Sedgwick's reading of her object (Jane Austen's novel *Sense and Sensibility*): in one bedroom scene, she establishes how sisterly (arguably homoerotic) tenderness between Elinor and Marianne overlaps with unrequited hetero-desire; how a lonely (yet acceptable) articulation of passion for a man intersects with a displaced, same-sex passion. These forbidden attachments (between women, between sisters, within oneself) are structuring absences in Austen: Sedgwick therefore suggests that uncoupled longing is both easily assimilable to virginal proprietary logics *and* that it confuses object-based sexuality. Unlike her earlier formulation, the political status of autoeroticism is left uncertain, its relative conformity to gendered intimate patterns placed in suspense.

The following analysis locates a similar textual ambiguity at the heart of Wong's first major role in *The Toll of the Sea* (Chester M. Franklin, 1922),[3] an early two-strip (red and green) Technicolor film that retells the Puccini opera *Madama Butterfly* (1904).[4] Here, Wong plays the Chinese Lotus Flower, whose life is defined—and then undone—by her love for a stranded white American man, Allen Carver (Kenneth Harlan), whom she discovers floating in the water near where she lives. As can be intuited from such a short description, this work has been primarily understood through its crystallization of regressive, tragic tropes related to Asian/white interracial intimacy: it crystallizes a normative narrative wherein such romances can only lead to the Asian woman's self-abnegation. While I do not necessarily want to dismiss this realm of critique, I think that the film's seeming collusion with hegemonic forms may help illuminate its paradoxical relationality: the manner in which its erotic strangeness, its queer autoerotic potential, is couched in bonds that are quite generic and conventional. Crucially, this article proposes that the film's novel illustration of color and its conceptualization of Lotus Flower's desire must be formulated *together* and that its ornamental flourishes cannot solely be understood as Orientalist gestures. Therefore, I argue that the manifestation of color in the film is inherently linked to its portrait of interracial relations and that, by extension, it becomes a vehicle for articulating the same racialized isolation and impossible bonds that Wong expressed in this article's epigraph. I propose that the inseparability of the film's sexual politics and its formal affinities does not simply reiterate an equation of color and otherness foundational to discourses of racial evidence and presentational aesthetics: it also redirects color away from *racialized bodies* and toward what I call *interracial autoeroticism*. In this formulation, Carver—and the WASP masculinity he represents—is an initiating point for Lotus Flower's desire, but he is also marginal to its illustration (both by law and by the film's visual strategies): her erotic life is thereby best understood as a (non)partnership with herself, as a more dissonant object that confounds the separation between interracial and intraracial. Color articulates this unrequited, incipient longing, rather than the permanent, self-evident racialization of Lotus Flower (or by extension, Wong) herself.

Contrary to a certain strain of representation-based Asian American studies, this article charts a series of interactions between color, racialization, and communal extrication that situate Wong's performance neither in the realm of positive reclamation nor in the rejection of retrograde cultural tropes. Instead, this essay articulates how the film uses its aesthetic register to encode the forcibly uncoupled intimacies both she and Lotus Flower occupied; in so doing, the film also reexamines interracial desire neither as inauthentic betrayal nor bridging of difference but as an unresolved relay between unactualizable contact with otherness and self-constitution. In this context, autoeroticism emerges not as a condition of abstinence or celibacy (conscious

Figure 2. Lotus Flower and Allen Carver (Kenneth Harlan), *The Toll of the Sea.*

refusals) but as a sexual condition informed by legal blockages to consummation. The color palette that surrounds Lotus Flower is thus not a marker of her essentialized Asianness but rather simultaneously illuminates her interracial desires as a conceptual impossibility *and* returns her longing to herself, thereby obscuring the boundary of other (and self-directed) attachment. Here, I argue that color as a property of disenfranchised bodies has often been emphasized to the neglect of its role in demarcating improper desires. Lotus Flower's colors are not solely a means of rendering her decorativeness for a white gaze: they correlate instead to an ambiguous formal autoeroticism that couples her with Carver even as it articulates her solitary, unrequited sexuality.

This article proceeds in three sections, each of which explores this problematic of interracial autoeroticism through a different aspect of *The Toll of the Sea*'s construction. The first explicates the film's aesthetic system and how its usage of nonrealist, excessive color differs from the portrait often given to such displays in anti-Orientalist critique. The second examines work in Asian American studies focused on both Wong and the Madame Butterfly narrative: here I will establish how these literatures simultaneously secure Orientalist frameworks and gesture toward more nuanced negotiations of racialized isolation. The final section explores anti-Asian immigration and miscegenation law in the early twentieth century, providing a historical grounding for both the film's depiction of interracial impossibility and its concomitant investment in autoeroticism. Although each of these sections are separate in their methodological commitments, they are aligned in their evocation of racialized autoeroticism as a site of unconsummated strangeness, albeit one that attests to pain and frustration alongside delight and invention. Rather than a focus on sexual norms and their opposition, this article attests to how they are often embedded within each other, suggesting that the colorful exertions that illuminate Lotus Flower's erotic life are both a symptom of racist prohibition *and* figures that elaborate possibilities beyond them.

COLOR'S RELATIONALITY

In *Toll of the Sea*, the central couple do not so much develop a relationship as Lotus Flower becomes obsessively fascinated, elaborating a crush in her separate space without many partnered scenes. Due to antimiscegenation cultural ideals (albeit not, in a pre-Code universe, legal prohibitions), the two do not spend much onscreen time together, and Lotus Flower herself begins to take on a curious linkage of object and subject status. On the one hand, the film's intertitles (filled with broken English), its Orientalist mise-en-scène, and its portrait of sacrificial maternality (Lotus Flower kills herself after giving up her son to Carver's wife) fix Wong's character to a stereotypical portrait of Asian femininity.[5] Yet on the other, Lotus Flower could easily be established as the film's central figure through a myriad of tropes: the frequency of facial close-ups, her amount of screen time, her actions motivating narrative progression, the existence of multiple scenes of herself alone (which will prove crucial to this analysis). By contrast, Carver remains an abstraction: sexless, distant, dull, and without any individualized traits. Here the political complications of the film's relational color begin to emerge: in the confluence of melodramatic tropes (including sacrificial suffering) and Carver's lack of particularization, Lotus Flower's desire for him can appear like a longing for whiteness itself; a longing for the destruction of racialized selfhood (or, conversely, rejection of racialized belonging). Yet I also want to make the claim for a slipperier reading, one that illustrates Lotus Flower's protagonist

Figures 3–6. Contrasts between women, *The Toll of the Sea.*

status—and the queerness of interracial impossibility—not through spectatorship or narrational/affective networks but through the film's formal schema and the way color formulates a portrait of her isolation as a desiring mode.

In one sequence in *Toll of the Sea*, a conversation between Carver and two friends about the prospect of him returning with Lotus Flower to the United States is juxtaposed with Lotus Flower longingly appreciating a photograph of Carver. Although the scene explicitly foregrounds racial difference—with the film dismissively contrasting, through the men's conversation, a poor Chinese girl and a rich white woman (sharing, notably, a similar pale teal)—what is more provocative here for a politicized color analysis is the manner in which ornament arguably becomes a function of interracial autoeroticism more than racial essentialism. Perhaps the most colorful scenes in the film (showcasing the full extent of the red and green palette) are not those that Lotus Flower shares with Carver but those in which she is depicted alone in a grove of flowers and trees: color is made to correlate with relational potential—it tends to blossom and cede depending on Lotus Flower's emotional state—and with an interracial erotic pull that is dependent on Carver but that also configures him as an inaccessible object. Thus, in a cinematic paradox that is unique to forbidden

Figure 7. Lotus Flower in her garden, *The Toll of the Sea.*

interracial arrangements, Lotus Flower's eroticism is only really demonstrable without the interceding of Carver: her attachment to him possible solely through autoerotic longing.

For Rosalind Galt, the denigration of ornamental forms and the suspicion of "Oriental" subjects are inextricable, particularly alongside an axis of neoclassical taste that aligns depth, seriousness, and even moral truth with ascetism, balance, and artistic streamlining. In her words, "the classical binary of Attic authority versus overly flowery Asian rhetoric links decorative style both to the non-Western and, in the binary's modern forms, to effeminacy and sexual perversion" (Galt, 20). In this phobic system, the East functions as a figure of antirational, excessive femininity and perhaps the imagistic impulse writ large: representing all that is deceitful, masquerading, or cosmetic about the realm of the visible. Aiding Galt's thesis is David Batchelor's articulation of Western aesthetics' systematic devaluation of color, which he suggests is accomplished alongside two axes: its assignation to a dangerous, foreign body—under whose providence he includes "the feminine, the oriental, the primitive, the infantile, the vulgar, the queer or the pathological" (Batchelor, 22–23)—or its formal relegation to a

Figures 8–10. Lotus Flower with Mrs. Carver (Beatrice Bentley) and Little Allen (Priscilla Moran), *The Toll of the Sea.*

supplementary position distinctly subordinate to architectural or linguistic functionality. Whiteness is thereby affirmed both corporeally and psychically: color standing not only for the visibly abject but also for an object without immediate use value, for impulses and embodiments that exceed imperialist instrumentalization or that (to follow from Edward Said) elaborate imperialism's reach over even that field of subject-destabilizing eroticism.[6]

Read straight, *Toll of the Sea* buttresses Batchelor and Galt's theories of racialized color through its costume and set design, wherein whiteness is generally accompanied by a beige tint in dress or décor: this differential framework signifies Lotus Flower's ostentatiousness as a kind of excess-in-lack, less a perverse or immoral Orientalist presentation than one of pathetic overcompensation, marking the absence of erotic lure. In contrast to Lotus Flower's flourishing, jewel-tone costumes, the Carvers are presented in modest attire (and when Mrs. Carver's [Beatrice Bentley] dresses are colored, they are shown to be pastel rather than saturated in color) thus reflecting their own subjective rationalization—their incompatibility with Lotus Flower's naked emotionality and developmental backwardness. The antimiscegenation logic is confirmed when Lotus Flower's son, Little Allen (Priscilla Moran), is depicted in similarly uniform colorless clothing during the scene where she denies her own parentage: here, as well as throughout the film, color acts as a synecdoche for racial separation, his familial disavowal also requiring a ceding of his formal ties to the Asian mother. However, it is also possible that the collapse of style and bodies elaborated by Batchelor and Galt produces its own pernicious logic of racial divide, even upon a field as presentational and flouting of authenticity as their formulations are: color in chromophobic, antiaesthetic theory is equated with the stain of visibility, reducible to categorization (racialized, gendered, queer, etc.) and thus rendering whiteness again as tabula rasa, even as it supposedly reveals its covert operations. Would it be possible to instead envision color not as a property of social groups (claimed or not) but as a relational structure that negotiates the limits *and* reach of identity? Could color then be illustrated within a chain of desire, one that cannot simply be assimilated to constant poles of domination and submission?

While the above dynamic would appear to imply that color is used to mark a racial binary (and thus the impossibility of consummation between Asian and European people), I suggest that the color in the film is aligned with Lotus Flower's impossible union with Carver and that racialization is present less as a collapse between "Asianness" and ornamentation and more through the autoerotic, uncoupled position that she is forced to occupy throughout the film. To follow from Tom Gunning, color in the film illustrates a space of fantasy: a portrait of relational and aesthetic possibility beyond self-evident givens.[7] This fantasy is inevitably racialized but not necessarily in the exotic, "othering" fashion that is so common in critiques of Orientalism, simply because this fantasy is produced through Lotus Flower's doubly objectified (through race and gender) sexual subjectivity. While this formal presentation does not immediately eliminate the possible (and likely) collusion of racial fascination and color technology as an impetus behind the making of the film, it echoes the political contradictions inherent in Madame Butterfly narratives, and locates in autoeroticism an alternative aesthetic (and perhaps historiography) of interracial impossibility. This paradox of color as simultaneously Lotus Flower's means of expression and her subjective confinement is itself mirrored in the film's title: water is the site of her eventual self-abnegation in the face of racist familial (and national) consolidation, but it is also— if we are to take her name literally—the fount of her birth and transformation, the imaginative flux that enables her eroticism, both in that it brings Carver to her but (perhaps more crucially) that it also takes him away.

In her reading of M. Butterfly (David Cronenberg, 1993)—a revisionist take on the trope of Asian/white interracial tragedy—Rey Chow proposes that anti-Orientalist critique is often insufficient in theorizing intercultural relationalities. While she is sympathetic—as am I—to the work of interrogating the embeddedness of race in aesthetic processes, she suggests that a post-Said vision of prescriptive Orientalism possesses limitations: both as a political project and as an account of interracial desire. On the first account, she argues that this genre of scholarship presumes that the West's fetishization of the East is decadent and scopophilic, simultaneously erasing other forms of ossified idealization (her example being the French Maoism of the 1960s), and depicting display itself as an idol that must be destroyed. As a consequence, anti-Orientalist critique treats fantasy solely as a remnant of false consciousness—a relic of white mastery—and therefore, Chow demonstrates, it remains incapable of deconstructing the subjective ideations that crystallize East and West in the first place. She urges critics interested in these questions to go beyond the "debunking" maneuvers of bad representation "by continually problematizing the presumption of stable identities, and also by continually asking what else there is to learn beyond destabilized identities themselves" (Chow, 61–62). According to Chow, anti-Orientalist critique can profess too much faith in an authentic Asianness that exists outside the confines of Western illusionism, one that implicitly disavows spectacular pretense in favor of an unmediated core. At the same time, she also suggests that deferring racial legibility—of either an Orientalist or anti-Orientalist persuasion—invites broader speculation into the psychic mechanisms of erotic desire, not simply advocating for postidentity flux, but rather attempts to locate "the fundamental misrecognition inherent to processes of identification" (66). Following mostly from Laplanche and Pontalis's understanding of fantasy as mobilizing "the variable positionality of the subject, whose reality consists in a constant shifting between modes of dominance and submission" (63), Chow articulates a project of racial constitution that is based less on visible evidence or the recourse to verisimilitude and more upon the Lacanian conceptualization of the lure, which she describes as operating "as a snare over the field of encounter, ensuring that the parties meet at the same time that they miss each other, in a kind of rhythmic dance" (70). Instead of the reveal of the Other's truth, an unearthing of what has been repressed, or the marking of Asian authenticity in the face of Orientalist obscurity, Chow's fantasy paradigm emphasizes the immanent processes of presentational disguise within interracial bonds.

Although Chow ultimately suggests that fantasy is illuminated by acts of impersonality and misrecognition, she does not quite make the theoretical move of having such ideas resonate with a queer critique of the conjugal promise. Through this optic, Chow's vision could be extended thusly: if all interracial desire (indeed, perhaps all desire in general) contains a kernel of antirelational projection, then erotic intimacy is also bound to isolation. In other words, dyadic coupling is simply a mask for autoerotic longing, albeit a prop that is neither supplement nor deception but constitutive of the romantic scene writ large. In this light, the subjunctive reverie of Lotus Flower's moments alone speaks fervently to this conceit, the candy profusion of magenta flowers and teal fabrics purportedly conveying an attachment to Carver, yet perhaps more convincingly elucidating the character's secluded gratification. This does not remove the specter of racialized entrapment: that is, her enclosure in a simplified manifestation of Asian femininity as patient, passive, and pretty (she is named after the ornamental objects she is surrounded by, after all). Nor does it eradicate the context that such uncoupled fantasy arises specifically because Lotus Flower *cannot* consummate her fascination (either within the narrative or onscreen). What the shift from misrecognition to autoeroticism does perform is a slight contestation of Chow's project, conceptualizing not an absence—of fulfillment, of actualization, of mutuality—but an ambivalent presence that is not the negation of the couple but the fostering of fantasy with the couple as an ambient afterthought.

Early in the film, an intertitle adorned with blooming flowers states that "the garden knew she loved him, for her laughter stirred the rose leaves." In this traditionally romantic—yet also quite ornamental and strange—scenario, Lotus Flower's desire seemingly produces the blossoming of her environment and therefore the film's most glittering displays of color. In these sequences, Lotus Flower is framed off center in a medium shot, fostering an impression of the pink, shimmering, indistinct foliage as overwhelming and abstracting

Figure 11. Garden intertitle, *The Toll of the Sea.*

her situatedness. She and the roses become one and the same. While Carver is supposedly the originating source of this fecundity, the wording of the intertitles suggests that Lotus Flower's joyful singleness has the capacity to transform her surroundings: a closed bubble that encases her in heterosexual, Orientalist fascination while also rendering her longing quasi-distinct from her beloved.[8]

In his book on Technicolor aesthetics, Scott Higgins notes that the subtractive process used for *Toll of the Sea* had a limited representational range, with "flesh tones and saturated primary hues" (Higgins, 4) being difficult to render. While I am struck here by the acknowledgment that the film's cyan and magenta color base seemingly controverted racial-epidermal schemas—elaborating a speculative approach to race alongside a uniquely cinematic color palette—Higgins's description of the above scene is also worthy of note. Considering the mise-en-scène primarily through complementary shades of red and green, he suggests that "the image is strongly stylized as romantically glamorous, and careful composition lends it a sense of completeness—it militates against the feeling that something is missing" (4). While for Higgins the design of the sequence compensates for the absence of certain color gradations, these comments could also be read in terms of assumptions regarding dyadic intimacy. In other words, what is "missing" is not a more capacious color palette but rather the coupled actualization of Lotus Flower and Carver: the heteronormative sense of union as completion. In either case, color is understood as papering over a lack, of disavowing an obvious gap between coherency (of relationality or representation) rather than elaborating a stranger, less self-evident presentation of racialized isolation.

This phenomenon is articulated most clearly when Lotus Flower is approached by two other Chinese women (Etta Lee and Ming Young)

Figures 12–13. Other Chinese women (Etta Lee and Ming Young), *The Toll of the Sea*.

while in her secret grove. Not only are they costumed much more plainly in lighter, grayish greens, but a shot from their perspective indicates that the colorful profusion is localized heavily around Lotus Flower: from this vantage point, the frame elaborates a vast array of grass that is vaguely dotted with occasional flowers. This arrangement of color simultaneously suggests that presentationality is not inherently equated in the film with Asianness *and* that Lotus Flower's auto-erotic desire seems to bring at least some of this embellishment into being. The progression of the scene is intriguing for what it conveys about assimilation, passivity, and the notions of illegitimacy that undergird narratives of white/Asian romance in this period. When the two women approach Lotus Flower, their speech is expressed in the intertitles as characters that eventually fade into Orientalized script (English words with a hatched, vaguely "calligraphic" font). Other than the obvious assertion of the women's otherness for a non-Chinese audience, this moment is notable for Lotus Flower's response: she claims that she is Carver's wife and that by extension she will only speak "in American language" (her intertitles are in the same font as other English dialogue and narration). Not only do the women reject the validity of her marriage, they reinforce the cultural boundaries between Americanness and Chineseness that Lotus Flower had herself established in

Figure 14. Carver with other white men, *The Toll of the Sea*.

her retort. One of them jokes that she has had four American husbands, while the other states that Lotus Flower has only been married "in Chinese fashion": they mock her naïve virginity, but they more significantly establish her isolation, her incapacity to be either fully Chinese or fully American.

Their sentiments are reflected in the following scene, which similarly triangulates Carver between two white male friends, albeit with remarkably different blocking. Here, the three men are seated in white-gray tones with Carver in the middle: their equality, balance, and implicit normativity ensured through the composition. In their conversation, they affirm Lotus Flower's absolute difference, compare her disparagingly to a white woman, and admonish him not to take her back to the United States. Crucially, this sequence is intercut with more shots of Lotus Flower in the secret, colorful grove, her isolation once again secured by the film's form: she is visually articulated as a person who only belongs here (and who can only partake of Carver's presence) through a treasured photograph. Interestingly, Lotus Flower is last pictured in this section calling two Chinese children into her space of autoerotic fantasy: simultaneously aligning her with youthful, potentially perverse play (Wong was only seventeen when she made the film) and foreshadowing the structures of racialized futurity that will soon be closed to her. In the following fade to black, Carver will decide to leave China, and Lotus Flower will become Butterfly.

TOO ASIAN, NOT ASIAN ENOUGH

Asian femininity is often positioned in critiques of Madame Butterfly narratives as a substitute for the act of being colonized: a collapse of psychic, economic, and physical degradation with the self-destructive masochism of the Butterfly character, rendering her a symbol of Asian helplessness and susceptibility to Western influence. She is thus both indicative of Asian essentialism and not Asian at all. For instance, Gina Marchetti proposes that the Madame Butterfly story constructs a social universe wherein the title character is "saved either spiritually or morally from her own "inferior" culture, just as she physically saves her lover from her own people. Ideologically, the narrative can be looked at as either a liberal call for assimilation or as a portent of the annihilation of a conquered people" (91). Marchetti carefully acknowledges that the melodramatic nature of the story frustrates easy identification with either Butterfly or her white lover, as the choices for the audience member are balanced precipitously between suicidal naïveté or willful cruelty (81).[9] However, Marchetti's formulation of assimilation/eradication as the options for Butterfly and the feminized Asian subject risks occluding the story's biopolitical portrait of elided or impossible couplings. In other words, to forgo her own racialization is never a possibility in Butterfly's case. To paint her struggle in these terms presupposes a (misplaced) agency that is counterintuitive to its imagining of interracial romance or to the historical conditions that motivated that sense of impossibility. Such a portrait may also elide any recognition of Butterfly's pleasures: not as a consequence of either self-affirmation or destruction but those that are ambivalently contoured alongside interracial prohibition.

By contrast, Marina Heung proposes that these portraits of sacrificial Asian women present a doubled, contradictory politics that simultaneously binds Butterfly (and her descendants) to white-centered, conventionally heterosexual desire *and* provides a means for her to articulate her own discursive place. Noting the story's reliance on masochistic emotionality as a tool for identification, Heung suggests that

> while this reveals, on the one hand, the pervasive reach of patriarchal definitions of femininity that apparently recognize no national or racial boundaries, one would still have to acknowledge that *Madame Butterfly* provides a rare instance in which the "other" woman is envisioned as possessing selfhood and agency, even if these qualities are at once diluted by their being subordinated to notions of women's place. (Heung, 164)

With regard to this assimilation of Butterfly to deracialized femininity, the very qualities that render her an improper erotic figure (affective flourish, immediate intimacy, excessive attachment) are paradoxically what configure her as the mother par excellence. Heung describes how the Butterfly story often uses miscegenation to elaborate a Freudian conceptualization of the family romance, wherein a patriarchal crisis is resolved by the return of the son to the "proper" purview of the father, undergirded not only by a classed elevation (archetypical in Freud's telling) but also the polarity of East and West. Heung proposes that Madame Butterfly stories—several of which precede Puccini's opera—do not so much foreground interracial romance as they do the replacement of a transgressive scenario (miscegenation) with the white, nuclear family: Butterfly's demise is thus heralded not by her white lover's rejection but by the arrival of his wife. Heung's conceptualization of the story in terms of lost or mistaken paternity suggests that the family romance of Madame Butterfly is centered not on her motherly sacrifice but in the righteousness of white expropriation: the intimate mirror of colonial resource extraction. Such a narrative structure simultaneously entails that her erotic life be iterated almost exclusively through maternalism and that her claim to parental status be effectively erased by the appearance of racially respectable alternatives.[10]

Adhering to Heung's reading, Little Allen in *Toll of the Sea* is presented as a spectral reminder of his father (sharing his name, his whiteness) and thus almost becomes a ghost-child: he is simultaneously produced as evidence of his parents' consummation and also seems strangely (even before she relinquishes motherhood) to never have belonged to Lotus Flower at all. The film seemingly relies upon a visual logic of race—separate but also entwined with the color question—wherein the boy's seeming whiteness guarantees his reappropriation into a proper familial unit. His raced ornamentation (indicated through elaborate Chinese clothing) is a marker that can be shed at will, whereas Lotus Flower's "American outfit" brands her as both out of time and out of place. Her clothing here is a muddy, plain green-brown rather than her usually luminous pink and teal, suggesting that color inherently marks her inability to assimilate into Carver's WASP-y milieu. Compounding this lack of racial/cultural fluidity is the fact that at the moment of Carver's rejection, the color is drained from the mise-en-scène in general: an aesthetic choice that illustrates color as a relational

Figures 15–16. Lotus Flower's last meeting with Carver, *The Toll of the Sea.*

object, while never entirely extricating it from racialized logics. Here and throughout the film, color stands for a condition of desire—a desire that both belongs to Lotus Flower (as, following Heung, she is the only character in the film with an inner life) and that confines her as an othered object, as a racialized nonperson who cannot fully attain selfhood as it is mediated by bourgeois whiteness.[11] While both Heung and Marchetti suggest that Butterfly is redeemed by her incorporation into white, middle-class familial ideology (and her implicit communion with her son's eventual adoptive mother), this formulation would seem to deny the melancholic *inability* to incorporate that forms the institutional blockage on that very union.

Although melancholy is traditionally posited in relation to loss, rather than something that was never possessed, the "neither/nor" quandary that seemingly dictated Wong's conjugal options suggests some resonances with what Anne Anlin Cheng has called the "melancholic narrative" of race relations in the United States. In Cheng's account, American national subjectivity must consistently misremember the legacies of racialized exclusion in order to accommodate teleological exceptionalism (in other words, the postracial state). Yet, such racial melancholy also affixes itself to minoritarian subjectivity, describing not so much a suicidal impulse (i.e., a longing for whiteness) but a doubled incorporation of the embodied expectations dictated by whiteness *and* a recognition of the absence wrought in their wake. Not simply mimicry or acquiescence to a normative standard, such racialized grief settles within any attachment; the grief does not dissipate merely by recourse to more "authentic" or less contaminated figures of being. Cheng's intervention here is not just to propose that a melancholic model of racialized ego-formation—wherein an excluded other becomes the ghostly (yet also opaque) foundation of selfhood—is a precondition of all identity declarations but also to complicate acts of supposed self-renunciation vis-à-vis race. "If the melancholic minority is busy forgetting herself, with what is she identifying? We have all heard the wisdom that women and minorities have internalized dominant cultural demands, but do we really know what that means?" (Cheng 1997, 54). It is not enough, Cheng urges, to posit such racial melancholies as the result of interiorized self-hatred, as if positivity itself can quell the attractions of "unmarked" embodiment or mitigate every painful consequence of racialization.

Cheng postulates instead that unconscious forgetting is a consequence of *all* personhood, and that Asian American theory (among others) consistently locates minority identifications with self-abnegating —or, contrariwise, racially fetishizing—forces inside the dynamics of coercion and assimilation. In contrast, Cheng's racial melancholy permits an engagement with the more difficult and uncomfortable aspects of Wong's racialization, but perhaps more importantly, she invites the problematic of *desire* back into the equation. As with Chow, a substantial section of Cheng's analysis hinges on *M. Butterfly*, yet Cheng is interested in the specific appeal of such fantasies to Asian subjects. Is it possible to view self-Orientalism—if, indeed, this is the precise term— neither within an appeal to white mastery or as a form of self-possessed critique but as a melancholic absorption of racial difference? While Cheng's argument is underwritten by a universalizing negation (proposing that love-attachments are premised on illusions for *all* subjects), she inquires into—but never resolves—the loneliness of paradoxical over-legibility (as racialized Other) and illegibility (the fostering of difference through realms of artificiality).

Anna May Wong's early life was marked by this very contradiction, with her career being defined not just by the supposed incommensurability of white/Chinese miscegenation but also by a form of transnational nonbelonging informed by her second-generation, English-speaking childhood. She was named Huáng Liushuang at her birth in 1905, but according to biographer Leong, U.S. Census records indicate that she was already going by "Anna" at age five (59). Unlike many Chinese Americans—a highly precarious identity in the early twentieth century—living in Los Angeles at that time, Wong did not grow up in Chinatown but just along its edges in a neighborhood populated by mostly European and Mexican immigrants. Leong's narrative of Wong's childhood notes many painful incidents of racist aggression, but it also suggests that her relative mobility outside Chinese-specific communities was permitted by her work delivering clothes from her parents' laundry. These details enable the flowering of a butch rebel in Leong's portrait: skipping school, playing baseball, and (most crucially) not getting married. One of Wong's favorite activities while playing hooky was to visit movie shoots taking place within Chinatown, a practice that was common throughout her teen years for the environment's associations with criminality and decadence.

Likely inspiring her entrance into film acting, Leong succinctly notes the paradoxes such an origin story presents: "Ironically, Wong's very American choice of an acting career developed because of Hollywood filmmakers' stereotypical ideas about China and Chinese people" (62). In other words, the same performance space that enabled Wong to skirt one portrait of (married, passive, devoted) Asian femininity was also the site of a regime of visible evidence predicated upon her "looking Oriental" and playing into another version of (seductive, dangerous) Asian femininity. The accusation of inauthenticity that would also haunt her career (particularly from Chinese nationalist authorities invested in uplift) arises from the same paradox: she was taken to be indexical of a racialization that was both read on her body, and that had no correlation to "real" Chineseness. As is often the case with prominent minority figures, Wong was always too Asian *and* not Asian enough: her uncoupled sexuality simultaneously a figure of unknowable otherness and overly knowable stereotype.

These qualities are perhaps best exemplified in Yiman Wang's exploration of Wong's mirrored abjection, wherein she was viewed in China as a proliferator of bad images and in the United States as an indexical, if glamorous, representative of Asian mystery. Wang therefore objects to attempts by Asian American cultural writers and artists

Figure 17. Shosho (Anna May Wong), *Piccadilly.*

to reincorporate Wong under their own provenance, insightfully suggesting that such labeling denies the ruptures in both terms (Asian and American) embodied in her persona. Wang rightly proposes that these recuperative efforts avoid a confrontation with the politics of hybridity and the layers of authenticity baked into these formulations of ethnic identity. Instead, she suggests attention be paid instead to Wong's hyperstylized form of screen passing, or "her ability to act and *over*act in a wide variety of racialized roles, by which she brings to the fore the stereotypical and Orientalist underpinnings of these roles" (160–61). In this way, Wong is recontextualized by Wang as self-consciously performative but in a manner that is rife with ambivalences, compromises, and thwarted agency. In a particularly emblematic passage, Wang suggests that although the popularity of art deco aesthetics (which borrowed from numerous sources, including Orientalist exoticism) should have secured a place, however tokenistic, for Wong as a symbol of Ameriasian modernity, that she was instead viewed as too rigidly Chinese for such a plastic masquerade. In this sense, the ironizing qualities that Wang detects in some of Wong's performances—her deliberately artificial flirting with racist caricature—must be understood not solely as knowing gestures of self-determination but also as a necessarily constrained means of negotiating competing essentialisms. In this portrait, she was either responsible for perpetuating derogative images (being "true Chinese" and not a yellowface performer), or she was presumed to possess access to Chinese interiority (despite the fact that "China" had been a mediated object for her entire life). If Wong's acting style can be considered camp—or even, perhaps, as a form of racialized drag—then Wang cautions that such bravura irrealism arose from an industrial context in which Wong was affixed to not only an illusionary Asianness but also barred from Orientalism's chic cachet. In Wang's portrait, Wong's denaturalized racialization was less a reclamation—a liberating contestation of the punitive discourses that had defined her—and more a making do, a send-up of mimetic clichés (from China *and* the West) that slips away from contemporary attempts to make her respectable. While *Toll of the Sea* is bereft of irony and difficult to incorporate within the above terms, Wang permits Wong's acting to be understood as a site of doubleness, fakery, and melancholia rather than either an affirmation of Asian American dignity or a bad image to be exorcised with historical hindsight.

In a similar vein to Wang, Cheng argues for a modernist interpretation of Wong's acting style, using her work in *Piccadilly* (E. A.
Dupont, 1929) to elaborate a theory of the performer-as-object, a means
of maneuvering around what she calls critical race theory's tendency
"to reproduce the raced body's irreducible visibility and materiality"
(2011, 1023). Against the positing of a racial epidermal schema, Wong
in *Piccadilly* becomes a luminescent bauble, her radiance explicating
an encrusted shimmer rather than an ontology of Asian skin. Cheng is
especially drawn to the moments of nightclub spectacle in the film,
wherein Wong's character Shosho comes to stand in for both the affirmation *and* the undoing of ornamental nonpersonhood: the super-
fluousness of exotic decoration and the exteriority that refracts any
"deeper" correspondence between surface and essence.

> Wong's refusal of the human produces a notion of inanimacy critically
> different from the laden, passive, or regressive corporality often associated
> with the (good or evil) "Oriental beauty" . . . we are given the fascination
> not of a darkened or exposed body, or of one penetrated or ruptured by
> the gaze, but of a body clad in resistant and mobile gleam. (1031)

Here, Cheng diverts Wong's racialization from a matter of corporeality, exhibitionism, and revelation to one of fortified shininess: a presentational glitter that aligns her with design and dazzle itself rather
than any transparent truth. Cheng's work carefully illustrates how
impersonality and incandescence can be used to dispel the self-evident
inscription of racial difference on organic skin. Instead, she suggests
that Wong in *Piccadilly* possesses a "cellophane glamour" (1031), one
that simultaneously aligns her with sleek commodities and offers some
respite from petrified embodiment. Here, Cheng proposes that ornamentation can be imagined not just as an art deco fetish but also as a
queer elision of selfhood: thingness becoming less the enforcement of
insensate Asian femininity and more a means of negotiating illegibility, of being released from "natural" materiality.

Yet in rendering this specific film as an object of interest, Cheng
is not necessarily forced to reckon with Wong's relationship to racial
types, unless they can be reconfigured under the premises of super-
luminosity, impenetrable adornment, or surface-based irrealism. In
transforming Wong from a bad representational object to a neutral
antirepresentational one, Cheng usefully removes the actor from paradigms of racial evidence, but her theory is not as easy to square with

Figure 18. Shosho's performance, *Piccadilly*.

a role like Lotus Flower: one whose artificiality, transgression, and surfeits of desire take on a less obvious shape.[12] I argue that the two-tone contrasts of the subtractive Technicolor system obviously do not elaborate a sense of visual transparency (indicating a reveal of Asianness) but by the same token, the colors also do not necessarily connote an eroticized excess, a voiding of visibility, or the self-objectification of jeweled prostheses. The decidedly messy nature of *Toll of the Sea*'s racial politics cannot simply be relocated through ostentatiousness or hyperbole, and thus the film repeatedly risks (perhaps even invites) a more simplistic Orientalism, one defined less by its aesthetic flourish than its portioning of agency. As defined by the film, Lotus Flower's erotic life is primarily nonsubjective and devoid of a certain kind of feminist self-presence. Her sexuality is isolated by political circumstance; it thus remains—in Cheng's marvelous terminology—at the level of it (passive objectness) that cannot attain It (what she calls "ultrapersonality" [103] or the divestment of individuality in service of glamorous surplus). At the same time, while Cheng's analysis privileges a role whose self-reflexivity is far from *Toll of the Sea*'s melodramatic sincerity, she also provides a frame for negotiating the film's color system outside the poles of Orientalist complicity or sovereign oppositionality. Describing a moment in *Piccadilly* wherein Shosho signs a contract

Figure 19. Shosho signing the contract, *Piccadilly*.

with Wong's given name, Cheng suggests that "throughout the film, some form of substitution comes into play whenever we are supposed to be witnessing authentic personhood" (1032). For Cheng, this surrogate collapse of actor and character is both a self-inscription and an act of misrecognition—one heralded by the exchangeability of Wong's character and shiny trinkets in the showgirl sequences. Lotus Flower has none of Shosho's affinity for the starry (in shine and in celebrity), but her autoerotic colors possess a similarly frustrated relationship to property and to the gestures of an individualized self: they both emerge from her and indicate a parameter elsewhere—the aesthetic as escape and the aesthetic as capture. What Wang's account of doubly racialized abjection and Cheng's elaboration of disembodied shininess ultimately articulate is this very edging of limitation, the border upon which actualization and denigration were precariously negotiated by Asian women in the early twentieth-century United States.

THE LAW CANNOT ACCOUNT FOR EVERYTHING

In 1922 (the year of *Toll of the Sea*'s release), the United States Congress passed the Cable Act, a piece of legislation that simultaneously decreed

that (white) women could not lose their citizenship through marriage to a noncitizen *and* thereby made it difficult for Asian immigrants (especially women) to attain citizenship through marriage or
the naturalization of their husbands. Laura Hyun Yi Kang suggests
that the Cable Act effectively rendered assimilation impossible and
that "such a state-enforced procedure of Asian women's 'denatural-
ization' further rebukes the naturalizing metaphors of national affiliation in terms of both territorial birth and familial bloodlines" (141).
Examining the often geographically fractured familial structures that
resulted for Asian immigrant communities, Kang concludes that this
policy was inseparable from a xenophobic biopolitics that did not just
attempt to limit the Americanization of the Asian individual but that
formulated the problematic of citizenship alongside the interruption
of recognizable, reproductive eroticism. Therefore, despite the fact that
the intimacies being regulated were purportedly straight, such legislation often had the purpose of securing the continuance of white conju-
gality and thus produced the unintentional consequence of queering
racialized sexuality.

For instance, Susan Koshy argues that unlike other statutes against
interracial intimacies, Asian/white miscegenation laws were "shaped
by a need to police the sexuality of a primarily male immigrant labour
force; the laws worked to impede their incorporation into America
through marriage or through the creation of a subsequent generation of American-born citizens" (Koshy, 6–7). Noncitizenship for Asian
immigrant men in the late nineteenth and early twentieth centuries
was dependent on the mandated contradiction of (low-wage, feminized) capitalist labor and reproductive labor. In this context, questions
of political or national belonging cannot be severed from forcible isolation and the divisions of racialized subjects based on gender or sexual capacity. At the same time, the barring of this homosocial male
collective from a scene of national incorporation and hetero-fecundity
may have also enabled sexual possibilities unimaginable by the origi-
nators of such laws. By extension, it is likely that these circumstances
cultivated same-sex intimacies, both out of necessity and—more crucially for my argument—pleasure. As David L. Eng notes, "Physically,
socially, and psychically isolated, these segregated bachelor communities might easily be thought of as "queer" spaces institutionally
barred from normative (hetero)sexual reproduction, nuclear family

formations, and entitlements to community" (18). Despite its aspira-
tions to omnipresence, the law can never account for everything.

The queer resonances of Chinese women's immigration to the
United States are trickier to chart, perhaps because they were often
haunted by the specter of (straight) miscegenation: first in the 1875
Page Law (which banned Chinese sex workers) and then through the
prevention of conjugal unions ensured in the 1882 Chinese Exclusion
Act. The former was instituted following a conjoined moral and public health panic in California, and Kang proposes that "from cloistered
spectacle to public obscenity to a more penetrating contagion, Chinese female bodies pose a counterreproductive threat to the national
citizenry through its most prized and hopeful embodiment in and as
youthful white masculinity" (123). While the justification for the Page
Law hinged on a coupling of Chinese women and uncleanliness, the
real threat according to Kang was the potentiality for white/Asian
miscegenation—particularly the sexual corruption of white boys by
coercive, immoral Chinese. She goes on to suggest that the Exclusion
Act—which made exceptions for merchants, teachers, and students—
was thoroughly bound to an ideology of class replication, wherein Chinese laborers were prohibited from forming permanent bonds in the
United States and thus excluded from a national promise of futurity
or familial continuance detailed by Koshy. Here, once again the question arises: Which intimacies are lost in such an exclusion? And which,
by extension, are also created?

Perhaps most significantly for *Toll of the Sea*, the promulgation of
this rhetoric through the Immigration Act of 1924—which barred the
entry of all aliens ineligible for citizenship—marks the period of the
film's release as one in which the conflation of "Asian" and "without family" was allowed to persist. Although this does not confirm
any self-conscious parallels between the film and immigration legislation on the part of the filmmakers, it does make clear that there
were numerous statutes and cultural attitudes in place at the time that
insisted on the impossibility of white/Asian miscegenation, at least
within the borders of the United States. Koshy suggests that such part-
nerships were often more common extra-territorially (especially in
American colonies like the Philippines) offering a standard narrative
wherein "sexual contacts between white men and Asian women overseas emerged largely in the context of the sexual license and power

afforded white men in treaty ports, military bases, or as occupying forces in Asia" (11). Koshy thus acknowledges that the commonality of these relationships was itself dependent upon the judicial—and perhaps also fantasmatic—forbidden quality of such unions in the United States, that their appeal and availability required a level of illegality at home. Yet she does not necessarily examine what the attraction to such relationalities may have been for the women involved—or what would have happened to Asian women left overseas when their husbands immigrated for work. Asian femininity remains in these accounts a barrier to the indexical, seeing as how the existences of these women are less easily tracked through labor or military records. By extension, the very mechanisms used for evidence are insufficient in detailing a potentially oppositional field of fantasy: an erotic space that is not necessarily bereft of male intermediaries but one that is definitely placed at a distance from physical men.

In this sense, Koshy and Kang's readings of these laws are hampered by a reliance on normative constructions of sexuality, in particular heterosexual inevitability and the centering of the family unit. The isolated relationalities produced through legislation are treated as barriers to a more fulfilling consummation—either of Asian American community building or patrilineal continuance—rather than as means to think relationality differently and to consider what kinds of eroticism were produced through the impossibility of sexual unions. However, as Koshy recognizes in a footnote, homosocial bonds and same-sex eroticism have often been pathologized in Asian American discourses because they supposedly affirm a discourse of Asian male effeminacy and undesirability: masculinism thereby confers the dignity that was denied within the bachelor paradigm (and that defines contemporary sexual racism). At the same time, such an insistence on tradition and gendered respectability secures straightness at the core of Asian American identity, making race rhetorically inseparable from hetero-uniformity (and, as its specter, queerness affiliated with whiteness). Koshy clearly does not endorse this view, stating that these intimate figurations "offer a rich ground of investigation for the production of alternative subjectivities and social units that enabled immigrants to survive the economic and social pressures of poverty and displacement" (165 n.28). But in articulating these bonds—both of documented bachelors and often-undocumented Asian women—mostly as survival mechanisms, she elides any impression of erotic investment. These phenomena remain of interest mostly for what they communicate about communal resiliency, not the desires they instantiated or inspired.

A historiography of racialized autoeroticism, therefore, would not just entail being attentive to the manner in which Asian American subjects were queered by their lack of access to these very normative bonds but would also interrogate certain political strands upon which the evidence of such bonds is produced.[13] To return to the question of color, and the representational problems it inherently brings to the fore, it is my claim here that it is possible to understand formal elements as enacting historical work that is *linked* to these extratextual, judicial discourses without necessarily making them analogous to each other and without rendering them *intentionally* historical in the text itself. In this way, color in *Toll of the Sea* does not stand for race but rather enacts a consciousness about visibility that simultaneously exteriorizes an absent interiority (that of Lotus Flower) and ensures her lack of integration: her necessitated separation from whiteness and distance from the field of intelligibility. Yet it also indicates an erotic life; it suggests that speculative modes (in aesthetics and in intimacy) are formulated not just as acknowledgments of prohibition or limitation but as forms of sexual invention. Color is potential, and color is

Figure 20. Pacific Ocean ending, *The Toll of the Sea.*

also containment: in *Toll of the Sea*, it indicates neither formless eroticism nor the explicit marking of identity but instead gestures toward an absent presence, a longing that can never be consummated: the visible trace of an invisible intimacy.

The film's ending performs this absence on three fronts: the death of Lotus Flower, the ceding of color, and the disappearance of the ending itself. From a certain perspective, the ending of *Toll of the Sea* no longer exists: after being lost, it was reconstructed using the same photographic methods in 1985 by the UCLA Film and Television Archive and inserted back into contemporary versions of the film. Yet, this act of recovery cannot necessarily surmount the discursive negativity of the ending, its provenance (or, more precisely, lack thereof) in the film proper and the constituting absence that haunts Asian/white sexual relationality. The refilmed portions consist entirely of shots of the Pacific Ocean, drained of all red and green vibrancy, and iterated in a matter-of-fact, "naturalistic" register. At first glance, these images signify little, and an intertitle card directly depicting Lotus Flower's suicide is needed to signal her death. Yet there is also a way in which these final shots signify everything about the film and its relational politics, perhaps even more than would have been elaborated in the original ending.

In her theorization of nonextant and fragmented films (in her case, silent works associated with Black uplift), Allyson Nadia Field suggests that celebratory acts of archival excavation and rediscovery can sometimes overwhelm a reckoning with the nature of lost work. For her, this entails not just a historical attention to the spectatorial and political negotiation of these films before their loss but also reorganizing the status of the film object itself. She suggests that if a film is treated as a coherent, solidified artifact, then the lack of a surviving print necessarily becomes a lacuna that can be acknowledged, although it takes on the shape of a negation: a fissure that can only be resolved through narratives of miraculous recovery. Contrary to this logic, she argues that absence possesses materiality, that it not only signifies hierarchies of preservation but also requires close analysis: a recognition of the shape the absence takes and a reconsideration of how film historians tend to perpetuate a binary of lost and found. According to Field, "Instead of praying for resurrection, we should spend more time with absence. Absence is defined by the object it

regrets; it is marked by the location, position, positing, and emplace-
ment (both in time and space) of the missing piece . . . In a very real
way, absence has presence" (25). Unlike many of Field's objects, *Toll of
the Sea* is mostly extant with only a single missing element: it seemingly does not require the wholesale reevaluation of evidence that
Field recommends. However, I see Field's methodological concerns as
overlapping with the imperceptibility of Asian autoeroticism in the late
nineteenth and early twentieth centuries: not just in her attention to
the racialized elisions of archives but also in the particular relevance
of erasure to figurations of acquiescent, self-abnegating Asian femininity. Although Field would likely approach the film's "missing" ending from a more industrial or spectatorial framework than what I have
elaborated here, I think that her suspicions of recuperation and wholeness resonate with this article's investment in unrequited relations.
The import of this absence in *Toll of the Sea* is not that it precludes
access to the complete film but that it crystallizes the problematics of
erotic and racialized presence that echo through its surviving portions.

Without an indexical representation of Lotus Flower's death, her
being itself becomes a function of form—the relational color that has
embodied and delimited her throughout the film—wherein the negation of her existence can only be ascertained through the withdrawal
of stylistic presence, rather than through her onscreen suicide. The
ending's removal of color therefore echoes the earlier moment in the
film where Carver leaves—the ambivalent web of self-destroying, self-
defining desire that it uses to characterize interracial eroticism—but
here it also takes on layers of historical and material absenting that
transcend the diegesis. If this conclusion is meant to narratively confirm the impossibility of Asian/white miscegenation—in Cynthia Liu's
terms that Lotus Flower "conveniently "elect[s]" suicide so as not to
mar the future happiness of [her] white lover and [his] white fiancé"
(25)—then the fact of its "missing" status becomes a matter of some
political and aesthetic consequence, one that is further compounded
by the archivists' attempt to erase the gap produced in its wake.[14] The
lack of a conclusion—and the subsequent insertion of one that does
not include the film's purveying impression of color—invites not just
a reflection on absence itself (the way any lost artifact of the silent era
might) but specifically racialized and sexualized absence, one whose
tensions are locatable in the choice of imagery itself.

The film ends not just with water but the specific body of water that indicates the gap between China and the United States: the Pacific Ocean. Seemingly, Lotus Flower's demise in this symbolic passageway confirms the impression of interracial impossibility established throughout: the "toll" of her forbidden relationship being her consumption by the insatiable expanse that indicates the irreconcilable nature of racial difference. Yet the fact that this ending is both missing *and* present transforms the melodramatic pessimism and racist isolationism of the narrative itself, permitting Lotus Flower's death to itself become an absence, an unresolved impasse. In rendering opaque these final moments, her desire is not confined to the framework of racialized tragedy but reverberates instead within the gap between supposedly legible entities (continents, races, lovers). Here, her loneliness is finally iterated not as lack but as a constitution of form—an alternative to racial mimeticism and coupled completion. Here, Lotus Flower is also alone in a means continuous with Anna May Wong and her enforced singlehood, the Chinese women rendered over- or undersexualized by racist immigration policy, or Asian American theorists attempting to reconcile an absent archive with essentialized passivity. This is a loneliness fostered not in the grand, Orientalist tragedy alluded to in the film's second title card but rather in a mediation of unrequited longing and racialized blockages. Here at last, Lotus Flower's autoerotic potential is both demarcated *and* illuminated by color.

Erin Nunoda is a Ph.D. candidate at the University of Toronto. Her research examines queer loneliness, thinking about unconsummated eroticism as a function of film form, histories of asexuality, and theoretical approaches to frigidity. She is the comanaging editor of *Discourse*, and her writing has been published in *Velvet Light Trap* and *Feminist Media Histories*.

Notes

Thank you to Emily Barton, James Leo Cahill, Eli Jenkins, Charlie Keil, Cooper Long, Judith Lemieux, Cindy Liang, Angela Morrison, Kate J. Russell, Nicholas Sammond, Sara Saljoughi, Joshua Wiebe, and the two anonymous readers for generously giving feedback on this article in various forms and for deeply influencing its construction through their insights and support.

1. Wong in Leong, 71. Source originally from Helen Carlisle, "Velly Muchee Lonely," *Motion Picture Magazine* (March 1928): 41, 94, 101. It is not indicated in Leong's notes which page contains the original quote. Leong 185 n.46.

2. In fact, Wong broaches this subject later in the same interview, claiming against sociosexual caricatures that it was not passivity and effeminacy that turns her away from men of Asian descent but traditionalism and patriarchal control. "I have never found a Chinese man whom I could love. With us, the woman is slave, the man master. I've been educated as American girls are. My work has fostered independence in me." Wong in Leong, 79.

3. Her first role was uncredited in *The Red Lantern* (Albert Capellani, 1919), and her two credited roles preceding *Toll of the Sea*—in *Shame* (Emmett J. Flynn, 1921) and *Bits of Life* (Marshall Neilan and James Flood, 1921) are both in films considered lost.

4. In Steve Neale's account of the development of Technicolor, he quotes one of the company's founders, Herbert Kalmus, on the processes behind *Toll of the Sea*'s subtractive, "relief" system, which was first experimented on in 1919. Up until this point, color was applied directly using tinting, toning, or stenciling processes *or* generated through the less common additive method that involved the use of a light prism inside the camera. Therefore, one could argue that the actual process of obtaining color for *Toll of the Sea* mirrors the film's thematic concerns: involving an allegorical meeting of opposing reliefs rather than a unified whole or an indexical reproduction of extant color. See Neale, 14.

5. One could easily make an argument that the intertitles for the film are more directly Orientalist than anything that appears onscreen: not only for the ways in which they construe Lotus Flower's speech as unsophisticated or grammatically haphazard (in a manner that deliberately contradicts the lack of exaggeration in Wong's performance) but also for the pictorialist way they illustrate the narrative itself. Often, the intertitles are accompanied by drawings of flowers or stylized fonts that frame the story in a kind of stereotypically decorative aesthetic palette, thus interrupting the more complicated play with race/color taking place in the filmed sections.

6. One of Said's examples of Orientalist rhetoric is the objectified manner in which Gustave Flaubert writes about the Egyptian courtesan Kuchuk Hanem, in particular her paradigmatic lack of discursive control: "She never spoke of herself, she never represented her emotions, presence, or history. *He* spoke for and represented her" (Said, 6). In this way, Said characterizes Orientalism as an aesthetic practice that articulates the East through a sexualized, dominated femininity.

7. Here Gunning is referring to the usage of tinting, toning, and stenciling in preclassical cinema: colorization methods that he argues "rendered movies more vivid and more fantastic, thereby allying cinema to realms of dreams and fantasy, or to the striking and unusual" (19). While Gunning is using "fantasy" to evoke its generic qualities, or its capacity for nonnarrative astonishment, his evocation of color's "sensual intensity" may also suggest that these formal properties have erotic components, or a specifically antirepresentational drive.

8. In a brilliant reading of the film's color palette, Xin Peng suggests that the film's persistent association between Lotus Flower and flower gardens not only showcases the usage of Orientalized spectacle in 1920s color technologies but also collapses her body into the flora-based mise-en-scène, thereby affirming a model of eternal, naturalized Chineseness. Contra a racial epidermal schema, Peng proposes that Lotus Flower's racial difference is indicated through her positioning in the frame: "Rather than being foregrounded as a figure that is separated clearly from the background according to the norm of (western) perspectival composition, the aptly named Lotus Flower *is* part of the natural environment" (299).

9. One way of examining this would be through Lauren Berlant's genre of "female complaint," that is, stories that "tend to foreground a view of power that blames flawed men and bad ideologies for women's intimate suffering, all the while maintaining some fidelity to the world of distinction and desire that produced such disappointment in the first place" (2). Such narratives thus simultaneously navigate frustration with inequity or even critique certain aspects of the normative feminine world, while still on some level being bound to its sentimental attractions or its promise of romanticized transcendence from the ordinary. The question of how a spectator—Asian or white, queer or not—would have responded to this particular film is beyond the scope of this essay, but an account of racialized isolation (especially one so dependent on the antimiscegenation politics as I am describing here) would need to reflect the mediated position that the many iterations of this story have offered to women viewers/readers.

10. Heung situates these dynamics in terms of the lost masculinity of the post-Vietnam era, suggesting that this period symbolized a "pervasive social insecurity about maleness and paternal legitimacy that in turn mobilized an insistent, even obsessive, revalorization of the patriarchal nuclear family" (161). In this sense, while an aura of paternal crisis runs through all versions of Madame Butterfly, Heung is particularly invested in their revival (in both fictional representations like *Miss Saigon* and in the "reunion" of half-Vietnamese children with American soldier fathers) as a function of American military defeat in the 1970s.

11. While the film does not have the same equally developed relationship to camera distance as it does to color, this scene is also notable for containing one of its only close-ups while Lotus Flower is crying. Without drawing an overly simplistic analogy between identification and proximity to the apparatus, this decision does suggest an engagement with the personal/impersonal dynamics of desire that are being elaborated formally elsewhere.

12. At the same time, Homay King insightfully notes that Wong's initial performance in "the American outfit" melds together tragic anachronism with a measure of knowing cheekiness, "[inflecting] her fashion faux pas with irony" while "[strutting] regally with her nose in the air" (66). In this sequence, Wong *does* appear thoroughly campy and self-conscious, and her perverse delight in the dress's badness signals a flash of Cheng's shininess within a straightforwardly dramatic role. As with Peng, I unfortunately could not examine King's argument in detail within

this article (due to publication deadlines), but I am nevertheless indebted to their excellent scholarship on both Wong and the film itself.

13. Kang importantly notes (in a manner perhaps echoing Wang and Cheng) that this paradigm is itself disputable. For her, "Asian American" encompasses many different ethnic histories and immigrant narratives. It also retroactively asserts a consciousness about racialization influenced by contemporary identity politics, one that likely was not present among the groups under examination during the late nineteenth century. In her words: "The relatively recent composite category of "Asian women" is cast backward in historical time to point to and group together ethnically diverse bodies of women, who likely did not recognize themselves and each other as part of this collectivity" (151).

14. That being said, Liu also argues against what she calls "mimetic criticism's assumption that the primary task of filmic images—perhaps the sole task—is to reproduce the world faithfully" (26), suggesting similarly to Wang and Cheng that such theoretical gestures limit the production of racialized images to those deemed most authentic, incorporating an implicit appeal to authority that echoes patriarchal invocations elsewhere in society.

Works Cited

Batchelor, David. 2007. "Chromophobia." In *Chromophobia*, 21–50. London: Reaktion.

Berlant, Lauren. 2008. Introduction to *The Female Complaint: The Unfinished Business of Sentimentality in American Culture*, 1–32. Durham: Duke University Press.

Cheng, Anne Anlin. 1997. "The Melancholy of Race." *The Kenyon Review* 19, no. 1:49–61.

———. 2011. "Shine: On Race, Glamour, and the Modern." *PMLA* 126, no. 4 (October): 1022–41.

Chow, Rey. 1996. "The Dream of a Butterfly." In *Human, All Too Human*, edited by Diana Fuss, 61–92. New York: Routledge.

Eng, David L. 2001. *Racial Castration: Managing Masculinity in Asian America*. Durham: Duke University Press.

Field, Allyson Nadia. 2015. Introduction to *Uplift Cinema: The Emergence of African American Film and the Possibility of Black Modernity*, 1–31. Durham: Duke University Press.

Galt, Rosalind. 2011. *Pretty: Film and the Decorative Image*. New York: Columbia University Press.

Gunning, Tom. 2015. "Applying Color: Creating Fantasy of Cinema." In *Fantasia of Color in Early Cinema*, edited by Giovanna Fossati, Tom Gunning, Jonathon Rosen, Joshua Yumibe, 17–27. Amsterdam: Amsterdam University Press.

Heung, Marina. 1997. "The Family Romance of Orientalism: From Madame Butterfly to Indochine." In *Visions of the East: Orientalism in Film*, edited by Matthew Bernstein and Gaylyn Studlar, 158–83. New Brunswick: Rutgers University Press.

Higgins, Scott. 2007. Introduction to *Harnessing the Technicolor Rainbow: Color Design in the 1930s*, 1–21. Austin: University of Texas Press.

Kang, Laura Hyun Yi. 2002. *Compositional Subjects: Enfiguring Asian/American Women*. Durham: Duke University Press.

King, Homay. 2021. "Anna May Wong and the Color Image." *liquid blackness* 5, no. 2:59–73.

Koshy, Susan. 2004. Introduction to *Sexual Naturalization: Asian Americans and Miscegenation*, 1–25. Stanford: Stanford University Press.

Leong, Karen J. 2005. "Anna May Wong." In *The China Mystique: Pearl S. Buck, Anna May Wong, Mayling Soong and the Transformation of American Orientalism*, 57–105. Berkeley: University of California Press.

Liu, Cynthia. 2000. "When Dragon Ladies Die, Do They Come Back as Butterflies? Re-Imagining Anna May Wong" In *Countervisions: Asian American Film Criticism*, edited by Darrell Y. Hamamoto and Sandra Liu, 23–39. Philadelphia: Temple University Press.

Marchetti, Gina. 1993. *Romance and the "Yellow Peril": Race, Sex, and Discursive Strategies in Hollywood Fiction*. Berkeley: University of California Press.

Neale, Steve. 2006. "Technicolor." In *Color: The Film Reader*, edited by Brian Price and Angela Dalle Vache, 13–23. New York: Routledge.

Peng, Xin. 2021. "Colour-as-Hue and Colour-as-Race: Early Technicolor, Ornamentalism, and *The Toll of the Sea* (1922)." *Screen* 62, no. 3:287–308.

Said, Edward. 1995. First published in 1978. *Orientalism: Western Conceptions of the Orient*. New York: Penguin.

Sedgwick, Eve Kosofsky. 1991. "Jane Austen and the Masturbating Girl." *Critical Inquiry* 17, no. 4:818–37.

Wang, Yiman. 2005. "The Art of Screen Passing: Anna May Wong's Yellow Yellowface Performance in the Art Deco Era." *Camera Obscura* 20, no. 3:158–91.

Review Essays

POLITICALLY RED

THE BENJAMIN FILES
BY FREDRIC JAMESON
Verso, 2020

Eduardo Cadava and Sara Nadal-Melsió

What does it mean to read or to write? In what way are reading and writing a means of doing political work? Why is it that, in *Reading Capital*, Louis Althusser insists that "only since Marx have we had to begin to suspect what, in theory at least, *reading* and hence writing *means*" (16)? We could begin to answer these questions by considering the trajectory of Fredric Jameson's readings and writings for now more than fifty years, since he remains the most well-known and long-standing American Marxist critic. But it is even more interesting that, after his early essay on Walter Benjamin in 1969, after having written extensively on Theodor Adorno and Bertolt Brecht (as well as on several other thinkers associated with Benjamin), Jameson writes his first book on this rather singular reader and writer now—in a moment marked by the rise of both old and new fascisms. He even publishes it on election day, November 3, 2020. What is it that makes this particular act of reading and writing so necessary at this particular moment? And what does it tell us not only about Benjamin and Jameson—about Jameson's relation to Benjamin—but also about the political stakes of this act?

It is not surprising that in reading Jameson's *The Benjamin Files*—his latest and most extended reading of Benjamin—we discover several things about Jameson. What is more surprising is that the more closely we look at Jameson's book, the more closely we attend to his engagement with the strangeness of Benjamin's writings—even (and perhaps

Cultural Critique 118—Winter 2023—Copyright 2023 Regents of the University of Minnesota

especially) at the level of sentences —the more we can register the profound transformation in Jameson's writing that occurs because of this
encounter. Jameson's book is more "writerly" than any of his previous
books. There is a peculiar mimetic contagion that seems to infiltrate
his style, which helps account for the citationality of his text—itself a
kind of homage to Benjamin's own penchant for quotation. It is as if
this most recent encounter with Benjamin's writings transforms Jameson's mode of reading and writing.

This return to Benjamin enables Jameson to formalize things he
may have wanted to say earlier but could not until this latest passage
through Benjamin's writings. It also permits him to go further—in the
most dialectically materialist way possible—in the direction of exposing himself to the risk of reading and to the attendant risks that, for
him, are encrypted within any effort to bring about political change
through reading and writing. This is something he knows better than
most since he has had recourse to literary and philosophical texts in
order to do his political work throughout his entire career. We should
never forget that Marx himself was one of history's great readers and
writers and that he, too, often passed through literature and philosophy in his analyses of, among so many other things, capital, religion,
history, ideology, law, rights, nationalism, and various political forms
of social organization.

Jameson seems particularly aware of the risks of reading—and
perhaps especially the risk to himself of reading Benjamin—when early
in the book he suggests that reading involves "a physical displacement within the reading mind itself, a regulated spasm in which the
mimetic categories are unexpectedly substituted for one another like
the prestidigitation of a shell game or the unmistakable tremors of an
underground detonation. This writer has visibly tampered with our
mental infrastructure; his sentence has reached inside the mind with
an imperceptible violence that ought to be illegal and denounced as
such" (Jameson 2020, 22–23). He later refers to the violence of this "reading effect" as "an unusual pedagogy which has to do with the perceptual levels within the mind, a kind of pedagogical surgery that can be
characterized as a cultural revolution within the reading process" (35).
The more closely we engage with a text, the more extended our reading becomes and the more it affects not only our reading and writing
but also our capacity to remain just ourselves (and even just a body).

It is as if only in surrendering ourselves to the language of multiple others—none of whom are ever just one—can we begin to navigate our way through a text, as the archive of relations that we are and that we become. Reading and writing—like all political acts—reveal themselves to be entirely collaborative and collective. We can never enact them by ourselves, and this is why Benjamin resists—except in letters, he claims—using "I" in any of his writings and why we might say that Jameson, in his own engagement with Benjamin, can only begin to reveal the destruction (beginning with the destruction of the self) that is at the heart of all reading: what Benjamin called "the perilous critical moment on which all reading is founded" (Benjamin 1999, 463).

In the essay "Marxism and Historicism," Jameson already had formulated the impersonality of reading in a passage that describes both the reader and the writer whose work he or she engages as "different modes of production," and their encounter as an "essentially collective confrontation of two social forms" (1979, 70). There, he makes clear that the activity of reading not only transforms the reader but also judges him or her—as the "social formation" of which he or she is the living and constantly changing archive. We cite the passage at length since, in essential ways, our reading of The Benjamin Files will be nothing more nor less than a demonstration of its consequences for any understanding of a reading that would present itself as political and, in particular—we are speaking of Jameson, after all—as politically red. He writes:

> We must try to accustom ourselves to a perspective in which every act of reading, every local interpretive practice, is grasped as the privileged vehicle through which two distinct modes of production confront and interrogate one another. Our individual reading thus becomes an allegorical figure for this essentially collective confrontation of two social forms.
>
> If we can do this . . . [w]e will no longer tend to see the past as some inert and dead object which we are called upon to resurrect, or to preserve, or to sustain, in our own living freedom; rather, the past will itself become an active agent in this process and will begin to come before us as a radically different life form which rises up to call our own form of life into question and to pass judgment on us, and through us on the social formation in which we exist. At that point, the very dynamics of the historical tribunal are unexpectedly and dialectically reversed: it is not we who sit in judgment on the past, but rather the past, the radical difference

of other modes of production (and even of the immediate past of our
own mode of production), which judges us, imposing the painful knowledge of what we are not, what we are no longer, what we are not yet.
(1979, 70)

Jameson here reminds us—and this is perhaps the greatest discovery
of Western Marxism—that the base is intertwined with the superstruc-
ture in the mind and is inseparable from the shaping of subjectivity
through form, even if this form is in turn always in flux. Jameson has
been faithful to this discovery throughout his career and, indeed, following him, we can understand that Marxism is another name for the
act of reading. If this passage could just as easily have been written by
Benjamin, it is because both Benjamin and Jameson inhabit Marx's language in similar ways. Their abiding return to literature as a resource
for doing political work and the commitment to writing in a literary
style confirm their fidelity to Marx—to the Marx for whom literary
texts become writerly events. It is because neither Benjamin nor Jameson stop reading even as they write that we are privy to the effects of
reading in their minds but also in their writing.

Part of the wonder of Jameson's book lies in his insistence that the
reader never lose sight of Benjamin's strangeness, of the lateness and
anachronism of his literary taste, and ultimately of his style, especially
as it relates to the centrality of figuration in his thinking. Benjamin's
"canon"—which is part of his strangeness, including not simply names
we recognize but also a vast network of lesser known and even marginal figures—is more than a question of taste (Jameson refers to his
"private canon" as "totally unorthodox" (2020, 136). It signals a series
of structural choices—what Benjamin called "elective affinities"—each
of which, if read properly, allows us to trace Benjamin's active and
complicated relation to tradition: in the sense that what is at stake for
him is the possibility of activating what he inherits (the resources he
finds in *his* tradition of writers) in the direction of political work in the
present. If, as he puts it in his "Work of Art" essay, "the uniqueness of
the work of art is identical to its embeddedness in the context of tradition" (2003, 56) it is because its singularity—like that of Benjamin's
writings—emerges from its engagement with earlier works that, in a
real but unpredictable manner, prefigure and even destine Benjamin's
writings to realize their shape through various forms of displacement.
This is particularly legible in the violence structured into Benjamin's

POLITICALLY RED | 159

practice of citation, which involves the removal of words or sentences from their context and their unexpected reinscription elsewhere.

This activity of citation reenacts the displacements, the distances and separations, from which subjectivity emerges. Yet this is a subjectivity that has been subtracted in the service of making legible a deeper and more enduring version of time: one that, for Benjamin and Jameson, is destined to survive histories that presume linearity, causality, and continuity. Just as a room is better seen when its inhabitants have left, history becomes more intimate when the "I" has been removed, in this instance by embedding it in a tradition that works against tradition, even as it carries its most critical moments forward. According to Jameson, these writerly gestures maximize "the techniques of cultural revolution," since, among so many other things, they trace "the ways in which instruction comes to society." The figures in Benjamin's canon "are always the objects of pedagogy" and, Jameson adds, "this is the deeper secret of his political and aesthetic kinship with Brecht" (2020, 42). Benjamin's effort to extract, multiply, and fragment voices is not simply part of his "unusual pedagogy": it is also his way of mobilizing a certain version of communism against fascism, something that will be explored more fully in his later works, as Jameson himself does in the latter half of his book and especially in his chapters "The Hand and the Eye of the Masses" and "History and the Messianic."

As Jameson notes in his chapter "The Spatial Sentence," it is precisely Benjamin's passion for the "multiplicity" of voices that most interests him, and that is "yet another symptom of his not unpolitical fascination with the multiple, with the masses as such" (34). He goes even further when he insists that "[m]ass politics lies at the very center of Benjamin's thought" (207). If Benjamin and Jameson claim that there can be no Marxism without a conception of production and reproduction that is neither teleological nor a sign of progress—a conception that introduces imperfections and differences, fissures and breaks, multiplicities and pluralities, within these processes—it is because the end of capitalism must itself pass through reproduction as a technology and as a process of formation and transformation. In Benjamin's terms, the formation of a collective historical subject of history—what Jameson calls "a new structure of subjectivity" (193) and what Benjamin would call a *mass subject*—coincides with the end of aesthetics, or rather with its neutralization in the name of a politics of the masses. However, even the word "masses" has to be reconceptualized and distanced from a mass that would have an identifiable "face." In Benjamin, this work of reconceptualization—something that gets performed within the movement of his writing—and not only because for him the crisis of our existence is inscribed within "the very heart of language" (1994, 84)—is already a means of doing political work. In our present context, this suggests that technology becomes a means of engaging the historical "dialectic of the individual and the masses" (2020, 200), since it is capable of transforming consciousness through perception and the materiality of form. To be more precise, it puts perception through a process of "massification"—and this because it has always existed as a mediating force in our relation to the world (200).

From the very beginning of his book, Jameson identifies a pedagogical dimension in Benjamin, an "unusual pedagogy" that involves "the shifting of perceptual levels within the mind" in order to produce "a cultural revolution within the reading process" (35). Since pedagogy only works if it can be transmitted, Jameson actually confirms the efficacy of Benjamin's training manual for reading historically, especially in moments of danger, by transmitting the writer's concepts in his reenactment of them—in his extraction, selection, and presentation of Benjamin's most emblematic figures. Indeed, he enacts the act of reading as a form of transmission. As evidenced by Jameson's book, it is only when a reader is entirely embedded in the constellation of references and relations that form the physiognomy of a writer's corpus that he or she can even begin to read. Despite the rather extraordinary way in which Jameson—in this book more than any other in his vast corpus—takes on the concepts and even the cadences of the writer he is reading, Jameson nevertheless tries to resist being "boxed in" by Benjamin, even as we time and again witness his failure. What gets staged in this effort and failure are the risks and restrictions of embedding himself in the worlds of a writer and the reduced agency it entails. The more deeply a reader inhabits the works of a writer— the more deeply the reader enters a writer's words or sentences— the more profoundly he or she disappears in the writer's corpus. Similarly, within the trajectory of his book, Jameson increasingly disappears into Benjamin's figures, as Benjamin himself had disappeared into them, by withdrawing the "I" in his sentences so that someone else could one day inhabit them, take them over, and send them somewhere else, as Jameson does here. Indeed, Jameson moves through the various figures in Benjamin. He is the flaneur who, making his way through the streets of Benjamin's texts, the many paths and sentences the reader is asked to follow, understands, like the flaneur who writes with his gaze as he walks, that "[e]ach directed gaze is a sentence in the making, a formulation already virtual and implicit; the writing is already being done with the movements of the eye" (114). He is the gambler who takes his chances and makes his bets not only in relation to which texts he will attend to in order to reap the greatest gain but also in relation to yet another gamble, a temporal one, which "risks destroying temporality altogether" (93). He is the storyteller who pieces together the nonnarrative threads within Benjamin's corpus that, interrupting the linearity of any story, attend to the distance that prevents any story from being fully unfolded but that lead us to an exploration of what cannot be experienced in experience—*experience itself*. (166). He is the historical materialist who traces the relations between politics and theology through his passion for language and literature; the one who, engaging the relations between history and historiography and among the past, the present, and the future, registers the inevitability of a complicity that he associates with the always present danger of, without knowing it, reinforcing the very forms of domination he wishes to overcome and responds with an explosive force that, corresponding to a will to "expansion" and "intensification" (30), is most often legible in his writing. He is the insurrectionist who, like Blanqui, seeks to intervene in a context in which history repeats itself "over and over again in unimaginably vast cycles" (28) and does so from his own lifelong prison cell—a "prison-house of language," but one that Blanqui could also be said to have shared and in which style is inseparable from an insurrectionary politics and sentences are a form of action. What we witness is a Jameson whose singularity as a reader, writer, and thinker gets displaced—and even appropriated—by a series of mimetic contagions that eventually usurp the place of an argument or thesis in his book. The book reveals his full incorporation into an experience of reading and writing in which the words and figures of Benjamin—and the other readers and writers encrypted within Benjamin's "name"—move Jameson away from his "own" signature and into what he himself calls the "impersonality of reading." Jameson's acknowledgment that the language he uses is never just his is largely what motivates the form and content of his book, as—in a very Benjaminian gesture—he enacts, within the movement of his language, albeit a language that is never just "his," what he wishes to convey.

Indeed, in the rather striking opening of his book, entitled "Wind in the Sails," and taking its point of departure from Benjamin's famous claim that what matters for the dialectician "is having the wind of world history in [his] sails" and knowing how to set them, Jameson insists that thinking and writing are indistinguishable in Benjamin and that the movement between words and concepts in his work produces an uncertainty that makes it impossible to settle on any of them as key to his thought. If "history is change as such" (2), it is not surprising, he suggests, that the "changeability and variability" of Benjamin's vast reservoir of concepts is the writer's way of remaining faithful to the transience, fleetingness, contingency, "variability," and "historical ephemerality," that, for him, are history's signature and index (3). This is why the only works Benjamin can write are works that destroy themselves and can only appear as a process of destruction and bear the force of their own dissolution within them: as the cipher of the violence through which they are formed and deformed in the very movement of their coming into existence and as the consequence of all the multiple temporalities they contain. In Jameson's words, destruction is "a Benjaminian *gestus*," a "modus operandi" (7). This is why, he adds, Benjamin "could not write a traditional book": from the *Trauerspiel* to the *Arcades Project* and beyond (even if we consider *One-Way Street* his one "book," it is less a book than simply "the new form that the impossibility of the book brings forth in its place" [9]). This is largely because Benjamin's works carry the traces of their own finitude. Penetrated by a sense of finitude and violence, they are riven and interrupted by a force that prevents them from remaining identical to themselves.

This force of dissociation is legible in the way in which Benjamin's language immediately distances itself from itself. As Karl Kraus writes, in a sentence that Benjamin cites in the essay he devotes to the critic, "The closer one looks at a word, the further it looks back" (Kraus, qtd. in Benjamin 1999, 453). This sentence gives us a "formula" or "protocol" for reading Benjamin but also for his experience of language and of things in general. It suggests that every word or sentence in Benjamin has an entire network of other voices, of other words and sentences, sealed within it, even "behind" it. This is why he can never write as an "I": he can never speak only in his own voice. The act of reading becomes an involuntary conjuring of a distance, however close we may think we are to this or that text. Every word and every sentence shows itself to be a "constellation," in the strict Benjaminian sense, and the multiplicity this constellation brings together makes it, in Jameson's words, a "destructive weapon, an instrument to be wielded against system and above all against systematic philosophy" (2020, 4). It is because the words and concepts that circulate in Benjamin's works—among others, allegory, aura, citationality, dialectical image, experience, happiness, impersonality, legibility, masses, media, messianism, mimesis, monad, montage, multiplicity, origin, redemption, reproducibility, revolution, similitude, or theology—are intertwined and entangled and can never exist in isolation from the others, that, in the end, reading can only encounter its own incompleteness. This multiplicity of words and concepts belongs to what Benjamin—and Jameson—will later think in relation to the masses, the Baudelairean crowds, the redemption of the dead, and the still unthought collective that might help inaugurate a future that will not repeat the past (13). But it also registers the multiplicity of figures and voices within Benjamin's language, a multiplicity that keeps his language from ever being just his and that corresponds to an almost machine-like citational structure.

That Jameson finds himself inscribed within Benjamin's figures—that he finds himself scattered and extended across these different figures, each of which contributes to the dissolution of his own voice and his control over it—becomes a means of measuring the difficulty that structures the very possibility of insurrectionary political acts and the mediating conditions that restrain the voluntarism and agency of political action. While this is the question raised by Benjamin's angel—whose wish to stay, to waken the dead and restore what has been destroyed, is made impossible by the storm whose wind has "got caught in his wings" and has prevented him from being able to close them—Jameson prefers the more mobile figure with which he begins his book: that is, the "wind in the sails" that makes the work of the dialectician difficult. Like the figure of the angel, this earlier figure reduces the question of agency to that of directionality. What is at stake for the dialectician is the possibility of setting the sails in such a way as to take advantage of the force of the wind of world history—to enable it to move things in an emancipatory and revolutionary direction. But he needs to consider not just the wind but also the always moving and often turbulent undercurrents beneath the boat that, unseen and uncontrollable, intensify the precariousness of his task. In this scene, the chance that for even a brief moment the sail, the wind, and the undercurrent can align themselves in a direction that might offer a revolutionary opportunity demands that the dialectician be prepared, at that very moment—which "flashes up" (391) in this moment of danger: to "blast open the continuum of history" (396) and to seize the opportunity and work to maximize its consequences. The question of directionality has a political valence in Benjamin—especially in relation to its utter incalculability, its radical unpredictability—and it should be understood in temporal terms.

This directionality is also an element in the pedagogical impulse that he develops and enacts throughout his life: an ever-widening constellation of emblems, concepts, and figures that requires an exercise in the reading of history as an enigma. This pedagogy prepares us to engage a world that is always transient, metamorphosing, and unfolding in multiple temporal directions. These shifting traces—exhibiting the discontinuities and the processes of "perpetual translation" (2020, 3) that together inaugurate a force of destruction—are mobilized within Benjamin's writing against any form of identity, intentionality, and capitalized indebtedness. It is precisely through the withdrawal of the individual into the impersonality of their many figurations that Benjamin hopes to ready us for the emergence of the fleeting and transient moment of political possibility and historical intensity. Removing his individual self for the benefit of a figure, however withdrawing this figure might be, he frees up a negative space for others to occupy and inhabit: a space that belongs to the uncertainty of a political future. The intensification of relationality Jameson uncovers in the Benjaminian sentence strives to interrupt, displace, and transform the "guilt-nexus of the living" by moving us to *choose* a debt to the future rather than to the past. Here, directionality and temporality become complicit in the topological undoing of the nexus that binds capitalism to religion, and in this way, they transform the certainty of indenture into the indeterminacy of hope, neither one of which can ever be disentangled from the other. This new nexus offers the possibility of a destructive force whose pessimism can enable a more energized future (2020, 80) and whose sense of defeat can become the catalyst for revolutionary events (93). But even here, the task of the dialectician—of both Benjamin and Jameson—remains risky and unpredictable in relation to several intersecting temporalities. In the end, there is no calculus for the political in either Benjamin or Jameson; the multiplicity of their figures remains a site of political incalculability, and this is because the absence of the individual self corresponds to the intensification of historical contingency.

Indeed, what characterizes the interior mechanism of Benjamin's language—what Jameson calls his "style"—is the way in which its figures cinematically fade out into one another before they can assert themselves. They are evoked only to be transformed by different figures or mobilized into different contexts in a violent movement of extraction and displacement. As we have noted, the shifting movement that we understand as the signature of Benjamin's language is his way of remaining faithful to a process of destruction, what Jameson identifies as the "violence of [his] critical practice" (29). This violence is at the heart of Benjamin's citationality, something that is already evident in his earlier essays but that gets its first extended enactment in his 1928 *Trauerspiel* book, the subject of Jameson's fourth chapter, "Nature Weeps." According to Jameson, Benjamin's *Trauerspiel* tells us that history can only *be* history as long as it is the withdrawing trace of its own transience. Only when it is no longer history—that is to say, no longer an empirical, historical fact among others—can it survive as history and as the possibility of history. This is why the *Trauerspiel* presents itself as an anthology of baroque figures, a history of the surviving linguistic figures of the past, and, in particular, of the linguistic emblems of a literary past. If Jameson's arguments hinge on the unstable relationship between figuration and the transience of legibility, it is because, like Benjamin, he wants to point to the necessity—the political necessity—of training new collective subjects in reading the images, figures, and emblems of history and, in particular, of the reproducibility inscribed within them.

As Benjamin demonstrates, the baroque's emphasis on the inevitability of repetition, on the citational and scriptural character of history, suggests that the notion of an original work of art is almost as difficult to sustain in the German baroque mourning play as it will be with the emergence of photography and film. Indeed, the *Trauerspiel* should be read as a self-proliferating recitation of history—in particular, of a pre-bourgeois history—and, more provocatively, as a violent masterpiece of unoriginality (Jameson himself refers to it as "a tissue of citations" [35]). Benjamin's language surrenders itself to innumerable others— a Shakespeare, a Calderón, a Gracián, or any number of the baroque writers he considers here (and later a Marx, Blanqui, Baudelaire, Proust, or Kafka, or any of the other voices encrypted in his sentences)— whose language enters his text fragmentarily through a process of extraction that is violent and destructive. Once gleaned from a histori-cal text, this fragment, or even just a word, enters into a logic of anal-ogy with other fragments and other words. The mechanism of analogy becomes an antidote both to causality and to a naïve understanding of creativity; it underscores the fact that history is only political if it is simultaneously form and the breaking of form. The similitude or conceptual affinity that travels from one text to another signals the movements of what can become legible, which appears as a series of endless emblems carrying enigmas across several different temporali-ties. As Baltasar Gracián puts it in his definition of *conceptismo*, they are inscribed within "un acto del entendimiento que expresa la corre-spondencia que se halla entre los objetos" (within "a mental event that expresses a correspondence between objects"), and their itinerancy relies on the intensification of polysemy, allegory, paradox, emblem, enigma, and ellipsis (55). Gracián can illuminate the past insofar as his writings can be read as contemporary through a logic of analogy that bypasses literary history—a paradoxical refracting technique that freezes their contextual history to reveal structural similarities that dialectically illuminate the simultaneity of past and present. It is in the possibility of our being able to read this relation and difference that we can begin to register what Benjamin means by history as a path-way to politics, which is always his absolute priority, especially when his approach often seems so curiously abstract. If Benjamin returns to Gracián and other baroque writers, it is certainly in recognition of their inescapability for his thought but also because, wanting to spec-ify the means of his analyses (what makes them possible but also what in them may help us bear witness to an uncertain and open future), he wishes to release and mobilize the resources and critical potential he finds there in order to realize the promise of transformation—of revolution, of a future, of a potential redemption—in his present moment. Benjamin writes in the hope that, if he can transform our relation to language, to even words or phrases, he can perhaps change not just language but also the relations in which we live. Jameson reminds us that Benjamin gifted a copy of Gracián to Bertolt Brecht and, with this detail, underscores not only the philological origin of the playwright's *gestus*—an embodied emblem of sorts rather than an action—but also the act of transmitting a text from one context to another, from one person or one social form to another. This act of transmission belongs to Benjamin's commitment to the circulation and recirculation of texts—a gesture he understands as political—and to his insistence on what we used to call "intertextuality." In Jameson's words, this passing of the book from one to the other "alerts us to the attention in both to this rarely formulated level of intercourse, which eludes the visibility of history and yet remains undetected on the level of individual subjectivity" (2020, 11).

But it is not what art and literature in themselves are that interests Benjamin but rather how they operate in the mind and shape subjectivities. Aesthetics, understood as a repository of beauty and a space of contemplation, is always regressive and compensatory and, for Benjamin, authoritarian and even fascist. It is exactly the relation between aesthetics and fascism that will later prompt his reconceptualization of the work of art as an impersonal masslike object that can more easily resist its instrumentalization by fascism. In his *Trauerspiel* work, Benjamin had already noted that the baroque spectacle depends on a manipulation of the aesthetic for the sake of political legitimation. Baroque sovereigns domesticated the aesthetic in order to secure their own position and Gracián's *Agudeza y arte de ingenio* (Subtlety and the art of genius) is a *conceptista* training manual for the development of a strategic and political defense against such royal abuses. Absolute sovereigns instrumentalized public spectacles in order to control the emergence of new concepts of secularized power and political autonomy in all their contradictions. The rise of European fascism during the 1920s and 1930s urges Benjamin to return to this conceptual and figural armature and to seek similar resources that can become weapons against the present rise of fascism. In its most extreme formulation,

Benjamin's work understands the very grounding of action in figuration as an instance of political work. Figuration emerges throughout as a historical and concrete abstraction of phenomenological essences that evades both philosophy and aesthetics.[1] In Jameson's reading the secularization of religious abstractions traces the conceptual movement of Benjamin's historical figurations and often in strange and unexpected ways.

Messianism may be the most important of this secularized religious abstraction. It is because the messianic refers to the transience, transformation, and change that structure existence that it bears constant reference to the experience of an emancipatory promise—but a promise that, remaining open, promises what cannot be promised and therefore is unrealized. That the messianic promises a futurity that is open to something else means for Benjamin that we must oppose any effort to predict or organize the future. "Whoever wants to know how a 'redeemed humanity' would be constituted," he warns us, "under which conditions it would be constituted, and when one can count on it, poses questions to which there is no answer. He might as well ask about the color of ultraviolet rays" (1974, 1232). We might recall here, as Benjamin does, Marx's claim in an 1869 letter to Edward Beesly that "whoever drafts programs for the future is a reactionary" (1977, 194). This is why, Jameson reminds us, Benjamin's angel of history "cannot turn its face toward the future" (2020, 219), but this is also why, insisting on what Benjamin gains by never letting go of the language of theology, he adds, "[t]he theological code . . . has one particular conceptual space in which it proves to be the privileged instrument in what is, in any case, an impossible situation: and that is the realm of the future" (231). Indeed, "[t]heology reserves a uniquely specific virtue for the domain of the future: it is called hope" (240) and, as we have seen, "hope is the sign of a future for those who are hopeless" (242).[2]

Jameson insists throughout on the centrality of theology for Benjamin's political thinking, yet he goes further than anyone else and turns Benjamin himself into an awkward theological emblem, a baroque figuration that contains a political enigma we must decipher anew in every act of reading, a reading at risk of getting lost amidst the force of Benjamin's figurations. While many critics have identified Benjamin with his angel of history, Jameson tells us that the angel is "the awkward Benjamin himself" (220). Whether wittingly or not , he qualifies Benjamin with a word that, in its late Middle English origins, combines "awk"—which means "backward" or "wrong way round"—with "ward," and, in doing so, suggests a *moving in the wrong direction*. This Benjamin-angel moves backward—is pushed backward by the *"storm of progress"*—into the future, which is of course Benjamin's own signature gesture and one that, no doubt to his great pleasure, would have satisfied Gracián's criteria for *"ingenio."* Benjamin everywhere looks backward in order to think about his present. He draws resources from a past that, in his hands, becomes a kind of lens through which he can view his particular historical moment since one of his most fundamental axioms is that every moment is already full of time: it can only be thought by considering the past, the present, and the future all at once. In turn, Jameson's book offers us an awkward Benjaminian lens through which to consider a Marxist practice of reading that reminds us that our only hope is in what Marx famously called "a poetry of the future" (18).

The close kinship between Marx and Benjamin—and of course between Jameson and these two political readers and writers—is demonstrated throughout *The Benjamin Files*. That Benjamin is a brilliant close reader and active interlocutor of Marx's texts is legible in all the ways in which his language is entirely infused by Marx's language, images, and conceptual movements, and by how much his analyses absorb the lessons of Marx's writing. As Jameson would have it, Benjamin returns us to the full complexity of Marx's worlds by refusing to read him ideologically and instead by taking the more difficult and indirect path of finding what is most political in Marx in the movements and images of his sentences. For Jameson, it is in this act—an act not unlike that of Jameson's insistence that we stay close to Benjamin's sentences—that Benjamin makes all of us (including Jameson), better readers of Marx.

Eduardo Cadava is Philip Mayhew Professor of English at Princeton University.

Sara Nadal-Melsió is a NYC-based Catalan independent scholar and curator.

Notes

1. With regard to the centrality in Jameson's book of the question of aesthetics—and to the issue of Benjamin's "anti-aestheticism"—the diminished role of Adorno is rather remarkable. In general, Adorno appears mostly as a figure of contrast and counterpoint in order to distance his strategic preservation of the "autonomy of art," as the locus of independence and differentiation required to articulate a political critique, from Benjamin's antiaestheticism and, indeed, from the latter's willingness to do away with such autonomy altogether. The Jameson we encounter in this book seems less willing to engage in polemics and much more invested in his full immersion in Benjamin's language and thinking—an approach of which one can easily imagine Adorno being highly critical but that Benjamin, and now Jameson, view as the only way to point to the social relations that subtend the artwork and also subjectivity itself.

2. Given the importance of Carl Schmitt's political theology in Benjamin's *Trauerspiel*, his absence from Jameson's book is striking. It is as if the echoes and corrections of Schmitt's theory of baroque sovereignty already contained in Benjamin's secularization of theology—as mediated acts of incorporation and mobilization—had, at least for Jameson, somehow transformed the centrality of Schmitt in favor of Benjamin's much more uncertain and fugitive historical categorizations. On the closeness and distance between Benjamin and Schmitt, see Samuel Weber's "Taking Exception: Walter Benjamin and Carl Schmitt," Diacritics 22, no. 3/4 (Winter 1992), 5–18, which is still the richest account of the vexed relation between these two thinkers. Jameson's silence in regard to Schmitt here, though, signals his stance of whom he believes is more politically revolutionary.

Works Cited

Althusser, Louis. 1971. *Reading Capital*. Translated by Ben Brewster. New York: Pantheon, 1971.

Benjamin, Walter. 1974. *Gesammelte Schriften*. Vol. 1. Edited by Rolf Tiedemann and Hermann Schweppenhäuser. Frankfurt am Main: Suhrkamp.

Benjamin, Walter. 1977. *Gesammelte Schriften*. Vol. 2. Edited by Rolf Tiedemann and Hermann Schweppenhäuser. Frankfurt am Main: Suhrkamp.

———. 1994. *The Correspondence of Walter Benjamin, 1910–1940*, edited by Gershom Scholem and Theodor Adorno, 84. Translated by Manfred R. Jacobson and Evelyn M. Jacobson. Chicago: University of Chicago Press.

———. 1999. *The Arcades Project*. Translated by Howard Eiland and Kevin McLaughlin. Cambridge, Mass.: Belknap Press of Harvard University Press, 2003.

———. "The Work of Art in the Age of Its Technological Reproducibility." In Vol. 4 of *Walter Benjamin, Selected Writings, 1938–1940*, edited by Howard Eiland and Michael W. Jennings, 256. Translated by Harry Zohn and Edmund Jephcott. Cambridge, Mass.: Belknap Press of Harvard University Press.

————."Karl Kraus." In *Walter Benjamin, Selected Writings* vol. 2: 1927–1934, edited by Michael W. Jennings, Howard Eiland, and Gary Smith, 453. Translated by Harry Zohn and Edmund Jephcott. Cambridge, Mass: Belknap Press of Harvard University Press, 1999.

Gracián, Baltasar. 2001. *Agudeza y arte de ingenio.* Madrid: Castalia.

Jameson, Fredric. 1979. "Marxism and Historicism," in *New Literary History* 11, no. 1 (Autumn 1979): 70.

————. 2020. *The Benjamin Files.* London: Verso.

Marx, Karl. *The Eighteenth Brumaire of Louis Bonaparte.* Translated by Daniel De Leon. New York: International, 1963.

PARTING WAYS: WITH WERNER HAMACHER

GIVE THE WORD: RESPONSES TO WERNER HAMACHER'S
95 THESES ON PHILOLOGY
EDITED BY ANN SMOCK AND GERARD RICHTER
University of Nebraska Press, 2019

Kevin Newmark

~

Wer spricht, wer sich ausmacht, wer seinen Namen, seinen Ort, sein Wort
vermisst, der entmisst *sich, verliert seinen Ort an der Verortung, sein Wort an die*
Entwortung und (ist) entwo

—Werner Hamacher, "Amphora"

The prominent place accorded to philology by Werner Hamacher is remarkable for a number of reasons. Among the most eye-catching would doubtless concern the way that, for him, philology can be assigned no place; it is only by virtue of philology taking place that the world becomes a place in the first place. "Philology is not a part of this world," Hamacher writes in the eighty-ninth of his *95 Theses on Philology*, "it is the movement of the world itself: it is the coming into the world of the world" (Smock and Richter, liii).[1] Such an affirmation would not be the most predictable one to derive from the canonical concept and practice of philology. If philology today seems mostly antiquated, that is because we have lost touch with what, through a return to philology, the same name might have been—and still be—able to point toward. Philology as we know it has succeeded in becoming rigorous enough as a historical and hermeneutical discipline to have made us forget what a philology of the term *philology* might otherwise be able to disclose. And it would be toward allowing such an *other* philology to emerge from the crusty layers of *philology* that Hamacher devotes his *95 Theses*. For, if philology names a certain attentiveness to language, and if language consists first of all in those acts that open a "place" in which names can begin to function as names, then a particular kind of attentiveness—call it *philia*—to language (call it "philia-logy") could by the same token bring about an attentiveness to the way the world will have become whatever we think is meant by that term, *the world*, only through the philological fact of its having been so named. One of the innumerable merits of Hamacher's *Theses* is to have been able to generate from this situation sufficient attentiveness among scholars of philology, literature, and philosophy for another publication to have resulted from it: *Give the Word: Responses to Werner Hamacher's* 95 Theses on Philology.

In many respects, *Give the Word* is a peculiar volume. It is composed of a third reprinting of Hamacher's *95 Theses on Philology*, this time in both English translation and German, followed by a short introduction by coeditors Ann Smock and Gerhard Richter, which leads to the Responses to the *Theses* written by eleven scholars, most (but not all) of whom are affiliated with U.S. universities. Following these eleven Responses—anywhere between six and nearly forty pages in length—there is another text by Werner Hamacher, "What Remains to Be Said," which responds at surprising length to the preceding essays on his *Theses*. As the editors point out in their introduction, extracts from the *Theses* first appeared in English translation as part of a 2010 special issue of *PMLA*, "Literary Criticism for the Twenty-First Century" (Hamacher 2010b, 4).[2] "As the beginning of a response" to that publication, the editors specify, they organized two panels at the 2013 MLA Convention in Boston and then followed up on that first initiative by compiling the volume of texts that now appear in *Give the Word*.

It is worth noting, however, that Hamacher died in July of 2017, two years before publication of the volume. Something of a disjunction, if not a dissonance, is produced as soon as one notices that Hamacher's Response to all the other Responses now has, or has been given, "the last word" in a way that could not have been registered at the time he wrote the essay "What Remains to Be Said" in 2016. In the interval between Hamacher's writing "What Remains to Be Said" and its publication in *Give the Word*, lies an event—Hamacher's death—that from now on cannot help but leave its mark on the essay: on what it says and what remains to say in response to it. One of the contributions, "Language-Such-That-It's-Spoken," by Michèle Cohen-Halimi, contains a citation from the poet Francis Ponge that takes on an uncanny resonance when it is made to refer to Hamacher's signature on "What Remains to Be Said." Ponge is using the French word *chose*, "thing," but in this case the "thing" at issue would be the larger question— *die Sache*, the matter of our concern and attentiveness—of just how to understand Hamacher's essay in relation to his existence as thinker, writer, teacher, friend. "It," the thing we are talking about, Ponge writes in the citation included by Cohen-Halimi (and which I am now turning toward Werner Hamacher's life, death, and writings), "should be described *ex nihilo*, but so well that it could be recognized only at the end: so that its name would be a little like the last word of the text and not appear until then" (Smock and Richter, 35). Hamacher's name has from now on been definitively separated from the one who called himself and whom we called by that name. Out of this *nihil*, or more precisely out of the fatal break of this nihilation—and out of it alone—can Werner Hamacher's name now appear and be recognized, precisely at the end and as the last word of all the texts by which that name has so well described and signed itself.

A slight trace of these complications appears in the first words of the introduction, when the editors refer to "the late Werner Hamacher's *95 Theses on Philology*" and then go on to quote some lines of poetry "that perhaps Hamacher would have liked" (1). The lines that Hamacher might have liked have to do with the "breaks" the editors count among "the many beauties" of the *Theses*. Why, exactly, the "breaks" in the *Theses* should be characterized as "beautiful" is not elaborated upon in the introduction. And though it may seem like only a casual and passing remark, associating the motif of the break in Hamacher's *Theses* with the beautiful in this way would merit further attention and commentary. For the beautiful is an aesthetic determination, and since aesthetics belongs, even if problematically, within the precinct of philosophy rather than to philology properly speaking, it is worth asking how Hamacher's *Theses* relate specifically to the phenomenality of appearance without which no aesthetic theory could be formulated. "Philology," Hamacher's Thesis 56 reads, "multiplies a gap—an interval—into gaps—and intervals—that cannot be contained by any *topos* but hold open an *a*-topy or *u*-topy. The time of space is suffused with the time of spacing: time-spacing is no longer a condition of phenomenality but its withdrawal into the aphenomenal" (xxxvi). If the break that is written into and multiplied by Hamacher's *Theses* involves the withdrawal of phenomenality into the aphenomenal, then it would also serve to sever Hamacher's philology from aesthetics as such and from any coherent determination of "beauty" tributary to it.

On the other hand, one of Hamacher's most far-reaching gestures is to initiate the separation of philology from itself, to hold open a space within philology as we know it for an "other" philology, one that could no longer be relegated to "an ancillary discipline" dependent on philosophy, theology, historiography or jurisprudence, or to "a disciplinary technique in pedagogical institutions," or to the specialized domain of "literary studies" (Thesis 86). It could well be, then, that the attribute of "beauty" the editors associate with Hamacher's *Theses* might be read otherwise than from within a properly philosophical and aesthetic horizon of understanding. If one of the "beauties" of Hamacher's *Theses* is indeed the break they pursue between philosophy and philology, then it would become necessary, as an after-effect or consequence of Hamacher's text, to learn how to read "beauty" otherwise. It would be necessary, in other words, not to read the "breaks" of the *Theses* as belonging to a philosophical determination of aesthetic beauty; rather, it would be necessary to learn how to read the "beautiful" as another name for whatever takes place in Hamacher's text in the mode of a break, rupture, interruption, or blank. And first of all, the break that could open a space between an "other" philology and the philosophical determinations of being, meaning, history, and beauty to which the "ancillary discipline" or "disciplinary technique" of philology has always been subjected. Hamacher, moreover, has regularly displayed a special attentiveness to just such a scission between philological singularities and philosophy as both ontology and phenomenology. Insofar as philosophy has always determined "what is" on the basis of what comes to appearance and can as a result be brought to knowledge through language, it has always exhibited an inclination to treat language as being itself an object that could be known through its phenomenal attributes. Or, to put it differently, philosophy, in order to be the ontology and phenomenology that it constitutes itself as, must also be a phenomenology of language such that the devices of linguistic meaning can be grounded in its own phenomenality, that is, as voice or writing. Aesthetics, as the branch of philosophy whose role is to uncover and maintain a stable articulation between meaning and its phenomenal manifestation in works of art, would be perfectly compatible with, though subservient to, a phenomenology that surpasses the being of mere appearance by speaking it in a discourse of truth, as *logos*.

In this way, there would be a kind of symmetry, or ratio, established between language and the coming to presence of being that language alone can speak and thus make accessible for reflection. "The *logos apophantikos*," Hamacher (2019a, 143) writes in an essay on Paul Celan, "understood as demonstrative speech, was the privileged Organon by means of which phenomena might disclose themselves." What one could call the voice of reason—as distinct from the mere sounds attributed by Aristotle to animals—is constituted from out of this *logos apophantikos*. By stating "what is" by pointing out "*that* it is," and by further predicating the attributes of whatever is in the discourse of assertion, the logos apophantikos grounds its capacity to ascertain as well as communicate the truth value of all those phenomena it brings to manifestation, including itself.

But does all language speak apophantically? In other words, is there nothing but predication, demonstration, proposition, and manifestation in the saying of the logos? In the first chapter of *On Interpretation*, as Daniel Heller-Roazen's contribution to the volume reminds us, "Aristotle begins with a simple, yet perplexing claim: there are 'things in the voice' [*ta en te phone*] in need of investigation" (Smock and Richter, 195). *That which is in the voice*: how should we listen to it, what do we hear there? In Thesis 49, Hamacher speaks of hearing words "with a philologist's ear" (xxx). With a philosopher's ear, one should undoubtedly understand Heller-Roazen's comment to refer to an epistemological "investigation" that is not only announced in Aristotle's text but accomplished by it, a discourse able to subject whatever in the voice is not yet known to an analysis sufficient to disclose and communicate it. With a philologist's ear, on the other hand, one might hear Heller-Roazen's "in need of" another way, as an echo or announcement of radical neediness, unending indigence, lack, or even emptiness. But what would be a lack so lacking that it could not ultimately be determined as a "lack *of* x"—in this case, a lack "of being"? If such a pure lack were conceivable, then one would be hearing— though "hearing" would perhaps not be the best term here—that which in the voice would be so devoid of definitional potential that it could and should remain forever open to investigation. But precisely because of that, it could never be adequately made to manifest itself through the propositional language and investigations of philosophy. Such would be the indefinite spaces or lacunae opened by that which might also be heard in the voice: the speaking gaps to which the philologist's ear would never tire of responding. Out of those things that Hamacher's ear perceives in Aristotle's voice, in fact, emerges a kind of logos that diverges in just this way from apophantic speech.[3] It is this other way of speaking that, for Hamacher, marks a decisive break with ontology and the various phenomenologies to which it has given rise. Since the propositions in Thesis 8 lay out the terms of this break, which also functions in one way or another as a pole of attraction for many of the Responses to the *Theses*, it is worth quoting in its entirety:

> From the *logos apophantikos*, the discourse of propositions relating to finite objects in sentences capable of truth, Aristotle distinguishes another *logos*, one that does not say something about something and therefore can be neither true nor false. His only example is the *euche*, the plea, the prayer, the demand. Propositional discourse is the medium and object of ontology as well as of all the epistemic disciplines under its direction. Meaningful but non-propositional discourse is that of prayer, wish, and poetry. It knows no 'is' and no 'must' but only a "be" and a "would be" that withdraw themselves from every determining and every determined cognition.[4] (xiii)

To the degree that language speaks otherwise than in propositions, it breaks with apophantic speech, though such a "break" should not be taken to mean that apophantic speech in any way precedes the separation from nonapophantic speech that may constitute the divided "origin" of every language. As precisely such an inaugural separation from "itself," language would also name an ineluctable longing to pursue whatever, belonging to it, nonetheless and for that very reason withdraws from it: a longing to "be" what cannot but elude "being" in the very cleft of its longing. Language in love with its (own) interminable withdrawal: an other *philo logos*, loving what in itself is always only other than itself. "Language" says the first Thesis, "is archiphilology" (xi).

If language in this way always speaks the language of self-resistance, moreover, then the "privileging" of apophantic speech, by

which philosophy has defined itself at least since Aristotle, will also
have to include the desire, wish, or longing that it has in fact exhibited throughout its history: to subjugate nonapophantic speech to its
own forms of phenomenally determined knowledge. The history of
philosophy has therefore consisted in an unspeakable "philological"
enterprise, whereby the *euche* belonging to apophantic speech—the
longing to make the logos of *euche* belong to it, apophantic speech—
can claim satisfaction only by giving itself over to a way of speaking
that is other than and that thus alters it. But if apophantic speech loses
its "privilege" at the very moment it gives in to its desire to exercise
it, then the other mode of speaking—the *euche,* that speaks of what "is
not" and does not "have to be," and further, of what cannot even be
said demonstrably "not to be"—becomes the place where philosophy's
"secret" philology can be spoken, if not simply revealed in the mode
of apophantic "truth." Such a "place," since it cannot be phenomenally
determined by the ontological categories of time and space, could be
located only in a nonplace and a nontime: that of break, rupture, blank,
interval. It should come as no surprise, then, that the name Hamacher
reserves for this time and place that neither is nor is not—nor can it
be said in truth either to be or not to be—would be poetry. "Poetry
is the language of *euche,*" Hamacher writes, "poetry is *prima philologia*" (Thesis 13, Thesis 14, xvi, xvii). To suggest, as Hamacher does,
that poetry names a kind of speech that breaks with the ontological premises governing all apophantic discourse, would by the same
token serve to liberate poetry from the aegis of aesthetic experience. If
the attribute of "beauty" can still be given to poetry, then it would
have to be a kind of beauty devoid of any determinate relation to the
phenomenal dimensions of language considered as sound or visibility. Philology, the "other" philology, would as a consequence name
an attentiveness to "the beauties" of language that are not restrained
by ontological considerations and that are not constrained to speak
in the mode of what is or is not, or that it is or that it is not. Language
not restricted to meaning or not-meaning according to logical and
phenomenological criteria of truth, that would be the aphenomenal,
a-topic and ana-chronistic, intervals opened and developed in language
by poetry as *prima philologia.* "Language is only halfway an ontological process," Hamacher writes, "philology has to deal with the other
half too" (Thesis 48, xxx).

Whether or not the Responses to the *Theses* refer to poetry by name, each in its own way—uniquely, more or less attentively (in other words, philologically), responds to the poetic intervals that are opened in language whenever those elements that are not reducible to apophantic discourse are given leave to speak. Two essays in particular, however, refer not only directly to poetry but also to the gesture—philological in Hamacher's sense—that occurs in poetic speech as a remarking of the break with apophantic discourse that marks its inauguration as poetry. The first of these, "Language on Pause," by Vincent W. J. van Gerven Oei, reads together two very short Theses: Thesis 14 ("Poetry is *prima philologia*") and Thesis 46 ("Philology: in the pause of language"). Van Gerven Oei, interested especially in showing the consistency in Hamacher's thinking of poetry as another name for the "pause" of and in the *logos apophantikos*, cites in passing Hamacher's 1984 contribution to a special issue of *Yale French Studies* devoted to Paul de Man, "The Second of Inversion: Movements of a Figure through Celan's Poetry." What attracts van Gerven Oei's attention is the following commentary Hamacher offers Celan's poem "Counter-Light":

> This possibility of the impossibility of its own existence breaks open only in the dash. . . . in the interruption of tropic language . . . This graphic pause . . . opens in poetic speaking a hole that cannot be closed by the logic of inversion . . . This is the site of an absence that must still remain unreachable to every absence that could change into our own, into the presence of our language. (109)

The lines from Celan to which Hamacher's commentary is attached refer to "die grosse Blume," the large (perhaps even giant) flower: "It is not white, not red, not blue—yet you take it. / Where it never was, it will always remain." What Hamacher underlines is not the phenomenal absence—the pause—that would consist in the negation of the flower's presence, since that absence could always be inverted into a negation of negation, to become, or blossom into, a presence in its turn. The absence of *this* flower is not due simply to its not (yet/any longer) being there, present/absent to intuition. Rather, the absence—break, pause, interruption, interval—that this poem by Celan speaks and speaks of occurs in the "graphic pause"—dash—that separates determinate negation (*not* white, *not* red, *not* blue) from a flower that will remain forever where it never "was," precisely because it remains forever recalcitrant to all phenomenal determinations of being.[5] Something that van Gerven Oei does not mention here but that is not left unremarked in Hamacher's reading of Celan's poem, however, is the way this particular "flower" repeats a "graphic pause" that can be found everywhere inscribed in the poetry of Stéphane Mallarmé—and in his prose, too.

Mallarmé's flower, moreover, is given special attention in this anthology thanks to the contribution by Susan Bernstein, "The Philia of Philology." For Bernstein, the flower at issue is the one Mallarmé famously pronounces in the equally famous text "Crise de vers": "I say: a flower! and, out of the oblivion where my voice consigns every shape, inasmuch as something other than known calyces, musically arises, suave and sheer idea, the absent (flower) from every bouquet" (213).[6] It is this flower that allows Bernstein to make the associations that she will draw out of Hamacher's word, *philology*. Taking as its cue Thesis 9, Bernstein's essay, like nearly all of the Responses, is sensitive to the way that philology, for Hamacher, does not belong to the order of the *logos apophantikos* or to the epistemological disciplines governed by it. "Its name does not signify knowledge about the *logos*," Hamacher writes there, "rather: inclination, friendship, love for it" (Smock and Richter, xiv). Bernstein's essay goes to the heart of the matter when it establishes, however discreetly, a potential link and an exchange in Hamacher's texts between two different orders of philia. On the one hand, there is no disputing Hamacher's emphasis on the way the "philia" in philology is to be understood as an inclination toward—even a love for—language. In this respect, the "other" philology Hamacher inclines toward is to be distinguished as rigorously as possible from a primarily cognitive discipline or theoretical attitude. It is precisely because Hamacher's philology signals a break with the propositional discourse of philosophy that it tends to replace the terminology of inspection, analysis, and knowledge with terms more apt to be associated with *philia:* inclination, emotion, affection, friendship, or love. However, Hamacher is always careful to emphasize the way the *philia*, which in philology is directed toward language occurs and can occur only through and by language. "Therefore Philology," Hamacher stipulates, "is the inclination of language to language as inclination. It likes in language its liking, language's and its own. Language is self-affection in the other of itself. Philology is philophilia" (Thesis 25, xxi).[7] The crucial question that Bernstein's essay helps to disclose concerns the degree to which it becomes legitimate—even if it remains to some extent inevitable—to recoordinate the philophilia of Hamacher's philology with the kinds of personal and interpersonal relations with which notions like "emotion," "affection," and "friendship" are regularly thematized and understood both within empirical experience and in the discourse of philosophical reflection upon such experience.

One place the question surfaces in a particularly salient manner is when Bernstein has cause to speak of Hamacher's relation to Friedrich Schlegel. Schlegel, Bernstein points out, was "a powerful and consistent source throughout [Hamacher's] career, a close friend and companion" (185). The gesture, no matter how attenuated by the fact that, in this case, the "companions" joined in "friendship" would be able to encounter each other only in the linguistic space opened between Schlegel's texts and Hamacher's readings (and rewritings) of them, does nothing to eliminate the suggestiveness of the images employed here. It is echoed in the volume's introduction, when the editors refer to the "comradeship" and "friendliness" among the various interlocutors in Hamacher's *Theses*, or when they evoke the way several of the volume's contributions "converge around the emotion in philology, the *philia*, suggesting both in their propositions and in their style what work animated by friendship, rather than driven by the demand for results, might be like" (7).[8] And it is all the more noteworthy in that the last section of the introduction, moving from these references to friendship, comradeship, and work, leads to a consideration of the way philology and its possible futures must not "neglect the precarious political and institutional contexts in which [philology] is necessarily inscribed" (8–11). A "convergence" similar to the one named in the introduction reappears, moreover, in Bernstein's essay immediately after she introduces the citation of Mallarmé's flower. Mallarmé's flower, in fact, serves as the point of contact, the affective site of touching, where another pair of friends, or texts, are made to converge in order to set to work together. This time, their names are Werner Hamacher and Jean-Luc Nancy, and the motivation for them to appear at this point is provided by the way each of them, separately, has cited Mallarmé's flower in their writings. Saying again the "same" flower, Bernstein suggests, is a way for Nancy and Hamacher, each in his own language, to participate in the "philological process that moves from what has been said in general to the saying of the singular" (187–88). This kind of movement, "the process of gathering—the bouquet or collegiality," as Bernstein puts it, is also one in which her essay can be said to participate. Her essay not only gathers Mallarmé's flower together with Hamacher's and Nancy's citation of it but also goes on to say the flower anew, and differently, first by reading it against the ground of Heidegger's remarks on flowers and friendship and then by concluding with another, though seemingly related, pair of texts by Paul de Man and Maurice Blanchot (188–92). Clearly, the "collegiality" to which Bernstein alludes is not to be understood as an exclusively philological matter restricted to collections of words or flowers. Thanks in part to "the enumerative function" she finds operative in de Man's reading of Baudelaire, the list of flowers and plants gathered into what she describes as "the singular plural of philological community" will eventually expand to include the one species that, as her final citation from Nancy makes evident, will be granted the privilege of growing alongside and watching over all the others: "man and his inventions" (191).[9]

However, it doesn't take much attentiveness, philological or otherwise, to suspect that Mallarmé and his flower are perhaps not the best choices for making an argument about the formation of "philological communities" based on "collegiality," since it is precisely the way this flower is *not* gathered, *not* collected into any bouquet, "l'absente de tous bouquets," that is stressed in "Crise de vers." Rather, it is Nancy who has to go out of his way to give Mallarmé's words a twist that, on their own, they could hardly sustain. When Bernstein cites Nancy's claim that Mallarmé's flower is one "that is 'absent from all bouquets' only because its 'inasmuch as' [en tant que] is also the presence as such [comme tel] of every flower in every bouquet," she is no doubt putting her finger on something important that Nancy wants to say about language and community. But it remains an open question whether such an affirmation might retain any contact with whatever is happening in Hamacher's *Theses* on philology, never mind whether it comes close to grasping Mallarmé's evanescent flower and its reinscription, "where it never was," in Paul Celan's poetry. Mallarmé's flower, which does not lend itself to becoming a member of any "bouquet," nonetheless does exhibit a kind of "friendliness" toward another flower, the one to be found in the poem "Prose (pour des Esseintes)"

(28–30). That poem is especially pertinent here since, like Celan's "Counter-Light," it deals with the "je/tu" relationship that unfolds in proximity to the singularly poetic time and space where such flowers grow. The form of the "we" in "Prose," though, would be difficult to subsume under familiar models of friendship or community, all the more so because it is formed with a "sister" rather than a brother or a lover. Like "die grosse Blume" in Celan's poem, moreover, the flower that multiplies—enumerates—itself in "Prose" is qualified as *plus large*, "larger," and *trop grand(e)*, "too big"; a hyperbolic kind of flower, then, that *grandissait trop pour nos raisons*, "grew too much for us to comprehend." No matter how closely the "je" and "tu" of Mallarmé's poem converge, or appear to converge, they remain decidedly apart, and the ungraspable flower here does not help them merge into any community: *Nous promenions notre visage* / *(Nous fûmes deux, je le maintiens)*, "We went strolling our gaze / (We were two, I insist on it)." The spacing that regulates the "nous" in the poem does not in fact allow for the divisions between them to be bridged by either seeing or speaking the flower together; what is shared by them can be described in the poem only in terms of their "double lack of consciousness." As for the flower(s) in "Prose," each one, "chacune," the poem says, uniquely, *se para* / *D'un lucide contour, lacune* / *Qui des jardins la sépara*, "adorned itself / with a lucid contour, lacuna / That from the gardens separated it." The "aucun contour" named "l'oubli" in "Crise de vers" is repeated and maintained, though otherwise, in the verse poem, as a "lucide contour, lacune" separating the flower not just from all bouquets but also leaving it missing from any discoverable garden.

Nous sommes là avant la distinction entre l'amour et l'amitié . . . avant tout sujet, toute anthropologie, toute psychologie des passions.

—Jacques Derrida, "L'Oreille de Heidegger"

All the same, it would be difficult to imagine how anyone contributing to a book like *Give the Word* could avoid hearing in the *philia* of philology—and in Hamacher's association of this *philia* with movements of inclination, affect, emotion, and friendship—a call to think and write from out of the friendship one feels for Werner Hamacher himself, or, lacking any direct acquaintance with him, then for his work. But it would be equally (if not more) difficult to imagine how one could respond to Hamacher's *Theses*—to all of Hamacher's texts— without taking into account the force with which they resist translating such attributes directly back into the concepts and experiences we most readily associate with interpersonal friendship. And that goes first of all for using the first-person plural pronoun *we* to signify the most basic kind of "being with." For if Hamacher's philology—an other philology—occurs and can occur only as a break with ontology, and consequently only as a break with the phenomenological procedures of the *logos apophantikos* that are anchored by it, then it stands to reason that the concept of friendship that philosophical reflection, at least in its most dominant traits, has derived from empirical experience will have to be subjected to a thoroughgoing philological operation and displacement in its turn. To read the *philia* in Hamacher's writing of philology is necessarily to inflict a wound on it, to disfigure its familiarity, and to cut it off and allow it to separate itself from every known meaning and every known example of interpersonal "friendship." "Plato," Thesis 40 reads, "investigates the concept of *philia* under the title *Lysis*. Philology: attention loosened up. Shouldn't that *philia* loosen or even dissolve itself along the way?" (xxvi). Lysis, for Hamacher, would become in this way the (im-)proper name for a kind of *philia* to which access might be gained only by rupturing its tie with properly philosophical (ana-)lysis, only by dissolving its bonds and setting it loose from its reliance on the principles of apophantic speech, whose meaning, knowledge, and truth are always grounded in and constrained by the phenomenality of empirical data. For who has ever perceived "friendship" in the purity of its coming into being for thought? There can therefore be no knowledge of what is called *philia*—either as philology or as interpersonal relationships—that does not first have to pass through a rigorously philological attentiveness to that very term, including to its own "looseness" as a term, as well as to the further loosening up it has undergone through its subsequent transformations into the idioms of *Freundschaft*, friendship, and *amitié*, among others.

Considerations such as these, at any rate, help in beginning to account for the way Hamacher conducts his own Response to the other Responses to the *Theses* collected in this volume. Hamacher's essay,

"What Remains to Be Said: On Twelve and More Ways of Looking at Philology," constitutes a valuable little book all by itself. It comprises nearly 150 pages divided into eleven chapters, and it ranges over the full course of the eleven other essays as well as over the *Theses*, several important writers named in the *Theses*, several important writers not named in the *Theses*, and a good number of other texts by Hamacher as well.[10] The eleven chapters are numbered from I to XIII, but Hamacher has disrupted their sequentiality by putting chapter IX between chapters XII and XIII by skipping some numbers altogether, and by numbering both of the last two chapters XIII. If there is a compositional logic or signification to be derived from the numbering, it would have to take these interruptions of sequential ordering into account. A "key" of sorts is provided by the Wallace Stevens poem that Hamacher dismembers into his essay: "Thirteen Ways of Looking at a Blackbird." Each of Hamacher's eleven chapters thus begins with a numbered citation of the corresponding stanza from the poem's thirteen stanzas, which themselves are numbered sequentially with roman numerals by Stevens. The fifth stanza of Stevens's poem, number V, appears as or after the end of Hamacher's essay, under the Arabic numeral "5." That is the only stanza of the poem that contains the disjunctive word "or," and it contains it twice, making the echo-effect with the text's last word—*Or*—stand out even more. Theses 31 to 38—devoted to the incompatibilities between philology and narrative sequencing of any kind—would be a primary philological resource for whoever would read the typographical spacing at work in "What Remains to Be Said." To this should be added—though that is not quite the right way to put it—Thesis 54, which proposes a far-reaching speculation by Hamacher on the placeless site of the zero that has to factor into any philological endeavor.

Given the breadth of its concerns and the penetrating nature of its many philosophical analyses and philological (ana-)lyses, it would be impossible in the limited space of this essay to do more than touch upon several of its distinctive features. Still, if there is one motif to which Hamacher returns throughout, a motif that bookends his essay, it is the break, space, or interval that prevents the *philia* of philology, as Hamacher rewrites it, from being understood on the basis of any ontology or phenomenology: which is to say, ultimately, on the basis of subjective or intersubjective (and therefore personal) relationships.

To the degree that the relation we ordinarily call "friendship" would derive its meaning from interactions between those "living beings" to which Hamacher refers at the end of the first chapter of his Response, and further, that it would involve a determined form of "living-with-one-another (*Miteinanderlebens*)," then language could always be considered a merely subsidiary mode of such being-with-others, a being-in-common or community, which common terms for language— such as communication (*Mitteilung*) in the very first place—serve to suggest and confirm (2019c, 222/86). For Hamacher, however, language cannot constitute a mode of "being with," since, as language, there can be nothing ontologically certain about its "being," and consequently there can be no question of determining the relationships it makes possible by privileging a relation of "with" over one of "without." If friendship depends in any way on language, then by the same token it will necessitate a philological suspension of what "we" call "living beings" and their "living-with-one-another" in the "world."

"Language has something non-linguistic before itself," Hamacher writes, commenting upon his qualification in Thesis 4: "Philology: transcending without transcendence" (222/85). The ontological verb "to be" would remain inappropriate to language precisely to the extent that in order to function at all, language cannot "be" anything determinate; language operates by always referring to something else, something other, even when it would speak "of" itself, either in terms of being or not-being. An incessant motion toward alterity, language can never reach nor coincide with the "something non-linguistic" that must remain "before" and therefore outside of it. Such would be the death "of" language, the something else whose horizon is forever displaced in the very act of naming it, speaking of it with language. But on the other side, to name and speak with language of "living beings" would by the same token displace their horizon so as to render its ontological contours just as indeterminable. To speak with language of either dead or living beings could therefore never mean to speak "with" them, in the sense of reaching—beyond language—a transcendence in them or anything else for that matter. Language, in a peculiar fashion, can thus communicate properly neither with the living nor with the dead, at least not without, in its decease, ceasing to function as language. The "something non-linguistic before itself," the living and dead to and of which language always speaks, then, cannot fail to appear in the mode of a "with"—speaking with, living with, dying with—but the "with" in this case, Hamacher insists, must also mark an unbridgeable distance. "Being-with," when it comes to language, means a "speaking with" *without* common measure with whatever it would speak to or about. "And *with* that With," is how, near the beginning of "What Remains to Be Said," Hamacher will put it, "[whoever speaks] lets this very With become an other With" (217/81). The *other* "With" with which language speaks whenever it speaks with others, dead or alive, moreover, makes language always speak, Hamacher pursues, "*more* than one language" and, he adds, "perhaps something *other* than a language." To speak in this way *with* "more than one language" would also mean to speak *without* a language: without just one language for sure but perhaps even without anything we could—yet, still, or ever—determine with or as language at all.

How does Hamacher understand language in this way as a singular mode of "Mit-Sprache," a speaking-with, or participation, that having its say in other languages also—though without having any say about it—always "speaks with the Without-With of those languages that it is itself speaking" (217, 221/81, 84)? A language-speaking tainted at every moment by speaking with languages without any stable determinations as language. And more to the point, how would such a *Mit-Sprache* speak with "the Without-With" of precisely those other languages that it itself is speaking when, for example, it speaks them with the *philia* of what is called philology or friendship?

At various places throughout his essay, Hamacher repeats this reference to a speaking "with the Without-With" of other languages, and each time it serves to suggest how the *philia* of friendship could learn to speak with the *philia* of philology only by learning how to loosen its attachment to the "being-with," the being-in-common, proximity, or community, with which interpersonal friendships are most readily defined, and as a consequence endowed, empirically and philosophically, with meaning. To speak with what Hamacher calls an *other* philology, in other words, an other *philia*, or phil-*allo*-logy, friendship would have to learn how to speak with "the Without-With" that constitutes the distinctive trait, the *philein*, of philological "friendship."[11] Without exercising a sufficient degree of attentiveness to this particular trait of philology, moreover, a reading of the *Theses* could incline only toward misconstruing the singular way their language speaks

with other languages. A tendency to generate such "misunderstandings, distortions, and problematic assumptions," surprisingly—though
consistently—enough, is exactly what Werner Hamacher ascribes, "with
few exceptions," to the eleven Responses to his *Theses* collected in this
volume (225–26 / 88–89). That Hamacher feels obligated to point this
out, he suggests, results from "the regrettable concession that has to
be made to the form of responding to responses"; though he further
notes that such a concession is made "in all friendship and gratitude
for the friendship that announces itself in these responses." The concession to form on Hamacher's part, his responding to the Responses
by marking his distance from them, is to some extent inevitable; it
could not have been avoided short of making another, more serious
kind of concession. Rather than accumulate misconstrual upon misconstrual, to suspect Hamacher's Response to the other Responses of
lacking graciousness, or even of exhibiting haughtiness or arrogance,
one should ask how it is that a concession to form in writing a philological Response to these particular Responses to philology would
require Hamacher above all to identify and dwell on what they have
misunderstood or distorted in the *95 Theses on Philology*.

For what is at stake here is *phileîn*, the "affect" without which neither philology nor friendship—nor philosophy for that matter—could
be inaugurated in the "experience" of their very inaccessibility. If the
Theses speak with the *philia* out of which philology speaks, then they
cannot *not* speak with *philia* as it is also spoken in the languages of
friendship and philosophy and that always lies, like something non-
linguistic, before them as well. It is for this reason that Hamacher can
be willing to make concessions to form when it comes to responding
to the shortcomings of the Responses to the *Theses*. But for the same
reason, he cannot concede anything when it comes to responding to
philia, a call necessarily preceding and exceeding every response to
it. *Philia*—philology, friendship, philosophy—cannot be worthy of the
name if concessions to form or convention are made, since it would
itself be the "origin" of all possible philological, philosophical, and
amicable forms and conventions oriented toward and by it. It is therefore in the name of *philia*, for the sake of *philia*, that Hamacher will
acquiesce, albeit in a most unconventional manner, to a certain convention of responding—"in friendship" and "to the friendship that
announces itself"—by highlighting those places where the Responses

have failed to respond to the call of *phileîn* retraced in the *Theses*. Hamacher's essay, "What Remains to Be Said," should therefore be construed as a way of speaking with the eleven Responses that each time uniquely responds to what remains to say beyond what they have been able to hear: in other words, to repeat once more, otherwise, the *philia* that announces itself philologically in a singular fashion whenever language speaks.

The *phileîn* at the heart of philology would consist in an "experience" of longing, *Verlangen*, or *òrexis*, and that is why the language it speaks cannot be reduced to the *logos apophantikos* of mere statements about "what is" or "that it is" (Theses 8, 10b, 11, 16, 19). In this respect, *phileîn*, whatever else it names, would also name a kind of plea, request, or prayer; one that can occur only to the degree that it addresses itself to what remains other than and separate from the plea, request, or prayer with which it speaks. If this aspect of the *phileîn* in philology appears only fleetingly in the *Theses*, it is made abundantly clear at the start of the second chapter of Hamacher's Response. Immediately before conceding the need to respond mainly to the distortions and misunderstandings of the other Responses, Hamacher turns to Plato's *Phaedrus*, "a conversation about speaking and the love—*eros, mania, philia*—directed toward it" (223/86). Devoting several pages to Plato's text, Hamacher underlines the way neither *logos* nor *philia* functions in the dialogue independently of the dramatized relation acted out between them. The "philo-logos" relation is therefore not determined by the one "with" the other, since neither *logos* nor *philia* has an assured conceptual meaning before they emerge little by little through their personified back and forth between Socrates and Phaedrus.[12] Their *philia* for speech, says Hamacher, is displayed in "this comportment towards the *logos*, the draw towards it and the distance that this comportment towards it simultaneously maintains in its separation from it" (224/87). As for the friendship, made possible for Socrates and Phaedrus through their relation to the *logos*, Hamacher goes on to demonstrate, this *phileîn* does not emerge as anything other than the *logos euche*. By pleading for friends and friendship, the *logos euche* pronounced at the conclusion of the dialogue discloses only the interval that continues to separate them from Socrates and Phaedrus. Taking leave of each other, Socrates and Phaedrus do indeed speak with one another but precisely in the mode of "without." Socrates requests that

Phaedrus join him in addressing a prayer to *phile Pan,* making it "a prayer for *philia,*" which must be lacking in order to be prayed for. And Phaedrus "pleads that Socrates pray for him as well (*syneuchou*), since all is common among friends—*koina gar ta ton Philon*" (224/87). The *philia* shared in this way through the speaking (*logos*), concludes Hamacher, takes place exclusively as "a pleading for befriending and a longing after it." For the same reasons, the "being-with" (the *syn-*, *co-*, *cum-*) of the *koinon*—community prayed and longed for by the friends who, solely through it, will have been defined *as* friends—remains precisely that which cannot be made presently accessible to them in anything other than their prayers.

Hamacher's insight is at once an acknowledgment and a further insistence: if every *philein* consists originally in a movement toward the other—if as a result it always issues in an address, a call, a plea to the other—then what of *this* pleading that occurs first of all as language, an appeal or *euche* without which no language could accede to speaking at all?[13] Does language not constitute this inaugural act of *philein,* a plea in which pleading language, from the instant it speaks, longs for, and gives itself over to what is other than its plea? The plea inside language would consist before all else in a longing "for" language, in other words, for that befriended language which, by virtue of the *philein* from which it necessarily proceeds, it can never reach in another (or even its "own") tongue. Such an inaugural appeal can therefore speak only with "the Without-With" of other languages—as well as with the other of language—with which it will in fact have always been already speaking in its self-divided origin. In this way, philology, for Hamacher, would name the *philein* that occurs first within language as an incessant and errant movement of self-alteration, as a longing for that which remains indefinitely and infinitely beyond and other than what it, language, without the affect of such constitutive *philia,* might have been able either to reach or relinquish—and thus able to be or not to be. Precisely this "incessant and errant movement of self-alteration," which constitutes the relation of *philein* without which no *logos* would come to speech, is also that which makes language into the placeless "site," or interval, of a time forever in flight. The *philein* of language marks time as a longing, and that is what language can be said to "live" on: its longing to live. But by the same token, as such longing, language also makes life into a waiting for precisely that time that will have been always missing: a time—coming to life exclusively as this interval, both too soon and too late—with which nothing can ever quite coincide.[14] Thesis 19, which returns to the Aristotelian definition of the human, only to alter it beyond recognition, will put it this way: "The formula for the human as that living being having language—*zōōn logos echon*—can be clarified by the modification: to be a *zōōn logos euchomenon*: a living being pleading for language, longing for it. The longing for language is a longing that exceeds every given language" (Smock and Richter, xix). The reference to the human in this Thesis, of course, can always lead to misunderstanding and / or distortion. It can always be used to introduce— or reintroduce—a subjective and psychological dimension serving to reduce the originality of the *philein* that separates language at its very source. And it is precisely such a tendency to cover over that separation that accounts for many if not all of the misunderstandings and distortions in the Responses to Hamacher's *Theses*.

For Hamacher, language will not allow itself to become the means through which the human expresses its longing, or makes its pleas, be that only for a language in which to express its desire for friendship. Were that the case, then even if language could not be said to be the possession of human beings, the longing, the *philein* for it, still could. If, on the other hand, the *philein*—longing as incessant spacing— erupts first "with" language, then the "longing for language" with which Hamacher modifies the Aristotelian qualification of human beings could no longer be understood as an attribute of or on the basis of any kind of being, "human" or other.[15] Rather, it would be necessary to begin characterizing differently what, always and exclusively with language, is called human being. A first, philological, step: to refer "the human" to whatever might be affected by the errant spacing, or longing—*philein*—that announces itself originally only in and for language, and as a consequence, only as a withdrawal from any stable determination of it or anything else, including the human. "*Philein*," Hamacher points out in a decisive passage, "does not merely designate a belated relation to an already given language, but rather a relation such that language owes its being-given to it (*sondern ein solches Verhältnis, dem sich deren Gegebenheit verdankt*)" (2019c, 258 / 122). It is, therefore, *philia* that first initiates language, as a speaking out of a longing for whatever can be related to it in its withdrawal from it, and thus to speak with "the Without-With" of all these other languages. This would include even those languages that serve to designate— though aberrantly, since such designations would themselves constitute an effect of language's affect, or *phileîn*—the "speakers" and "addressees" of language. For this reason, the *phileîn* that Hamacher associates with the "archiphilology of language" (Thesis 1), cannot be taken to mean a "psychological or emotional inclination in the sense of a *psychologia rationalis* or psychoanalysis" (258/122). To take *philia* for such an inclination could end only by mistaking it for the self-sufficient positing of a subject, one that seeks a relation "with" another, although only in order to enter into "an exchange of the self with itself in the guise of another." Such a "movement," Hamacher concludes, "would be a return to the self, a self-givenness, but no giving" (259/122).[16] The giving of *phileîn* as Hamacher speaks it with an other philology, on the other hand, would be a giving over of language that gives (itself) away without limit, speaking only *with* a self-othering language that remains ineludibly withdrawn and therefore *without* possible return.

It should come as no great surprise that the most economical term Hamacher will find for designating the anthropomorphic gesture thanks to which the Responses, "with few exceptions," would misunderstand or distort, in short, recuperate the force of the *phileîn* at work in the *Theses* is also the one most consonant with the philosophically dominant concept of friendship as a type of fraternity: *genealogical* (225–31/88–94). To the degree that *phileîn* would be first of all "a linguistic behavior and a behavior of language" (258/122), it could never be legitimately subsumed under structures of proximity that rely on chronological, topological, or analogical lines of personal affiliations and lineages. Such lines of convergence and continuity will always privilege fraternal relationships of belonging, of "being-with" over all the ruptures of (being) "Without-With." In doing so, they will necessarily misconstrue the errant intervals that speak whenever the language of *philophilia* speaks in and is dislocated by other languages, as, for example, when the *sister*, "enfant-soeur," in Mallarmé's "Prose (pour des Esseintes)" speaks the word—*dit le mot*—that at the end of the poem lies "hidden" under the hyperbolic flower belonging to no garden. The displacement that Hamacher's *Theses* initiate, moreover— a displacement that effects a shift from a language of generation and generalization to the always singular "generation," or occurrences, of language—would result in anything but an operation of chiasmus. And so it could not become susceptible to the elaboration of symmetrical substitutions and exchanges required by all sequential narratives of a genetic and family type, even in their most elastic and modified forms.

"A new beginning in each of its moments, language must," Hamacher insists, "be a beginning without succession, an initium that does not condition its consequences" (259/123). Hamacher uses the German word *Nachfolge*, "ein Anfang ohne Nachfolge," a beginning without succession. But the slight mistake made by the English translation at this point, which reads "without a successor (*ohne Nachfolger*)," or without successors, is faithful to the thrust of the passage. For it suggests the way that every genealogical sequence draws surreptitiously on a law of causes and effects in order to mask the impersonal randomness of actual events, thereby reducing them to a coordinated network of anthropomorphic acts and their more or less programmed consequences. The rhythm of "What Remains to Be Said," is therefore discontinuous and repetitive. It sets itself the "it*errable*" task of interrupting (each time uniquely) the elaboration of whatever "family tree" might otherwise overshadow and supplant "the linguistic behavior" of a *phileîn* that occurs every time without determinate cause and without necessary succession, since it operates only as the self-altering longing that splits apart every effort at identifying and joining together causes and consequences. "Philology, phil*allo*logy, phil*a*logy" (Smock and Richter, Thesis 24, xxi). The *phileîn* of language makes language into the site of historical events such that the only mark of articulation adequate to the randomness of their occurrence would be the comma.[17] If *phileîn* emerges first of all as strictly linguistic behavior, then the philological practices proposed by the *Theses* will have to maintain a rigorous distance from all undue "personalizations," from the establishment of "ancestral portrait galleries," which in the last instance do nothing but distort the philological "experience" addressed in the *Theses* by making it into just another element within "a conjectural history" whose "causal laws" can always be shown to be purely illusory (Hamacher 2019c, 232/95–96). As unfamiliar, unsettling, and "unfriendly" as such a suggestion may at first appear, it remains an ineluctable corollary of every one of the ninety-five *Theses*. For Hamacher, philology's "affect" can in no way be determined on the basis of personal affects or affections. Rather, before drawing any line of genealogical filiation between the *philia* of philology and what we commonly understand as affection or friendship, it would be necessary to attend, philologically, to the *phileîn* that speaks with the self-splitting occurrences of language. Philology never speaks with the language of "an affective and familial relation" without having its say in and therefore altering it—to the point of making such filiations from now on unrecognizable as what we always, mistakenly, thought they were or wanted them to be. As a consequence, Hamacher's essay will develop according to a contrapuntal pattern, responding to the eleven Responses in the volume by resisting and contesting whatever would serve to make them legible according to genealogical laws of resemblance and continuity.

The law of philology knows no law of causality above or below it, before or after it; the history in which philology is inscribed—which occurs only as the divergent inscriptions left by philology—is not one of continuity and descent but rather one of rupture, of parting ways with the "With" that would cement every genealogical conjunction.[18] "The inner law of language," reads Thesis 35, "is history. Philology is the guardian of this law and this law alone" (Richter and Smock, xxv). Genealogical relations, Hamacher stresses, belong to mechanically reproducible processes of ordination and coordination. As such, "they also reduce whatever history, language, and philology could be to a quasi-causal sequence" (2019c, 226/88). As the guardian of the inner law of language—*history*—philology must respond to every impulse to misconstrue it as a lineage, a line of descendance and dependence, by puncturing it each time and rewriting it anew. Although Hamacher himself does not refer to this particular distortion of philology, it would not be illegitimate to read "What Remains to Be Said" as a way of responding to the always possible deterioration of philology into mere *filial-ogy:* genealogical filiations, determinable lines of descent and kinship, structures of paternity and succession, and all the subtle but imperious modes of a-philological authority that cannot help but function along with them.

The rhythm of Hamacher's Response is repetitive and discontinuous, but that does not prevent it from displaying a highly meticulous mode of singularity. Philologically speaking, the most scrupulous attentiveness to formal order, coherence, and coordination may also offer the most effective means of allowing the *phileîn* of language to resist and free itself from their usurped authority over it. It is perhaps just this kind of attentiveness on Hamacher's part that leads him to privilege Plato's *Phaedrus*—a dialogue about *philia, logos,* and friendship (in short, *koinon,* community)—at the beginning of his essay. And it could well be for the same reason that he will turn to Susan Bernstein's essay as a springboard into the concluding pages of his Response. For it is Bernstein's essay, "The *Philia* of Philology," that more clearly and resolutely seeks to connect "the affective relation," which opens the possibility of philology, with "the being-with" that, in all of its manifold versions, grounds the dominant philosophical and political concepts of friendship in terms of interpersonal inclination, affection, contact, camaraderie, and community. This is so not because Bernstein's essay explicitly develops or even specifies such a connection but rather because of the particular way it brings the *Theses* together with, joins them to, and makes them touch the other texts to which it also refers.[19] "The singular plural of philological community," which the essay evokes near the end, would thus be broad enough to include Schlegel, Hegel, Heidegger, Blanchot, de Man, Nancy, and Hamacher. But the very specific term "singular plural" used to name this singular community of proper names is not taken from Hamacher's language. The phrase is borrowed from a book, *Être singulier pluriel (Being singular plural),* by Jean-Luc Nancy, and it is this text that, in addition to Mallarmé's flower, is made to function in Bernstein's essay as a point of contact—friendship—with Hamacher's texts on philology (Richter and Smock, 186–91). Hamacher's Response to that gesture is attentive above all to the way Nancy's "being singular plural" can be shown to depend on a conjunctive "with" even where it is a question of "Without Being" (2019c, 330–36/193–98). This is necessarily the case since, according to the key citation Hamacher makes from Nancy's text, "Language is essentially in the with (*le langage est essentiellement dans l'avec*" (334/196). It is therefore language that would serve to gather even Not-Being and Without-Being together with Being-With; and that, for Hamacher, would ultimately make Nancy's thinking of community into a kind of coexistential and relational ontology of *Mitsein.* "The ontological minimum that Nancy insists upon," Hamacher concludes, "namely, the Being-With with others, is not the minimum of philology. Being-With cannot be deemed an irreducible universal foundation for philology; rather only a phase of thinking, a passage that becomes an impasse if it is not broken through . . . and opened up to what still remains to be said" (335–36/197). Only on the *other* side of thinking "Being-With" could an other philology—and politics—become accessible, a *phileîn* carrying language so unreservedly toward the other that it would inaugurate nothing but a placeless motion, an errant interval no longer determinable by any "with" at all. "The 'without' in 'With-without-With' is to be thought," Hamacher adds, "as inoperative negation, as 'without-without-without'" (336/198).[20] Nancy's "Being-With with others" would for Hamacher still name a relation of the "with" *to* the other; it would therefore remain a "with" unmoved by whatever might come and be received only *from* the infinitely indefinite other, which other, for the same reasons, could never be determined as (being) a relation "with" it.

True "mourning" is less deluded.

—Paul de Man, "Anthropomorphism and Trope in the Lyric"

Hamacher's compact but rigorous and persuasive response to the ontological residue that would prevent Nancy's relational ontology from becoming an other philology leads at last to a question that has been there from the start, or, in fact, even before the start. If the call to which the imperative of an other philology responds is the *phileîn*— the longing, appealing, begging—that opens every language to a speaking with the "Without-With" of other languages, then how should we speak of those other languages that, in one way or another, will have already been speaking with the "Without-With" of Hamacher's philology, although under a different guise, in another idiom, with someone else's signature? The Thesis with which Hamacher frames the last pages of his Response, citing it several times, is number 38, which refers to "the dark ground" on which philology trains its attentiveness and to which philology must remain just as attentive as to the figures eventually emerging from it (2019c, 330–36/193–98). Much earlier in his Response, Hamacher had cited the same Thesis, appending two new words to it, "contingency" and "coherence," in an effort to specify further the co-relation between the dark ground and whatever might, for philology, appear against it. "The ambivalent 'co-,' which contingency and coherence share with one another (*Das zweideutige 'Ko-', das Kontingenz und Kohärenz miteinander teilen*)," he wrote there, "is called in Thesis 38 the *dark ground* out of which phenomena, figures, and words rise up" (233/96). The "Ko-" at issue here is ambivalent precisely to the degree that *Kontingenz* and *Kohärenz* can "share *with*-each-other (*miteinander teilen*)" nothing but a relation *without* relation because contingency and coherence are grounded in mutually exclusive tendencies. One can relate to the other only by obliterating it, giving in either case precedence to the forces of *Kontingenz*, since the philological level on which Hamacher is posing their relation (the ambivalent prefix Ko-) will remain forever *Kontingent* with respect to their infinitely divergent meanings. And then, almost as an afterthought—or, as if to make his point more striking—Hamacher adds, though in a parenthesis that seems to emphasize even further its *Kontingenz*: "(This *dark ground* might also, without regard to Native American etymologies, be called *Connecticut*—Dieser *dunkle Grund* hätte auch, ohne Rücksicht auf indianische Etymologien, *Connecticut* gennant werden können)" (233/96).

Now the sudden appearance of the name "Connecticut" can become a very overdetermined and ambivalent circumstance or turn of events in this context. And that is not just because, taken "without regard" to Amerindian etymologies, it pretends to bring together, seamlessly in one word, the "co-" of "contingency" with the "co-" of "coherence," although signaling at one and the same time, impossibly, the way that at the very moment they appear to "connect" to each other they also "cut" any connection with each other in the most random and abyssal fashion.

Indeed, one might well wonder why "Connecticut," precisely insofar as it can function as another name for the "dark ground" of philology, should not, philologically speaking, be regarded here according to its Amerindian etymologies. For evoking the name *Connecticut* in this way, "*without* regard" to its etymologies, could of course always be regarded as a not-so-contingent gesture in its own right.[21] To take the name "Connecticut" *with* regard to Amerindian etymologies, on the other hand, would in fact confirm the way the history of Connecticut has itself been marked by a discrete series of philological ruptures, or "cuts," of speaking in very particular ways with the "Without-With" of other languages, including those Amerindian ones that have been

repeatedly misrecognized, disconnected, and displaced (if not altogether effaced) in a motivated attempt at piecing together a seemingly
"coherent" genealogy for the current state of things. If "Connecticut,"
regarded through the philological lens of its Amerindian etymologies,
is taken to refer to "the place of the long tidal river," *kwen ehtekw enk,*
then such a river could never be reduced to a simple "conduit," a convergence of tongues contributing over time to one "long" (never mind
continuous) space of shared connection, expression, and communication. The historical and philological "tides," regarded as the dark
ground on which the state of Connecticut has been constituted, moreover, would be neither natural nor symmetrical. Nor would they be
devoid of the many different kinds of violence implied by the term
"cut," whose legibility is brought out by Hamacher's philological attentiveness to the way this very name does in fact speak "more than one
language." But the overdetermination of the name *Connecticut* in this
particular context, its speaking more than one language or perhaps not
even one, is also, if not to say especially, due to the way that, sooner or
later, out of its dark ground, another kind of figure cannot fail to rise
up, *von dem dunklen Grund sich abheben.*

"With the relation of the *Theses* to the works of Paul de Man,"
begins chapter IV of Hamacher's essay, "the commentators have a
lot of trouble" (237/100). The trouble with de Man is easy enough to
identify: it is the trouble any commentator on the *Theses* will experience in attempting to circumscribe Paul de Man's place within the
Theses, or in any other text signed by Werner Hamacher for that matter. Hamacher's insistence that philology can take place only by breaking, or cutting, every connection with the "con-," or *with,* with which
all genealogies are constructed is entirely consistent with his suggestion that the philological operation of cutting connections could take
place only on the dark ground of somewhere called *Connecticut.* In
other words, to read anything by Hamacher as though it could simply
be connected and then illuminated through a mode of filiation or affiliation with the works of Paul de Man would be immediately to misunderstand and distort the writings and the names of both de Man
and Hamacher. If there is indeed a force of *philein* operative between
Hamacher and de Man, then one could begin to register it only by taking account of the cut through which their connection might become
open to something other than a series of crude narrative sequences

within a very predictable genealogical history or family tree composed of fathers and sons.[22] Hamacher himself, at any rate, displays no inclination in his Response to allow any such recourse to genealogical models of paternity or fraternity to stand unchallenged.

But how, exactly, does Hamacher's Response negotiate such a genealogical trap; how does his language speak with de Man's language without allowing its animating force of *philia* to lapse into a narrative of familial *filiation*? To take just one example—although an example that is not merely one among others—it would require no great effort to show that the "clear distance," *deutliche Distanz*, Hamacher will claim, at the end of chapter IV, to have put between his own work and that of de Man, as well as that of Derrida, on what he calls "the structure of positing" is, if not itself misleading or hyperbolic, at least more complicated than that. And, besides, what could "clear distance" mean when measured against philology's "dark ground"? What point could it make and what goal would it serve, philologically speaking? Some of the complication is caught in the German term, *Setzung*, which Hamacher uses as an equivalent for "positing" (237–48/100–111, passim). To have followed both Luther and Scholem in naming his *95 Thesen* with the Greco-Latin term, "thesis," in fact, helps to expose the difficulty at issue, since the term *thesis* can refer both to the act of positing, placing (*Setzung*), and to the fact of a given placement or position (*Stellung*). Is it simply possible to speak of drawing clear lines of demarcation and distance here, between a language of propositions (*Sätzen*) on the one hand and, on the other, a language of positing (*Setzungen*), which, to some extent like the *logos euche*, cannot be restricted to—or fully separated from—propositional discourse? And so it cannot be purely accidental that precisely at the point Hamacher draws attention to the "clear distance" between himself and de Man, he also twice mentions the possibility of misunderstanding (*missverstehen*) the very proposition (*Satz*) he had earlier used in responding to de Man's work on positing (*Setzung*) by taking a clear distance from it (247/110–11). Still, such a focus on the relative proximity or distance between Hamacher, de Man, and Derrida, at least when it comes to what Hamacher is here calling "positing," or *setzen*, could easily deteriorate into mere quibbling if it did not at some point become attentive to another, though not wholly unrelated, feature of Hamacher's response to de Man in this essay.

It should be granted that Hamacher is right: no one is entitled to read an "other philology" as though it could be simply treated as a genetic offshoot or progeny of either a "grammatology" or what Hamacher refers to in this same chapter as a "rhetorology" (245/108). Of course, the term "grammatology" is a name actually used by Derrida, and it is put to work by him in a very precise and even philological manner. "Rhetorology," on the other hand, is not a term used anywhere by Paul de Man; rather, it is introduced in this chapter by Hamacher to distinguish his own thinking of an "*other* philology" from what he calls "the reduction of philology to a rhetorology of topoi and tropes," a reduction that he appears, in this sentence at least, to attribute unreservedly to the works of de Man.[23] The implied dismissal of de Man, here and elsewhere in the chapter, is too categorical not to raise our suspicion that something else, something more original and far-reaching, is happening between Hamacher and de Man, between the philological language Hamacher is speaking with (and without) de Man and the language with which de Man speaks of positing.[24] While the name "rhetorology" may have very little pertinence when it comes to a genuine engagement with de Man's work, there are other names that appear in the course of this chapter of Hamacher's essay that tell a far different story. And that story, which includes the act of naming—of calling, of being called by, and of responding to the name—is one in which the *philia* of language can be shown to play a singular and irreducible role.

Chapter IV of "What Remains to Be Said" begins with the simple assertion that the relation between the *Theses* and the works of Paul de Man gives the commentators in this volume a lot of trouble (237/100). But it passes very quickly from there to a consideration of Thesis 54, which itself begins with a reference to Roman Jakobson and ends without mentioning Paul de Man (Smock and Richter, xxxiv–v). The Thesis deals with a radical break, rupture, or blank that, without possessing any structure of its own, structures the differential relation between the two axes of language-functioning that, in the wake of Saussure, are juxtaposed by Jakobson: the axis of substitution (equivalence) and the axis of combination (contiguity). The two axes—famously correlated by Jakobson with the rhetorical tropes of metaphor and metonymy—are not entirely unlike the ambivalent "co-" shared between "coherence" and "contingency," and whose "dark ground" Hamacher had just a few pages earlier also called *Connecticut* (2019c, 233/96). The "cut" in the geometrical model adopted by Jakobson will occur, Hamacher had specified in Thesis 54, where "both axes cross in a null point (*Nullpunkt*)" (Richter and Smock, xxxiv). At this null point, Hamacher writes, the linguistic axes "follow at once a logic of substitution and contiguity, of poetic and prosaic functions, as well as neither of the two." The development Hamacher will give to this Thesis in his Response stresses the way the "null point"—belonging to neither one nor the other and yet to both axes at once—can be accounted for only by what he calls "a zero-rhetoric." "Zero-rhetoric" has its own genealogy, it seems, which Hamacher retraces by reference to a host of proper names, including Frege, Gauthiot, Bally, Jakobson, Lévi-Strauss, Lacan, Derrida, and Deleuze.[25] What not all of the above-named authors saw clearly, Hamacher notes, is a special peculiarity about the "zero," since it has to function both as a mark and as an absence, or suspension, of marking. "In the 'zero,'" Hamacher specifies, "the minimal marking required for language to function divides itself into a marking of absence and the absence of a marking, relates itself as a consequence to the posited and the unposited (*bezieht sich somit auf Gesetztes und Ungesetztes*), is relation and reference to the withdrawal of every relation (*ist Beziehung und Bezug zum Entzug jeder Beziehung*)" (2019c, 241/104). Jakobson, for instance, would not have been among those sufficiently attentive to this split, and so he would not have registered the zero as the "site" for "an absence of marking," the "unposited," and the "withdrawal of every relation." "The zero-sign," for Jakobson, then, would be "the name for the absence of any sign that could stand in opposition to another sign"; as such, "it marks even the absence of oppositions as a significant or signified absence and thus as linguistically posited" (239–40/103).

Hamacher's reference to "zero-rhetoric," on the other hand, would indicate and carry out an "extension that is not congruent with Jakobson's use of zero-compounds," one that would deviate from Jakobson in two decisive respects: "Zero-rhetoric is no rhetoric of positing and opposing, and for that reason refers not so much to an 'empty-place' as to a 'placeless vacancy'" (241/105). The German word for "empty-place" here is *Leerstelle*, and like "blank," "blank space," or "gap," its use is idiomatic and familiar; one could call it the zero-desinence form. The other term that Hamacher uses, however, not so much to oppose it as to expose it to a philological deviation, is *Stellenleere*, a term whose signifying force derives from its marked divergence from the zero-desinence *Leerstelle*. The deviation indicated would be one that forestalls ontological recuperations of the zero through understanding it according to any kind of logical, topological, or phenomenological coordinates. Like the *entwo* in Celan's poem, Hamacher's zero-rhetoric would take place only as an errant interval, an "unwhere," forever out of time and out of space, accessible only through the philological *cut*, or zero, that marks its turn away from all conventionally marked "linguistic, arithmetical, or logical usage" (242/106). In Hamacher's own gloss of the play opened up by the zero between "blank space" and "placeless vacancy," he explains what he wants to say this way:

> The formulations of this Thesis thus attempt to say something in the language of positing-rhetoric (*Setzungs-Rhetorik*) that is resolutely excluded from this language, which however, even in order to be thinkable and indicatable (*denkbar und andeutbar*), must nonetheless remain open as a free-space (*Spielraum*) for alterations in that positing-rhetoric (*Positions-Rhetorik*). Such a free-space is given wherever a place, even an empty-place, is displaced into the absence of place: a placeless-vacancy (*Einen solchen Spielraum gibt es, wo eine Stelle, und sei sie Leerstelle, in die Abwesenheit einer Stelle, eben eine Stellenleere, versetzt wird*). (242/105)

"Zero-rhetoric" would therefore name the displacement that occurs whenever "positing-rhetoric" (*Setzungs-* and *Positions-Rhetorik*), which marks the zero of a semantically determined empty-place (*Leerstelle*), speaks with the zero's absence of marking; the *without*, then, of a placeless vacancy (*Stellenleere*) thinkable solely by altering the positing-rhetoric from which it withdraws.[26] Thesis 54 says, and Hamacher repeats in his Response at this point: "*Only the philology of the zero would be the Origo of philology*" (xxxv, 242/106).

It would appear, then, that the detour through Roman Jakobson— along with the subtle but crucial distinction it allows Hamacher to make between the empty-place (*Leerstelle*) of the posited zero and the zero of a placeless and therefore errant vacancy (*Stellenleere*) withdrawn from all positing (and opposing)—converges neatly with his insistence at the end of this chapter on the "clear distance" he has developed between his work on positing and Paul de Man's. The shrewdly pointed commentaries Hamacher offers on two important essays by de Man also seem to go in this direction. Keenly attentive to de Man's recourse to "the vocabulary of positing," Hamacher will suggest how such a vocabulary imposes upon de Man a "correspondence-scheme," *Korrespondenz-schema*, one that leads inevitably to his privileging "a symmetry" between "language-positing" and "language-privation," or between "figuration and disfiguration" (242–43 / 106–7). In the end, de Man's stress on positing would "maintain a balance" (*die Waage hält*) between "figure-elaborating and figure-effacing" acts of language (248 / 111). Since, however, language does not stand in equilibrium with itself, it already initiates a breaking off from and alteration of such balancing acts.[27] "Insofar as language posits," Hamacher cites himself, "it sets forth, *Sofern Sprache setzt, setzt sie fort.*" Setting forth from the balancing act carried out by de Man's positing, only an other philology could respond (*entsprechen*) to "something other than a positing," which would also entail "setting away (*sich absetzen*) from itself and exposing itself (*sich aussetzen*) to another—unposited and unpositable (*Ungesetzten und Unsetzbaren*)." Such an other, over which positings would hold no power, Hamacher concludes, "can always remain a nobody and nothing (*kann immer auch ein Niemand und Nichts bleiben*)" (247–48 / 111).

Whether or not one finds Hamacher's treatment of the role played in de Man's writings by the positing-function of language sufficiently attentive to them may ultimately be of less philological interest than the stark reference he makes here in passing to such a "nobody and nothing," two ineradicable possibilities to which an other philology, and perhaps only an other philology, will have been able to remain attentive. For, in addition to the way, like a certain zero, they recall the possibility, in all language, of a "relation and reference to the withdrawal of every relation," they also point back to the blank space—and more precisely the *Stellenleere*—inscribed in Thesis 54, to whose further development this chapter of Hamacher's Response is devoted. Just how is it, then, that Paul de Man, whose name in fact appears nowhere in Thesis 54, will return in chapter IV of the Response, specifically in these pages where Hamacher elaborates more precisely how and why "only the philology of the zero would be the Origo of philology" (237–48 / 100–111)? At the start of the chapter, Hamacher takes to task two of the Responses in particular for having difficulty relating the *Theses* to the works of Paul de Man—the essays by Vincent W. J. van Gerven Oei and Jan Plug. In both cases, Hamacher characterizes their difficulty as a mistaken attempt to identify de Man as one of the "sources" (*einer der Ursprünge*), or even the "original" (*das Original*), in relation to which Hamacher's philology would be merely derivative, functioning only as a kind of placeholder, or "prophet" for de Man (238/100–101). The zero, then, and emphatically not Paul de Man, would be the Origo of Hamacher's philology. Moreover, to place de Man's name in the *Stellenleere* of the zero, according to Hamacher, is possible only by means of a philological procedure of effacement (*Löschung*), one that would include the suppression (*Ausblendung*), denial (*Verleugnung*), or blotting out (*Übermalung*) of precisely those remarks made by the *Theses* in this regard. Such an effacement, Hamacher concludes, pertains yet again to "a not, or a nothing."

It is at this point that Hamacher turns back to Thesis 54, the one that begins with a reference to Roman Jakobson's opposing of a "poetic function" to one that could be called "prosaic" (Smock and Richter, xxxiv–xxxv). The basic operation treated in Thesis 54, Hamacher now states without further ado, is the differentiation between two fundamental functions of language—selection and combination. This distinction can be further correlated to the one between metaphor and metonymy. And it is in respect to distinguishing between selection and combination, as well as their correlation with the rhetorical figures of metaphor and metonymy, that Hamacher picks up and develops the reference to de Man. Unlike Lévi-Strauss, Lacan, and Genette, says Hamacher, de Man did not adopt the scheme of differentiation proposed by Jakobson without altering it, without undermining and radically subverting it. The most prominent example of such a subversive gesture on de Man's part, according to Hamacher, was to make both language-functions—as well as the tropes correlated with them—depend on a rhetorical "figure" capable of destabilizing every distinction tributary to it. Hamacher identifies this "sub-figure" as *prosopopoeia*: "the figure of figuration, the trope of the production and assignation of tropes, and thus the fundamental trope for the arrangement of the world (*die Fundamentaltrope der sprachlichen Weltzurichtung schlechthin*)" (2019c, 238/101). Now the name "prosopopoeia," unlike the name "Paul de Man," does make an appearance in Thesis 54, and it is a prominent one: "The rhetoric of metaphor and metonymy . . . relies upon a zero-rhetoric with a zero-function for which not even the figure of prosopopoeia can render account, since prosopopoeia consists in a positing rather than in no positing" (xxxiv).[28] The divergence, or cut connection between Hamacher and de Man, would therefore depend on a possible distinction between a rhetoric of prosopopoeia and a zero-rhetoric. That is why Hamacher will insist on the place of "a not or a nothing" in delineating his separation from de Man. Prosopopoeia consists in a power of positing, whereas a zero-rhetoric would consist neither in positing nor in opposing; rather, it lies in a not-positing, a withholding, or a-positing, which would necessarily precede all positing, one in which nothing would (yet) be either posited or opposed. *Stellenleere:* a turning away from the act of positing, from the place of positing in Paul de Man's "rhetorology," and so a dis-placing of it toward "the opening for place" in Hamacher's "phi-lology of the zero."

What should give one pause here is not so much the intricacy of the propositions with which Hamacher articulates this divergence between an "other philology" and the texts of Paul de Man, an argu-ment that he makes with considerable resourcefulness. A question may arise, however, precisely where a kind of prosopopoeia is enacted by Hamacher's own text. For it is Hamacher who, in his Response, goes out of his way to endow the rhetorical term *prosopopoeia* with the power to perform the very act by which its meaning was regu-larly characterized by de Man. Prosopopoeia is a figure that lends the power of speech to an entity deprived of it because it is inani-mate, imaginary, dead, or simply absent. In other words, no matter the underlying cause, prosopopoeia serves to make (*poiesis*) whatever is not there, whatever is nothing present and therefore not available for knowledge, appear as though it had a face (*prosopon*) that could be recognized and known as such. For example, Paul de Man—the name, the face, the person—is wholly absent not only from Thesis 54, but also, as Hamacher himself at one point emphasizes, his name is never once mentioned in any of the *95 Theses* (226/89). It is Hamacher who, despite this absence, makes de Man appear, gives de Man a face, and lends him speech retrospectively in the Response by having the term *prosopopoeia* in Thesis 54 function as though it could restore de Man's voice precisely where it remains missing, a true "nobody and nothing." Prosopopoeia, Hamacher declares flatly at this point in the Response, should be recognizable as another name for Paul de Man and for all that his texts say about and give to prosopopoeia as a positing power.

"Since prosopopoeia owes its analysis to de Man," Hamacher writes, "its name in Thesis 54 can point to his (*kann ihr Name auf den seinen hindeuten*): the name for figure-making to the name of the one who gave it its sharpest profile" (238/101). How can Hamacher have recourse to the positing power of prosopopoeia in the very place, Thesis 54, where he appears to turn away from and displace it toward the *Stellenleere* of zero-rhetoric? In other words, how can his text speak *with* prosopopoeia at the instant it would determine *Stellenleere* as a *without*-positing?

Paul de Man, then, according to Hamacher, is the one who gave prosopopoeia a face: "the one who gave it its sharpest profile (*der ihm das schärfste Profil gegeben hat*)." And so the name of that face-giving operation—*prosopopoeia*—can be used by Hamacher as a means to reconstitute both the missing face (or the profile), and the name of Paul de Man behind it. Nonetheless, at the very moment he addresses de Man, in the displaced name of the prosopopoeia inscribed in Thesis 54, Hamacher will have been compelled to remark an unconditional risk of failure inherent to this very operation of face-giving. The reference—*prosopopoeia*—to Paul de Man, his name, his face, his texts, can always miss its mark and remain, as in this specific case, unrecognized, "a not and a nothing," with no assignable place. Immediately after identifying Paul de Man as the one who gave prosopopoeia its "sharpest profile," Hamacher adds this: "Whoever is familiar with the field of literary and cultural studies should not be capable of failing to recognize this reference (*sollte dies Hinweis nicht verkennen können*)" (238/101). The prosopopoeia—the term as well as the act—that Hamacher writes into Thesis 54 was supposed to restore de Man's face and voice, but it failed; he went unrecognized there, and Hamacher himself draws attention to this fact by complaining about it. The unavoidable possibility of just such a failure of recognition—no matter how familiar or family-like the characters are with each other—is accentuated here by Hamacher's use of the negative modal "should not." It *must* be possible for the reference (*Beziehung, Bezug, Hinweis*) to be capable of remaining aberrantly blank, "a nobody and nothing," for such a possibility to be enunciated in this way as a prohibition. What Hamacher, intentionally or not, has succeeded in demonstrating—this time in the mode of an example rather than just an argument—is that all reference, all language, all philology is prosopon-poetic. Language, at bottom, is therefore a kind of abyssal prosopopoeia, the lending of a virtual "recognizability" to every conceivable name, mark, or trace of absence. But every prosopopoeia, every such act of philological reference, partakes at one and the same time of a zero-rhetoric in which all the prosopopoeia of language, along with any definitive recognition of them, will have been suspended in the very act of positing (themselves). Could it be that Hamacher's insistence on marking a divergence between de Man's prosopopoeia of positing and his own philology of the zero has led him ineluctably into a failure to recognize just such a zero degree of prosopopoeia inscribed already in de Man's texts?

There is, in any case, at least one place in chapter IV of Hamacher's Response where he drops his insistence on finding prosopopoeia function in de Man exclusively as a means for achieving a kind of "consolation" (Trost) through the production of textual effects like "balance," "symmetry," "correspondence," and "reciprocity" (242–45/106–9). That is when he comments at length on de Man's laconic assertion in "Autobiography as De-Facement"—"Death is a displaced name for a linguistic predicament." The name "Death," then, that "something non-linguistic" that language always has before itself, though without ever reaching it, will be taken by Hamacher to mark a moment in de Man's text when the positing power of prosopopoeia becomes once and for all "unsettled." According to Hamacher's gloss of de Man's sentence, "death" does not consist in any positing; rather, "'Death' is never posited death, without the de-posing of the entire order of positing, poiesis, and performing acts" (245/108). Hamacher goes on to suggest, however, that—at least in de Man—the de-posing (Entsetzung) of the order of positing (Setzung) carried out by the name "death" would remain somehow incomplete, only a sub-version of "opposition" (Entgegensetzung) still held minimally in balance with positing, and therefore, ultimately, still symmetrical to the figure of prosopopoeia.

But is the deposing of language's power to posit not precisely what de Man's texts will have so insistently documented as the necessary corollary of prosopopoeia in the first place? Hamacher cites de Man's reference to prosopopoeia in "Autobiography as De-Facement" in order to underline the close connection de Man draws there with positing. "When Paul de Man characterizes prosopopoeia," Hamacher writes, "he privileges, in accordance with this figure of figure-making, the vocabulary of positing: 'the figure of prosopopoeia, the fiction of an apostrophe to an absent, deceased, or voiceless entity, which *posits* the possibility of the latter's reply and confers upon it the power of speech'" (242/106; Hamacher's emphasis). More remarkable still than even its positing, or at least more disruptive with respect to its supposed power to posit, would be the appositive qualification de Man attaches to the figure of prosopopoeia in this sentence and that Hamacher does not mention or read. Prosopopoeia, before being able to posit anything at all, is made by de Man to pass through the appositional phase of what he calls a *fiction*. For de Man, prosopopoeia would be not just a fiction but the fiction of an apostrophe, the power to address. It is by means of a fictive apostrophe, addressing itself to the voiceless other, that prosopopoeia would first assume as its own the power to posit. But if the prosopopoeia's power to posit depends in this way on a fiction, then just what kind of power could such a figure actually be taken to possess? In other words, the displacement of the positing power of language—its deposal, its appositional and unpositionable vacancy, or zero—occurs as soon as it is supposed by Paul de Man to take place in the mode of *fiction*. For the positing power of prosopopoeia to be that *of* fiction would make it by the same token into a very shadowy power indeed, since, as we all know, there is no positive mark—figure or face—that, all by itself, ever belongs properly to fiction. To be fiction means: to depend—for the power to be called and as a consequence to speak in the voice of fiction—on an external and more powerful authority, which must have somehow granted fiction that name and authorized it to speak as such. In other words, to be able to be addressed and responded to as fiction will always have meant to call upon, or apostrophize, a more effective and out-of-reach place of power. This is made clear when, in the same citation, de Man goes on to say that the apostrophe apposed to the positing power of prosopopoeia serves merely to displace and break its connection to what it only ever feigns to call forth. The fiction of apostrophe is always in fact the attribution of power to the inaccessible other: it is able to confer "the power of speech" exclusively on an absent, deceased, or voiceless entity whose actual reply—or lack of reply— remains undecidably suspended. It constitutes, in other words, what Hamacher calls the "zero," insofar as it, too, precisely as fiction, always marks the place of "relation and reference to the withdrawal of every

relation" (241/104). The "positing" power of prosopopoeia is therefore doubly duplicitous in its fictive pretension to possess power. The
apostrophe on which it relies is first of all a fiction, a simulacrum; and
further, this fictive apostrophe, in the displaced name of prosopopoeia,
then pretends to confer a power that could never legitimately belong to
it.[29] In this way, language gives what it does not possess to an "entity"
that, however much it is lent the power of speech, remains inaccessi-
bly absent. The dislocation of any possible "symmetry" or "balance"
between language-positing and language-deprivation takes place in
de Man's texts from the moment prosopopoeia has to function as both
a positing and the appositive exposure of its powerlessness ever to
accomplish such an act of address. And this happens at its very Origo,
in the zero-rhetoric of what de Man calls its status as "fiction."

The prosopopoeia inscribed in Thesis 54 is therefore not to be
taken as one deluded enough to believe that, in its own name, it could
ever possess the power to posit and therefore address and speak with
the other who is not there to respond. The prosopopoeia intertwined
with philology throughout Hamacher's writings would rather be the
one of true "friendship," the necessarily fictive apostrophe of a *philia*
coming from the wholly other, the one to whose language an other
philology cannot fail to respond, even if, or, especially when, it remains
unnamable and thus unrecognized. Such a failure to recognize would
in fact be another way of referring to the other "as such," since it would
consist in speaking with the "Without-With" of the other's language,
which can always remain a language of no one, or none at all. "Philology is Nekyia, descent to the dead" Hamacher writes, "it gives some
of the life of its language away, in order to bring those underground to
speech (*um diese Unterirdischen zum Sprechen zu bringen*) (Smock and
Richter, Thesis 71, xlii). In that way, the same Thesis says, "it dies in
order to help one or another of those many to an afterlife for a while
in its language." That dark underground out of which one or another
can be helped to speak in a language dying, philologically, to give some
of its life away to an afterlife for them, could also be called, along with
Werner Hamacher—though each time differently, only for a while, and
from now on without him—*Connecticut*.

Kevin Newmark teaches literature and literary theory at Boston College.
He is the author of *Irony on Occasion: From Schlegel and Kierkegaard to*

Derrida and de Man and *Beyond Symbolism: Textual History and the Future of Reading*. He is currently completing a book called *Who Needs Poetry: Baudelaire, Mallarmé, and the Right to Literature*.

Notes

1. Here and throughout, I have modified published translations.
2. The special editors of the *PMLA* issue were Cathy Caruth and Jonathan Culler, not, as indicated by the editors of *Give the Word*, Cynthia Chase and Jonathan Culler (4).
3. The German word for ear is "Ohr." With a philologist's ear, one can always hear—or read—in the German "Ohr," an English "or" or a French "or." Now, Hamacher's "last word," literally speaking, at the end of the essay, "What Remains to Be Said," is: *Or* (340). One can take it as his signature, "in more than one language," as he says. Where, or *où?* There, for example: Hamacher (1993;1994).
4. The reference in Aristotle can be found in Barnes. Hamacher could have also heard Aristotle's reference to the *logos euche* repeated in Martin Heidegger's voice. "This mode of making manifest in the sense of letting something be seen by pointing it out," Heidegger says of the *logos apophantikos*, "does not go with all kinds of 'discourse.' Requesting (*euche*), for instance, also makes manifest, but in a different way." See Heidegger (1962, 56). Heidegger also refers, and in more detail, to the nonapophantic *euche* in section 72 of Heidegger (1995, 309–11). Jacques Derrida responds to the *euche* in many texts. One particularly sustained discussion, in which he is listening attentively to Heidegger's attentive listening to Aristotle, can be found in the eighth session of his 2002–2003 seminar, Derrida (2011, 202–30).
5. "The Second of Inversion" is now included in Fenves, 337–87. The citations in question come from pages 345–48; I have restored the second "our"— "of our language"—that is missing from van Gerven Oei's citation. In another essay on Celan, this time from 2014, Hamacher will return to the question of the aphenomenal "nowhere"—atopia and utopia, ontologically speaking—in which the poem takes place, emphasizing Celan's introduction of the "word" *entwo* (unwhere) into the poem "Deine Augen im Arm." See "Tò autó, das Selbe,—" in Hamacher (2019b, 181–208).
6. My translation. Hamacher not only alludes to this flower in "The Second of Inversion"; he cites it specifically in "Position Exposed," also in Hamacher (1999, 258).
7. Unfortunately, the English translation of the *Theses* provided in this volume follows the earlier translations in *Diacritics* and the volume called *Minima Philologica*, both of which omit the last sentence from this paragraph: "Philology is philophilia."
8. A possible tension is suggested in the way the editors make an implicit distinction between the "interlocutors" in the *Theses* (Aristotle, Kant, Schlegel,

Benjamin, Sappho, Ponge, Hölderlin, Nietzsche, Celan) and the contributors to the volume. The interlocutors whose "friendship" with each other occurs only in death is qualified: "the *uneasy* comradeship and *elusive* friendliness." No such qualification is attached to the contributors, who are described as *"animated* by friendship" (7, emphasis added). Salutary in this regard would be a careful reading of Thesis 71: "Philology is Nekyia, descent to the dead. . . . the society of philology is the society of those who belong to no society; its life a Living-Together with death (*ihr Leben Zusammenleben mit dem Tod)"* (xlii).

9. Unlike the texts by Hamacher, Nancy, Heidegger, and Blanchot that Bernstein cites, the one by Paul de Man does not make reference to "flowers." But Bernstein is right to include it here, since it is very much about how the substitutions and exchanges engendered within a tropological system, a collection or bouquet, of rhetorical figures, will expand without fail to include anthropomorphisms. What is in question is therefore not the "leap" from the *philia* of philology to the *philia* of human friendships. On the other hand, what is not to be taken for granted is its legitimacy and, especially, its legitimacy as a model for political and institutional analyses and interventions, much less everything that is left unquestioned about the "person" whenever friendship is allowed to define or be defined by its anthropomorphic reference.

10. The original German version of the essay, "Was zu sagen bleibt," now appears, along with "Für—die Philologie" and "95 Thesen zur Philologie," in Hamacher (2019c). Further references to the text will be made both to the English translation and the German original. I am especially grateful to Urs Engeler for helping me obtain a copy of the volume in German under very strict time constraints.

11. "With-Without-With": a variation of Hamacher's signature, a longer and more elaborated version of "or." There would be no *or* without establishing a relation "with" whatever relation the *or* intervenes within and splits apart. Furthermore, the relation of "with" established by the *or* would always be such that it could turn out . . . otherwise: such a relation with . . . or . . . (not). Such indefinability of the "with" established by the *or* could never prevent the lapsing of that very "with" into a not-with, or, a relation without relation. The "with-without-with" with which Hamacher signs—and countersigns—his signature is made even more pronounced by placing Hamacher's remarks on Aristotle's use of the word *hama*—which Hamacher translates into German as "Mit," or *with*—alongside Derrida's Latin translation of the same word as *cum* and *co-*. See Hamacher (2010a, 32) together with Derrida (1982, 55).

12. If, according to Thesis 1, "language is archiphilology," then it follows that the "philologist," *aner philologos,* is philo-philologist. And if man is defined in terms of language, then he must be defined in terms of that "love" that language bears (itself) as "archiphilology." In such a case, the human cannot be defined outside its relation to a language of love/love of language: philology. Hamacher says as much in a related text, which also makes reference to Plato's "Phaedrus": "Plato's 'philologist' is a friend and lover of speech about love that is itself loving speech. He is philo-philologist, because for him the logos is already love, and moreover the love of love. Language loves." See Hamacher (2015, 125).

13. The acknowledgment is not only to the *phileîn* that therefore operates in every *logos:* "Language is archiphilology" (Thesis 1, xi). It is no doubt also an acknowledgment Hamacher makes to both Heidegger and Derrida. For Derrida's part, see, especially, Derrida (2005, esp. 234–44).

14. Two of the eleven Responses, by following a singular path in each case, do a very fine job of picking out and developing this aspect of the *Theses* (see Smock; Schestag).

15. Hamacher touches upon this when he juxtaposes the knowledge-production of anthropology and the philological interrogation of anthropomorphisms: "Anthropology knows, in short, because it does not ask. But asking about man exposes this certainty to a language that offers no measure of man and thus no measure of anything at all" (Thesis 50, xxxi).

16. No doubt Hamacher has in mind here one of the classic philosophical definitions of friendship, proposed by Aristotle in Section 4 of Book 9 in the *Nicomachean Ethics:* "Therefore, since each of these characteristics belongs to the good man in relation to himself, and he is related to his friend as to himself (*for his friend is another self*), friendship too is thought to be one of these attributes, and those who have these attributes to be friends" (1166b2–116b24; emphasis added).

17. The comma, a kind of syntactical "or," separating what it serves to join by placing a potentially limitless abyss between them. A speaking "com," or *with,* though one that speaks only with the "Without-With" of another language, *ma,* that may not even be one. On the philological and therefore historical significance of the comma, see Thesis 92. Only the slightest fold separates the "com" of the comma/Komma from the French word *comme,* and all the resources—similitude, analogy, metaphor, symbolization—it holds in abeyance for both philosophy and philology, as well as for the history and politics that always go along with them.

18. "*Was geschiet,* what happens," says Thesis 34, "*ist Abschied*—is Separation" (xxv). For an incisive account and development of this Thesis, see Mendoza-de Jesús, 287–318, esp. 308–312. Hamacher will also highlight this Thesis in his Response (231–34/95–7).

19. Ronell not only makes the connection between philology and friendship explicit; it becomes the essay's focus—but exorbitantly so. In Ronell's case, understanding Hamacher's philology on the basis of interpersonal relations of friendship occurs under the sign of "misprision," or, in other words, "the dropped call" (131, 137). Personal and linguistic "affects" do not ultimately coincide; they "I'anguish" along the way to broken connections (134). The genealogical tree is put to work but ultimately unable to do its job: each of its hanging limbs, only a "phantom member" (156).

20. See Thesis 17: "Philology is not a theory in the sense of an insight into that which is. Nor is it a praxis that is guided by a theory or that has a theory as its goal. It is—if it *is*—the movement (*die Bewegung*) of an attentiveness to that which comes to its attentiveness and slips away from it, collides with and misses it, what attracts and, by attracting it, withdraws from it. It is the experience of drawing into withdrawal. The movement (*Die Bewegung*) of a search without predetermined

goal. And so without Goal. And so without the Without of a goal. Without the Without of ontology" (xviii). For the necessary extension of *philological* movements "Without-Goal" to *political* movements "Without-Rights," see Hamacher (2018).

21. I thank Liesl Yamaguchi for making me more attentive, philologically and historically speaking, to Hamacher's use of the word "ohne," *without,* in his reference to Amerindian etymologies.

22. Whether or not the privilege granted here to Paul de Man is a merely contingent effect of Hamacher's having called the dark ground of Thesis 38 "Connecticut," should remain an open question. What goes for Paul de Man goes, each time uniquely, for the "co-" with which Hamacher's language speaks with—longs for—the "Without-With" of the languages of Maurice Blanchot, Paul Celan, Jacques Derrida, *or* any number of other proper names that do and do not appear in *Was zu sagen bleibt* (What remains to say). Suffice it to say that chapter VI of Hamacher's Response, dealing with the "Without-With" speaking in the interval between Hamacher's and Derrida's language, would easily give as much to say as chapter IV. One is IV de Man; the other IV Derrida, etc.

23. It is not insignificant—far from it—that the term "rhetorology" was coined by Wayne Booth. "So we need a new term, *rhetorology,* for this deepest practice of Listening Rhetoric: not just distinguishing defensible and indefensible forms of rhetoric but attempting to lead both sides in any dispute to discover the ground they share" (10). Needless to say, Paul de Man would have had very good grounds not to have recourse to such a term.

24. A certain categorical rhetoric—propositionally imperious, unhesitatingly apodictic—is a curiously notable feature of Hamacher's writing. Curious, because it is precisely anything having to do with the Aristotelean categories that Hamacher tends so categorically to dismiss. This appears to be the case even with Hamacher's reaction to one of the Responses that suggestively argues that Aristotle's categories may not have been as categorically categorial as they have most frequently been taken to be over the course of their reception. See Fenves, 171–81.

25. Conspicuous by its unmarked absence from this "family" of proper names is the one that, perhaps more than any other, assigned and inscribed a certain *"or"* as the zero, or null point, where the geometrico-linguistic axes of selection and combination, or prose and poetry, are crossed and undone. And this precisely at the point where the crucial difference between the number and the letter, zero and o—zeRO OR o—becomes undecidably imperative for the functioning of every language. See Mallarmé, « Or »: "Le numéraire, engin de terrible précision, net aux consciences, perd jusqu'à un sens . . . si un nombre se majore et recule, vers l'improbable, il inscrit plus de zéros: signifiant que son total équivaut spirituellement à rien, presque" (245–46).

26. Much remains to say of the place occupied here by the German root-words "Stelle" and "stellen" Hamacher uses to mark the decisive divergence for a "zero-rhetoric" between *Leerstelle* (empty-place) and *Stellenleere* (placeless, errant vacancy). In short, it would require an extensive engagement with the appearance and

function of the syntagm "stell" in Heidegger, especially as it will crystallize around his rewriting of *Ge-stell*. For a helpful preliminary sketch, see Lacoue-Labarthe).

27. The two essays by de Man that Hamacher considers were first published in 1979 and can now be found in De Man (1984). They are "Autobiography as De-Facement" and "Shelley Disfigured." Later in his response, in chapter XI, Hamacher will come very close to taking back his earlier dismissal of de Man, though it will now include a qualification overtly genealogical in nature: "De Man's formulation ['language posits and language means (since it articulates) but language cannot posit meaning']—despite its not being understood by some of his disciples (*von einigen seiner Adepten*)—amounts to an unambiguous retraction for the theorem of language's consistent figurality, as well as for the theorem of its positing character" (276/139). It could well be, then, that the "clear distance" that concerns Hamacher is less the one between de Man's treatment of linguistic positing and zero-rhetoric than the one between de Man's texts and the misreading of them Hamacher attributes to some of his disciples.

28. "Prosopopoeia" appears, it seems, only to disappear, without end. The most stunning example of the "dark ground" on which the "co-" of "contingency" collides impossibly with the "co-" of "coherence" concerns the inscription-effacement of this very name, *prosopopoeia*, in Hamacher's Thesis 54 and the remarks he devotes to it in his Response. In the three published English translations, Thesis 54 reads: "a zero-function of which not even the figure of prosopopoeia can render account." In its first German edition, it appears this way: "eine Zero-Funktion . . . von der nicht einmal die Figur der Prosopopöie Rechenschaft ablegen kann." However, in *Give the Word* and in the volume, *Was zu sagen bleibt*, the German of Thesis 54 at that same point now reads: "eine Zero-Funktion . . . von der nicht einmal die Figur der *Katachrese* Rechenschaft ablegen kann" (xxxv/65; emphasis added). How could "catachresis" come to have filled the place left empty by "prosopopoeia"? Nothing—*zero*—anywhere in Hamacher's text points to this absolutely contingent substitution of one name by the other in Thesis 54. And yet, anyone who is familiar with the name, Paul de Man, should not be capable of failing to recognize a certain "coherence" in such a substitution. As if catachresis always left a *Leerstelle* into which prosopopoeia were just waiting to erect the vacancy—*Stellenleere*—of its name. As if the language of prosopopoeia were always calling to and speaking with the Without-With of a catachresis not yet, or, no longer there. Nothing—*zero* again—can reduce such an accident to the coherence of anything more than the repetition of this "as if."

29. The relationship of prosopopoeia to apostrophe in de Man is complex enough to demand its own analysis. An essay in which their intertwining plays an equally crucial role is "Hegel on the Sublime." Here, too, it is the face-giving power of prosopopoeia that is made to depend on apostrophe, and the apostrophe on which the prosopopoeia depends is once again characterized as a kind of fiction, or illusion: "the device of apostrophe as it allows for the illusion of address." The essay is all the more pertinent to this discussion insofar as it associates the illusory character of apostrophe with a possible "deposing" of the pretension to

possess the power of positing whose simulacrum it triggers: "The main monarch to be thus dethroned or desacralized is language, the matrix of all value systems in its claim to possess the absolute power of position." What de Man at that point goes on to refer to as a "critical power" would be the merely derivative power, by virtue of its very "namelessness," to undo "the claim to power." It would be just as difficult in this essay as in the others to maintain that de Man's reference to positing is governed by a simple or symmetrical opposition between positing and opposing. The essay is now found in De Man (1996, 114–15). Another essay in the same volume, "Pascal's Allegory of Persuasion," treats the indeterminable place and function of the "zero" in Pascal's model of language. Pascal's zero, which is not one that is mentioned (at least by name) in Hamacher's text, belongs, according to de Man's reading of it, neither to mathematics, nor to logic, nor to language properly speaking: "The zero is actually nameless, 'innommable'" (59).

Works Cited

Aristotle. 1984. *De Interpretatione*. In *The Complete Works of Aristotle*, edited by Jonathan Barnes, 17a8–17a9. Clayton, GA: InteLex.

De Man, Paul. 1984. *The Rhetoric of Romanticism*. New York: Columbia University Press.

———. 1996. *Aesthetic Ideology*, ed. Andrzej Warminski, 114–15. Minneapolis: University of Minnesota Press, 1996.

Derrida, Jacques. 1982. "*Ousia* and *Grammē*." In *Margins*, 55. Translated by Alan Bass. Chicago: University of Chicago Press.

———. 1993. "Heidegger's Ear: Philopolemology (Geschlecht IV)." In *Reading Heidegger: Commemorations*, edited by John Sallis, 163–218. Translated by J. P. Leavey. Bloomington: Indiana University Press.

———.1999. *Premises*, 337–87. Translated by Peter Fenves. Stanford: Stanford University Press.

———. 2005. *The Politics of Friendship*. Translated by George Collins. London: Verso.

———. 2011. *The Beast and the Sovereign II*, 202–30. Translated by Geoffrey Bennington. Chicago: University of Chicago Press.

Fenves, Peter. "The Category of Philology." In Smock and Richter, *95 Theses on Philology*, 171–81.

Hamacher, Werner. 1993. "Ou, séance, touche de Nancy, ici." *Paragraph* 16:216–31.

———. 1994. "Ou, séance, touche de Nancy, ici II." *Paragraph* 17:103–19.

———. 2010a. "Amphora." In *Wanda Golanka: Tanz Ensemble Modell*, edited by Elisabeth Schweeger, 32. Berlin: Theater der Zeit.

———. 2010b. "From *95 Theses on Philology*." *PMLA* 125, no. 4: Special Topic: Literary Criticism for the Twenty-First Century (October): 994–1001.

———. 2015. *For — Philology*. In *Minima Philologica*,125. Translated by Jason Groves. New York: Fordham University Press.

————. 2018. *Sprachgerechtigkeit,* Frankfurt am Main: S. Fischer Verlag.

————. 2019a. "Epoché Gedicht." In *Keinmaleins,* 143. Klostermann: Frankfurt am Main.

————. 2019b. "Tò autó, das Selbe." In *Keinmaleins,* 181–208.

————. 2019c. *Was zu sagen bleibt.* Schupfart: Engeler Verlag.

————. 2019d. "What Remains to Be Said: On Twelve and More Ways of Looking at Philology. In Smock and Richter, *95 Theses on Philology,* liii.

Heidegger, Martin. 1962. Introduction to "The Concept of the *Logos.*" In *Being and Time,* 56. Translated by John Macquarrie and Edward Robinson. New York: Harper and Row.

————. 1995. *Fundamental Concepts of Metaphysics: World, Finitude, Solitude.* Translated by William McNeil and Nicholas Walker. Bloomington: Indiana University Press.

Lacoue-Labarthe, Philippe. 1998. "Typography." In *Typography: Mimesis, Philosophy, and Politics.* Translation by Christopher Fynsk. Stanford: Stanford University Press.

Mallarmé, Stéphane. 2003. "Crise de vers." In *Oeuvres Complètes II,* edited by Betrand Marchal, 213. Paris: Gallimard.

Mendoza-de Jesús, Ronald. 2019. "Addressing Departure." *Discourse* 41, nos. 2–3 (Spring/Fall): 287–318, esp. 308–12.

Ronell, Avital. "The Right Not to Complain: A Philology of Kinship." In Smock and Richter, *95 Theses on Philology,* liii.

Schestag, Thomas. "Rereading *Tempus fugit.*" In Smock and Richter, *95 Theses on Philology,* liii.

Smock, Ann, and Gerhard Richter, eds. 2019. *95 Theses on Philology,* in *Give the Word: Responses to Werner Hamacher's* 95 Theses on Philology, liii. Lincoln: University of Nebraska Press.

Smock, Ann. "Einmal ist Keinmal." In Smock and Richter, *95 Theses on Philology,* liii.

BOOK REVIEWS

Cultural Critique's commitment to cultural and intellectual debate and discussion is bolstered by the regular inclusion of reviews of both new and not-so-new books. Generally, books reviewed will have appeared within the past three years, although reviews of older books that are emerging or reemerging in intellectual debates are also welcome. As an academic publication, *Cultural Critique* sees itself as having a responsibility to devote space to authors whose work may not be otherwise reviewed. For *Cultural Critique*'s special issues, book reviews should share the issue's thematic focus. *Cultural Critique*'s book review editors solicit writers, books, and ideas for future contributions to this section of the journal. Please contact the book review editors at cultcrit@umn.edu or *Cultural Critique*, Department of Cultural Studies and Comparative Literature, 216 Pillsbury Drive S.E., 235 Nicholson Hall, University of Minnesota, Minneapolis, MN 55455–0229.

"THE MAD (WO)MAN IN BLACK STUDIES"

BLACK MADNESS :: MAD BLACKNESS
BY THERÍ ALYCE PICKENS
Durham: Duke University Press, 2019

Megan Finch

Where, theoretically and in theory, do madness and Blackness meet? As an emotion, an exaggeration, and/or a generalization encompassing both cognitive impairment and mental illness, madness obtains a seductive inexactness in its archaism. Critical theory has positioned this madness not quite like its others as a site of potential epistemological critique since at least the earliest published work of Michel Foucault and Gilles Deleuze and Felix Guattari's writing on schizophrenia in the 1960s. While the combined influence of Foucault and Deleuze has not wrought a madness/mad studies[1] of an institutional breadth near that of sexuality or queer studies, madness has become the form of unreason associated—or, following Foucault's historicism, reassociated—with "the very heart of Reason and truth" (14). Still, whatever his continued impact on the field's trajectory, Foucault's history of madness is yet another example of his provincialism. As La Marr Jurelle Bruce notes, Foucault's ship of fools will remind the "scholar of black modernity . . . [of the] many millions of Africans abducted from their native lands and stacked in the putrid pits of slave ships" (303). To understand madness, Bruce and other scholars of its relationship to Blackness suggest that we both go beyond and decenter the stories of the explicitly white, and explicitly mad, men of Europe (and America).

At the same time, the mad Black figure, often female, waits at the edge of several works in Black studies published in the last ten years. There is the Black woman positioned at Columbia's gates, accusing non-Black "students, staff, and faculty of . . . having stolen her sofa and of selling her into slavery" in the introduction of Frank B. Wilderson's *Red, White and Black: Cinema and the Structure of U.S. Antagonisms* (and the Black man in his depiction of his own breakdown which opens the more recent *Afropessimism*) (1). There are the imprisoned, "idiotic" Black girls in Saidiya Hartman's *Wayward Lives: Beautiful Experiments* (and those Black girls sterilized for the same idiocy in Dorothy Roberts's earlier *Killing the Black Body)* (Hartman; Roberts). There is also the "mad" Serena Williams in Claudia Rankine's *Citizen*. And there is Aereile Jackson, the "former mother" carrying a baby doll that she knows is not one of her missing children, saying "I'm not mentally ill or anything like that" at the/as the ejection of capitalism in Christina Sharpe's *In the Wake* (Rankine; Sharpe). Some of these figures, like Wilderson's mad Black woman, suggest a madness retaining or more fully possessing the critical possibility that, for Foucault, the modern period precludes. Some, like Sharpe's non-mad mother, index madness's critical possibilities—including that of its own erasure—at its meeting with Blackness. For other mad Black figures, like the institutionalized girls in Hartman's *Wayward Lives, Beautiful Experiments,* madness in the form of discourses around cognitive lack or impairment renames and thus reifies the production of Black social death sans explicitly racial terminology while *also* being a site of potentiality for beautiful experiments in living. And, as in the case of Claudia Rankine's writing on Serena Williams, the mad Black figure can name the refusal to separate the ascriptions of a Black body labeled "too much" by the media from that body's potential to break with an atomizing and temporally linear Western epistemology that conceives of each sideline call and judge as separate and unrelated. For these scholars, "the slave ship," returning to Bruce, is the "urtext of abjected blackness in the West [that] commandeers the ship of fools, tows the ship of fools, orients Western notions of madness and Reason" (304).

Rather than attempting to enumerate all of the mad figures in Black studies, the archive assembled above betrays my own interest in how work that engages the incommensurability of Blackness and, at least, normative gender often also triangulates madness, un/reason, and Black women. If madness haunts the political and social lives and deaths of Black women in specific ways—as mental illness in the case of Sandra Bland, a Black woman who was pulled over for a traffic violation and purportedly committed suicide in her jail cell; or as fury in the case of Marissa Alexander, whose claim to a "Stand Your Ground" defense resulted in a twenty-year prison sentence for firing a warning shot out of "anger"—it produces different life outcomes for Black women. While the blurb on the back of Therí Alyce Pickens's *Black Madness :: Mad Blackness* never explicitly mentions gender, that the text engages the speculative fiction of three Black women—Octavia Butler, Nalo Hopkinson, and Tananarive Due—suggests that gender will be relevant to, though perhaps not constitutive of, how Pickens theorizes the intersection of madness and Blackness. How does unreasonable and/or "mad" Black female flesh—as characters, theorists, and as artists—interface with madness as conceived within disability studies? Amidst these renderings, Pickens's *Black Madness :: Mad Blackness* extends the discussion of contemporary Blackness in relation to the slave ship—the site that for many Black scholars continues to ground, though not necessarily totalize, Black life in the present—to the modern port of the ship of fools: disability studies.

Even before opening with an example of a particularly dated attempt to theorize the relationship between Blackness and disability from the (non-Black) disabled perspective, "a comparative analysis that does not work," Pickens's title stages the complex relationship between mad, Black, and their nominalizations (1). *Black Madness :: Mad Blackness*'s ostensible repetition, Pickens explains, calls attention to the insufficiency of analogizing theories that render the terms redundant, while the double colon serves to further "unsettle" rather than clarify the relationship between them. By acknowledging and juxtaposing each term as "description and category," Pickens shatters the stability of biological and discursive mad/madness Black/Blackness as they move in and out of putatively (white) mad and Black spaces and bodies (5). More significantly, Pickens's critical intervention suggests that mutual constitution, often the refuge of theoretical complexity, is also potentially reductive. While acknowledging that "mutual constitution impresses upon readers how these two discourses operate as interrelated and simultaneously present" (and seems to emerge in response to Christopher M. Bell's call for a critical engagement with the relationship between race and disability), Pickens argues that mutual constitution often amounts to throwing your hands in the air and saying, "It's complicated" (24). Fixing critical work at the poles of "retrieval and radicality," neither disability nor Black studies have thus far attended to the uneven temporality and (non)fungibility of white and Black mad subjects.

The insufficiency of these fields' engagements stems in part, Pickens argues, from the fact that disability studies often fails to interrogate its presumptive whiteness, even as it borrows from critical race theory and feminist studies. While Pickens notes that disability studies has often mobilized critical race theory to refuse narratives of disability as irrationality and cognitive decline, she also notes that this use fails to interrogate the normative whiteness of the field. Moreover, the field often constructs its refusals by instrumentalizing Blackness. Pickens opens her book with a discussion of the use of "the negro" and Fanon in Leonard Kriegel's 1969 essay, "Uncle Tom and Tiny Tim: Some Reflections on the Cripple as Negro." Conversely, the problem of the whiteness of disability studies seems to loom somewhat larger than the ableism of Black studies in Pickens's work. And I view this as being for at least two reasons. First, the language of disability studies, and even disability as a term, overrepresents the field of critical interrogations of madness. Pickens's wide range of references from Black scholarship and literature—from Henry Louis Gates's talking book and Audre Lorde's *Cancer Journals* to Harriet Jacobs's *Incidents in the Life of a Slave Girl*—locates madness outside the terms of mad studies, finding in their place terms for and internal to Black scholarship. The second (and perhaps most important) reason is that *Black Madness :: Mad Blackness* looks to Black speculative fiction writers for their theorizing on the "relationships between blackness and madness . . . [as] constituted within fissures, breaks, and gaps" of disciplinary engagements (3). Speculative fiction, Pickens reminds, is constructive for both Black and disabled people, making it a potential site of the critique of both whiteness and saneness. Black speculative fiction, Pickens argues, is a prime site for disrupting these multiply related discourses.

Pickens thinks with and in the literary disruption, fissures, and breaks staged by Black speculative fiction beyond mutual constitution by juxtaposing the work of Hortense Spillers, Gilles Deleuze, and Fred Moten. Deleuze's concept of the fold—a "space of various critical and creative possibilities" that offers but does not promise both possibility and erasure—provides a useful metaphor for conceptualizing the spatialized relationship between and within Blackness and madness and in the white and Black spaces of these texts (Pickens, 15). Yet, Spillers's famous theorization of the flesh—which indexes the slave's abjection as an "absence from a subject position" while offering the potential for "gaining the insurgent ground as female social subject"—both anticipates and exceeds Deleuze's conception (67, 80). By placing Deleuze second to Spillers, explicitly noting Spillers's anticipation, in 1982 and 1987, of his 1988 work on the fold, Pickens both deploys and "Blackens" the fold. Increasing this shade (obvious puns intended), Pickens ends the discussion of the conceptual tools with which she will engage the theory of Black speculative fiction writers with another Black scholar's concept: Fred Moten's "the break." While Pickens finds Deleuze's fold useful for its investigation of "the aesthetic praxis" of the "artist-theorist[s]" discussed, across her text the deployment of the fold seems most valuable in its ability to conjure the image of, without repeatedly describing, "a space not solely of possibility, but one that continually gets erased" (15, 16). Beyond this, the fold has what Patricia Hill Collins theorizes, in discussing intersectionality's potential as a critical social theory, a metaphorical utility. Utilizing the resources that Deleuze's easily visualizable concept makes available, Pickens's work also argues that Black theorists have anticipated and extended the fold with an attention to race. While, broadly speaking, Spillers's work is essential to critics and theorists in Black studies, Deleuze is fundamental to various strains of critical theory (and is also not absent from essential works by theorists of Blackness).[2] Pickens's containment of Deleuze highlights the fact that citing Black scholars, and particularly Black women scholars, is not simply a social justice practice. Spillers and Moten have simply done more by attending to the position of the unthought.

Pickens's placement of Deleuze and Spillers also sets the theoretical contours of this work in another way. While the relationship between madness and Blackness is neither simple nor linear, *Black Madness :: Mad Blackness* is nevertheless grounded in intersectionality. And though Black studies has not been devoid of intersectionality critiques,[3] the most prominent critical engagement emerges, as Jennifer Nash discusses in *Black Feminism Reimagined*, from Jasbir Puar's engagement with Deleuze and Donna Haraway. Reminding readers that Crenshaw's concept—despite its current uses and misuses in the academy—does not overdetermine the causes of disaster any more than Deleuzian "assemblages" or Haraway's cyborg, Pickens keeps focused on intersectionality's trouble in lieu of the supposedly less determinant alternative offered by Puar in "I'd Rather Be a Cyborg Than a Goddess."

Eschewing the linearity of chapters in this posttenure, mad Black book, Pickens stages a series of critical and literary conversations with the theorists of/in the break, for the most part Black female speculative fiction writers. In the first conversation, Pickens reads the interracial encounter between Blackness and disability theorized in Octavia Butler's *Fledgling*, which focuses on Shori, a "young"[4] Black vampire with amnesia, as an example of Black madness. Butler depicts Shori's Black madness as disruptive to norms of whiteness and ableism in both the human and the Ina (vampire) world. This disruptiveness, juxtaposed against and disturbing the "madness" of pedophilia and racism, does not, for Pickens, necessarily equate to liberation or agency for the Black mad subject. The space that Shori's Blackness and/as madness (as well as her madness and/as Blackness) folds or blackens in Ina (vampire) society is a provocation to confront its explicit ableism and disavowed racism. Yet Shori's "agency" is fundamentally limited to the procedures and limitations of liberal incorporation. The fold caused by Blackness and madness offers neither liberation from the social determinants of abjection nor full protection from its production of her bare life. The second conversation focuses on mad Blackness in the intraracial space of Nalo Hopkinson's *Midnight Robber*, theorizing the mad Blackness of two female characters inhabiting two different categories of madness: "cognitive impairment and mental illness" (Pickens, 51). Exploring the encounter between Blackness and madness in a Black world, Hopkinson depicts mad Black characters that—as Baldwin suggests is the key component for depicting humanity: "the relationship that Negroes bear to one another, that depth of involvement and unspoken recognition of shared experience which creates a way of life"—acquire their meaning and value within a Black social milieu (Baldwin, 36).

The relationship between Blackness and the human is exceeded by the nonhuman figure of mad (as excess) Blackness, the Granny Nanny system, an artificial intelligence that permeates, constitutes, and surveils the Black world in *Midnight Robber*. While Pickens's first two conversations focus on either the Black mad (Blackness in interracial spaces) or the mad Black (where mad is an intensifier of Blackness in intraracial spaces), the final two conversations complicate the project by depicting multiple mad figures with various relationships to Black life. In the text's third conversation, Pickens details how Tananarive Due's series, *African Immortals*, understands the challenges to the human offered from madness and Blackness within ableist and white supremacist frames. Finally, Pickens turns to Mat Johnson's *Hunting in Harlem* and to the genre of the novel more generally. Calling attention to the relationship between value and meaning, Pickens suggests that Johnson's depiction of mad Blackness/Black Madness places responsibility on the reader to determine how the mad Black/ Black mad figure comes to mean and be valued with/within the novel.

While Pickens's work stages these conversations separately from one another—hence they are not chapters—the final two conversations in particular point to the limits of this form as well as to possible congress between them. When discussing Due's work, the question of gender is at once insisted upon and elided. One paragraph discusses Fana as a "disabled black woman" while in the next she operates as a "mad black character" (89). Whether this is to follow Spillers's insistence that "we lose at least gender difference in the outcome"[5] or to avoid the (at least) three-body/term problem, the specter of gender in Pickens's volume puts pressure on Blackness and madness—through heteronormative gender performance and practice as well as gendered sexual violence that also creates and impacts madness and Blackness, the Black and the mad. In the final conversation on *Hunting in Harlem*, the form and genre of the novel are most fully discussed at the moment when focus shifts from speculative fiction and also with the introduction of the first Black male fiction author, Mat Johnson. The conversation grounded by Johnson's work—which ends Pickens's text—feels both necessary to the text's overall project while (and perhaps this is the point) opening out to an undiscovered constellation of relations, particularly those of gender and genre, in the fold rather than providing a period. Pickens's conversations invite thinking about the intersections of gender, madness, and Blackness in and as genre, but the use of discrete conversations does not seem to invite nor give rise to interstitial discourse. Compounding this absence is the lack of conversational space (a conclusion perhaps) in which to explore some of these meta-conversational threads. While undoubtedly productive features of the text, the intentional disjoint between the four conversations and the lack of conclusion nonetheless frustrate, as well as excite, some of this reader's desires.

Black Madness :: Mad Blackness models without (over)determining encounters between madness and Blackness. By stressing the inevitability of these encounters, Pickens demonstrates the necessity of her work for disability studies, mad studies, and Black studies. In foregrounding the work of writers like Butler and Due, Pickens's work also contributes to a growing list of recent critical texts that turn to Black speculative fiction as a site of theorizing.[6] And even though *Black Madness :: Mad Blackness* does not discuss gender as a theoretical category constitutive of the intersection of madness and Blackness, it does bring together two influential Black feminist theorists—Kimberlé Crenshaw and Hortense Spillers—who are not easily or often engaged both simultaneously and equally. Spillers's work problematizing the applicability of gender difference to Black flesh has been central to scholarship that has been critical, explicitly or implicitly, of intersectionality as a humanist discourse. Relatedly, an unscientific "study" of the indexes of recent works published in Black studies on my bookshelf suggests an almost zero-sum relationship between citations of Crenshaw and intersectionality and Spillers.[7] By reminding readers of the theory's potential to hold ambiguity, intersectionality's potential relationship to the flesh is afforded space.

Near the end of her introduction, Pickens offers a rich description of at least one aspect of the *Black Madness :: Mad Blackness* project: "To read within these faults points out how Blackness and madness exceed and shift the boundaries and definitions of human, specifically how the assumed subject position of knowable excess (that is, Black madness and mad Blackness) jeopardize the neatness with which we draw the line between self and other" (16). What the introduction insists— and what each conversation stages in different ways—is that we read madness and Blackness's complex interaction on the flesh in the fold. This insistence makes Pickens's work of criticism rare in that every conversation worries these lines and is a truly necessary read. Though a very different text, *Black Madness :: Mad Blackness* is as compelling an intervention into the relationship between Blackness (which should not be simply understood as a subcategory of race) and disability as, for me, Jasbir Puar's 2017 *The Right to Maim*. Had the latter been published a bit earlier, I wonder what, if any, additional conversations might have emerged. Even if my anticipation of a more thoroughgoing theorization of gender was somewhat frustrated, its inclusion in each of the conversations offers productive locations for thinking with and extending Pickens's work. In what strikes me as a brilliant performance of double voicing, the text says, in the middle of doing other work, "Be Clear." Whether this is the mad Black voice within an academic text that, by virtue of its inclusion in the genre, has no reason to be (clear) or the "sane" voice that calls attention to the potential madness of esoteric academic discourse, the text goes on to be necessarily mad, necessarily Black, and, clearly, necessary.

Megan Finch is assistant professor at the University of Minnesota. Her work focuses on contemporary Black women's writing on unreason.

Notes

1. In his later work Foucault places sexuality and madness alongside one another in the functioning of modernity. His 1975–1976 lectures, published as *Society Must Be Defended*, Foucault writes that "mechanisms of exclusion, the surveillance apparatus, the medicalization of sexuality, Madness, and delinquency, it was all that, or in other words the micromechanics of power that came at a certain moment to represent, to constitute the interest of the bourgeoisie" (32), and he revisits this connection in the 1978–1979 lectures, published as *The Birth of Biopolitics*—in which both are described as "regimes of veridiction" (35). Foucault's importance is thus (at least) twofold: his first major work, *Madness and Civilization*, published in 1961 and translated to English in 1965, attempts to historicize madness; it emerges and influences the period during which the literary texts under study here were written. Secondly, Foucault's later work on sexuality has been foundational to the establishment of entire disciplines (such as queer and sexuality studies), while madness, which was to Foucault coequal to sexuality in the functioning of biopower, has not achieved anything close to this level of prominence.

2. Nirmala Erevelles's Disability and Difference in Global Contexts is a foundational attempt to trace the Deleuzian strain of disability and to offer Spillers as a "corrective." Achille Mbembe's *Necropolitics* and Kara Keeling's *The Witch's Flight* are two works exemplifying the influence of Deleuze in Black studies.

3. In particular by Afropessimists and Black nihilists such as Patrice Douglass and Calvin Warren.

4. Though Shori looks like a young girl, she is in fact in her fifties.

5. I would suggest, however, that Pickens's use of "Interstices: A Small Drama of Words" along with "Mama's Baby, Papa's Maybe" suggests a move away from

the slave as identical with contemporary Blackness and thus to some notion of Black gender.

6. Kara Keeling's *Queer Times, Black Futures,* Alys Eve Weinbaum's *The After-life of Reproductive Slavery,* Sami Schalk's *Bodyminds Reimagined,* and Zakiyyah Iman Jackson's *Becoming Human,* among other works, take seriously the theoretical work of Black speculative fiction.

7. Nash discusses these as distinct strands of Black feminism.

Works Cited

Baldwin, James. 1955. "Many Thousands Gone." In *Notes of a Native Son,* 25–45. Boston: Beacon.

Bruce, La Marr Jurelle. 2017. "Mad Is a Place; or, the Slave Ship Tows the Ship of Fools." *American Quarterly* 69, no. 2:303–8.

Collins, Patricia Hill. 2019. *Intersectionality as Critical Social Theory.* Durham: Duke University Press.

Foucault, Michel. 1973. *Madness and civilization; a History of Insanity in the Age of Reason.* New York: Vintage.

Hartman, Saidiya. 2019. *Wayward Lives, Beautiful Experiments: Intimate Histories of Social Upheaval.* New York: W.W. Norton.

Nash, Jennifer C. 2019. *Black Feminism Reimagined: After Intersectionality.* Durham: Duke University Press.

Pickens, Therí Alyce. 2019. *Black Madness:: Mad Blackness.* Durham: Duke University Press.

Rankine, Claudia. 2014. *Citizen: An American Lyric.* Minneapolis: Graywolf.

Roberts, Dorothy E. 1997. *Killing the Black Body: Race, Reproduction, and the Meaning of Liberty.* 1st ed. New York: Pantheon.

Sharpe, Christina. 2016. *In the Wake: On Blackness and Being.* Durham: Duke University Press.

Spillers, Hortense J. 1987. "Mama's Baby, Papa's Maybe: An American Grammar Book." *Diacritics* 17, no. 2:65–81.

Wilderson, Frank B. III. 2010. *Red, White & Black: Cinema and the Structure of U.S. Antagonisms.* Durham: Duke University Press.

BOOKS RECEIVED

Adler-Bolton, Beatrice, and Artie Vierkant. *Health Communism*. Brooklyn: Verso, 2022.

Baross, Zsuzsa. *Living On/To Survive: Epidemic Writings*. Eastbourne: Sussex Academic Press, 2022.

———. *On Contemporaneity, after Agamben: The Concept and its Times*. Eastbourne: Sussex Academic Press, 2020.

Amin, Ash, and Michele Lancione, eds. *Grammars of the Urban Ground*. Durham: Duke University Press, 2022.

Berlant, Lauren. *On the Inconvenience of Other People*. Durham: Duke University Press, 2022.

Berry, Michael. *Jia Zhangke on Jia Zhangke*. Durham: Duke University Press, 2022.

Buller, Adrienne, and Mathew Lawrence. *Owning the Future: Power and Property in the Age of Crisis*. New York: Verso, 2022.

Burden-Stelly, Charisse, and Jodi Dean, eds. *Organize, Fight, Win: Black Communist Women's Political Writings*. Brooklyn: Verso, 2022.

Cecchetto, David. *Listening in the Afterlife of Data: Aesthetics, Pragmatics, and Incommunication*. Durham: Duke University Press, 2022.

Cifor, Marika. *Viral Cultures: Activist Archiving in the Age of AIDS*. Minneapolis: University of Minnesota Press, 2022.

Conley, Tom. *Action, Action, Action: The Early Cinema of Raoul Walsh*. Albany: State University of New York Press, 2022.

DiCaglio, Joshua. *Scale Theory: A Nondisciplinary Inquiry*. Minneapolis: University of Minnesota Press, 2021.

Grubbs, David. *Good Night the Pleasure Was Ours*. Durham: Duke University Press, 2022.

Hong, Renyi. *Passionate Work: Endurance after the Good Life*. Durham: Duke University Press, 2022.

Houellebecq, Michel. *Interventions 2020*. Cambridge: Polity, 2022.

Imhoff, Sarah. *The Lives of Jessie Sampter: Queer, Disabled, Zionist*. Durham: Duke University Press, 2022.

Kaplan, Dana, and Eva Illouz. *What is Sexual Capital?* Cambridge: Polity, 2022.

Kim, Jodi. *Settler Garrison: Debt Imperialism, Militarism, and Transpacific Imaginaries*. Durham: Duke University Press, 2022.

Lazarus, Neil. *Into Our Labours: Work and its Representation in World-Literary Perspective*. Liverpool: Liverpool University Press, 2022.

Linnemann, Travis. *The Horror of Police*. Minneapolis: University of Minnesota Press, 2022.

Lumba, Allan E. S. *Monetary Authorities: Capitalism and Decolonization in the American Colonial Philippines*. Durham: Duke University Press, 2022.

Malabou, Catherine. *Plasticity: The Promise of Explosion*. Edinburgh: Edinburgh University Press, 2022.

Moore, Kelli. *Legal Spectatorship: Slavery and the Visual Culture of Domestic Violence*. Durham: Duke University Press, 2022.

Nesi, Edoardo. *Sentimental Economy*. Translated by Antony Shugaar. New York: Other Press, 2022.

Olid, Bel. *Hairless: Breaking the Vicious Circle of Hair Removal, Submission and Self-Hatred*. Translated by Laura McGloughlin. Cambridge: Polity, 2022.

Parson, Annie-B. *The Choreography of Everyday Life*. Brooklyn: Verso, 2022.

Pratt, Mary Louise. *Planetary Longings*. Durham: Duke University Press, 2022.

Schaefer, Donovan O. *Wild Experiment: Feeling Science and Secularism after Darwin*. Durham: Duke University Press, 2022.

Sharma, Sarah, and Rianka Singh, eds. *Re-Understanding Media: Feminist Extensions of Marshall McLuhan*. Durham: Duke University Press, 2022.

Simone, AbdouMaliq. *The Surrounds: Urban Life within and beyond Capture*. Durham: Duke University Press, 2022.

Swan, Quito. *Pasifika Black: Oceania, Anti-Colonialism, and the African World*. New York: New York University Press, 2022.

Tremblay, Jean-Thomas. *Breathing Aesthetics*. Durham: Duke University Press, 2022.

Webb, Christopher. *Useless Activity: Work, Leisure and British Avant-Garde Fiction, 1960–1975*. Liverpool: Liverpool University Press, 2022.

Williams, Shannen Dee. *Subversive Habits: Black Catholic Nuns in the Long African American Freedom Struggle*. Durham: Duke University Press, 2022.

Wood, Jennifer Linhart, ed. *Dynamic Matter: Transforming Renaissance Objects*. University Park: Pennsylvania State University Press, 2022.